The Dreyfus Trials

1 *'Dreyfus crucified' Drawing by H. G. Ibels*

The Dreyfus Trials

GUY CHAPMAN

STEIN AND DAY/*Publishers*/New York

First published in 1972
Copyright © 1972 Guy Chapman

Library of Congress Catalog Card No. 71–18872
All rights reserved
Printed in Great Britain
Stein and Day/*Publishers*/7 East 48 Street, New York, N.Y. 10017

ISBN 0–8128–1487–8

Contents

The Illustrations

Acknowledgements

The Author and Publishers wish to thank the following for permission to reproduce the illustrations appearing in this book:

Photo Harlingue Viollet for figs 1–12, 16, 18 and 21
Mansell Collection for fig. 20
Radio Times Hulton Picture Library for figs 14, 15 and 17
Wiener Library for fig. 19

Preface

The Dreyfus Case is the classic case of miscarriage of justice: after fifty years we are only just coming to a full understanding of the triviality, the prejudice, the casual cruelty and the clannishness which sent a wholly innocent man to isolation on a bare Caribbean rock, kept him there for five years, and with a lack of scruple and a tenacity worthy of a better cause checked every move to re-open the case. The complications born of the sheer mass of evidence, genuine and invented, and of the equal mass of involuntary error and hard lying, are partly responsible for the fact that over a course of more than half a century minor details of this extraordinary case are still surfacing. Although a great measure of the heat engendered between 1894 and 1902 has evaporated, the passions of the past smoulder: there survive fanatical partisans of the original accusation, and infrequent vendors of new theories. The affair is unique in that a reference to it can still throw defenders of the *raison d'état* on to the defensive. It involved all the rival theories of the State, it disturbed profoundly the whole of France, and stirred sympathy in many other countries. The trouble from the beginning lay in the nature of the case itself. It affected not only the Army, it influenced powerfully the religious framework and organisation. It involved the other great organs of State, the Government, parliament, and the judiciary. It appealed in particular to the literate public, resulting in a 'tumult of the intellectuals' not yet entirely appeased. It cut across political affiliations, exacerbated personal loyalties and divided families.

In 1955 I published *The Dreyfus Case: a Reassessment*, an account based, so far as I then knew or could discover, on all the existing evidence, and on the contemporary political and social background. A year or so later, Messrs Plon published in Paris the *Journal de l'Affaire Dreyfus* by the late Maurice Paléologue, selected from the diaries he had kept during the heroic period of the case, before the suicide of Henry. Some critics believed he had manipulated them, but no one could be sure: there is, I think, no doubt that he had edited certain of the entries later. Apart from an entry, ostensibly of January 1899, in which he offers what he calls a constructive hypothesis that there were in fact three villains, Maurice Weil, Esterhazy, and a very high-ranking officer 'on whom no suspicion has yet fallen', the book raises no serious issues.

In 1961 there appeared *L'Affaire sans Dreyfus*, by M. Marcel Thomas, an acute and painstaking archivist. It revealed that many papers to do with the case, which I and others believed to have been destroyed, partly in September 1914 at the time of the Marne fighting and the threat to Paris, partly at the time of the collapse in June 1940, had in fact been preserved. They include the mass of documents accumulated and commented by General Gonse in 1898, and examined by the then Captain Cuignet, the first person to notice that the *faux Henry* was not a genuine document. M. Thomas's examination of these papers put beyond doubt the complicity of General Gonse, Major Lauth, and Staff-Sergeant Gribelin, in the whole complicated web of Henry's activities. He was also able to examine the private papers of the luckless du Paty, which reveal with great clearness how callously he was used by both Gonse and Henry.

Further search turned up, in the Historical Section of the Army at Vincennes, the original pieces composing the 'secret dossier' of the court-martial. Less important papers, discovered in the Bibliothèque Nationale, include the legacy of Esterhazy's letters left by the late Paul Desachy, compiler of the collection of documents of the case published about 1900 under the title of *Repertoire de l'Affaire Dreyfus*.

Various writers succeeded M. Thomas. None is of importance, but one might mention Madame Dardenne-Cavaignac's recent account of the case based on her father's papers, with the assistance of Lt.-Col. Cuignet.

A book published in 1962 has a special interest. This is *L'Enigme Esterhazy*, by Henri Guillemin. M. Guillemin is or was the cultural attaché at Berne. He has been described by a reviewer in the *Times Literary Supplement* as the 'enfant terrible' of French historiography. The book develops at length, with wit and intellect, the thesis that every previous investigator, including M. Thomas, has been misled or has misled himself, and that the real villain was Maurice Weil, in association with Saussier, the Military Governor of Paris, and his mistress, Weil's wife, an Austrian. He draws attention to the fact that at the end of 1897 Picquart was treated harshly by Saussier and Esterhazy with courtesy, but offers no evidence to support any conclusion as to Saussier's serious views. He concludes with the nonchalant confession that the whole argument is a 'reverie,' on which he does not, he says, insist.

After the publication of my book in 1955, Mr J. G. Wilson, of Messrs Bumpus, the London bookseller, allowed me to examine letters Esterhazy wrote after his flight to London in 1898. He had received them from the widow of the well-known publisher Grant Richards. Most of them were addressed to Esterhazy's lawyers and to Grant Richards, and related to his efforts to sell the world rights of his memoirs. Unhappily he had already disposed of the *Dessous de l'Affaire Dreyfus* to a French publisher, Fayard, and after a considerable amount of ill-tempered argument the correspondence ceased. It throws no light on the case. One small fact of interest emerged in that Esterhazy had already adopted the name of 'de Voilement' which is inscribed on his tomb at Harpenden. And he seems to have squeezed £1,000 out of Grant Richards.

I should add that, of the vast number of contemporary publications on behalf of or opposed to Dreyfus, one only, Joseph Reinach's *Histoire de l'Affaire Dreyfus*, six volumes, seven with the volume of index and corrections, is significant and indispensable. He was an ardent Dreyfusist, in the thick of the battle from the moment he became involved in 1895. Naturally, since he was writing almost day by day, he makes errors, but they do not diminish the supreme importance of his record, and the errors are on the whole minor.

Readers will notice that I have used the words 'Dreyfusist'

and 'Dreyfusard'. The first distinguishes those who almost from the beginning suspected a judicial error and attempted to secure a re-opening of the case by legal methods, long before it was brought into the political field. The word 'Dreyfusard', which was coined by the opponents of revision as a term of opprobrium, I have reserved for those who saw in the case an opportunity for political or personal advantage, the late-comers whom Péguy stigmatised as profiteers.

GUY CHAPMAN

Chapter One

The Bordereau

1

Auguste Mercier, the War Minister who was to play a major part in the Dreyfus case, was not a well-known soldier. A gunner, he had had a slow career: he had not been a member of the Staff Corps. He had served in the Mexican campaign of 1867 and the Franco-Prussian War, but he had only reached the highest rank in the French Army, Divisional General, in 1889. As a corps commander, he had done well at the manoeuvres of 1892. On the strength of this, coupled with a recommendation from the most famous soldier in the French Army, General de Galliffet, the then Prime Minister, Casimir-Perier, had selected him as Minister of War. Mercier had never meddled in politics; his reputation was entirely professional. He was no more than a conventional Catholic; indeed he was married to an English Protestant. A tall, slim man of sixty, with sallow skin and harsh features, a bitter mouth between a grey moustache and a grey mouche, he was reserved and courteous. Whatever other virtues he possessed, he had one to a marked degree: courage.

At first the Chamber had approved of him. He spoke clearly and plainly, and he led the Deputies to believe that so far as the Army was concerned, all was well. But in May 1894 he ran into unexpected trouble. An inventor named Turpin, from whom the State had bought certain rights in an explosive in 1885 and had decorated, had claimed that he was cheated by the Director of Artillery, and after much obscure quarrelling had eventually been given five years for espionage. On his release he attempted to sell another invention to the War Office. That department, having had enough of Turpin, closed its doors to him. He then publicly announced that he would take himself and his invention to Germany. Interpellated in the Chamber by the Extreme Left, Mercier mistook the temper of the members and failed to please. Nevertheless, when Casimir-Perier fell at the end of May that year, the only important survivor from his government was Mercier, who remained Minister of War in the new government of Charles Dupuy. This was on 30 May. Less than a month later an Italian called Caserio stabbed fatally the President of the Republic, Carnot, in Lyons. Much against his will, Casimir-Perier was elected in his place, over the head, among other rivals, of Charles Dupuy.

In July, Mercier had to deal with the indiscretions of General de Galliffet. Always reckless in speech, he was found to have made caustic comments on the state of the Army to a journalist. Questioned in the Chamber, Mercier made a spirited defence of his senior. Although he was cheered by the majority, he was assailed with violent abuse by the Left and by mischief-making journalists, in particular by the anti-establishment Rochefort of the *Intransigeant* and the anti-Semitic Drumont of the *Libre Parole*.

Less than two months later he clumsily laid himself open to further and more justifiable criticisms. On 1 August, after Parliament had risen, he published in the Official Journal a circular ordering the release of 60,000 men from the 1891 and 1892 classes in November. Save that it left the garrisons somewhat short-handed, it was not important. But he had failed to notify the Army commissions of the Senate and Chamber of his intentions, and moreover he had not even deigned to inform the titular head of the armed forces, the President of the Republic, whose first knowledge of the order was the circular in the Official Journal. Casimir-Perier for once lost his temper and summoned a Cabinet meeting, at which Mercier was told to draft an amendment to retain 20,000 of the 60,000 with the colours. Thus at the end of August Mercier's situation was far from secure. He had ignored the President; he had shaken the confidence of his Cabinet colleagues; he had snubbed the Army commissions; he had naturally, by his counter-orders, confused and enraged the Army and, perhaps worst of all, he had not only given a lot more ammunition to the Rocheforts and Drumonts, but had drawn acid criticisms from the sober newspapers. He knew that when Parliament met in October he would have to face the wrath of the commissions and the Chambers, and he could be quite certain that Charles Dupuy was not of the stuff to defend him. Only a happy accident could save him.

2

Parallel with the reconstruction of the Army after 1870, the reorganisation of the War Office was undertaken by the setting up of four Bureaux; the First covering Administration; the Second, Intelligence; the Third, Operations and Training; and the Fourth, Movements and Railways. Before becoming staff officers, the learners seconded to the War Office had to do six months with each branch, but in each year they must also be attached to units for three months.

The executive head of the War Office was the Chief of Staff, a position created in 1874. From May 1890 the post had been filled by General de Miribel, considered the best brain in the Army. The only criticism voiced was that he was, if not a Monarchist, at least a believing and practising Catholic, and inclined to select his staff officers on the recommendations o his confessor. Since the relevant accusation came from the Protestant General Billot, given in 1897 to the Alsatian Protestant, Scheurer-Kestner—'since Miribel's passage here, the War Office has become a Jesuitry'—in order to gain sympathy for himself, the statement is prejudiced: there were in fact few officers in the War Office who had been educated at the Jesuit school in the Rue des Postes.

Miribel had been selected as Chief of Staff by Gambetta in 1881, a choice which brought unsympathetic comments from the Republicans in the Chamber. Freycinet, during his tenure of the War Ministry from 1888 to 1893, had brought Miribel back from command of the VI Corps at Nancy to put through the reorganisation of the Army after the reduction of the period of service from five to three years. Miribel, an indefatigable worker, was inclined to take too much on his own shoulders. As his sub-chief, he brought back with him from Nancy his chief staff officer, General Charles le Mouton de Boisdeffre, a man from an old military family.

Joseph Reinach, author of the indispensable seven-volume *Histoire l'Affaire Dreyfus*, suggests that Miribel chose Boisdeffre because he was lazy and would not interfere. Boisdeffre,[1] a tall handsome man, with stately courteous manners, had been sent to Russia in 1892 to work out with the Russian staff the terms of the military convention which was initialled by the Tsar, Alexander III, in January 1894. When Miribel died of a stroke in September 1893, Boisdeffre stepped into his shoes. Like Miribel, he was a practising Catholic. His confessor and, it is said, counsellor, was none other than the well-known Jesuit preacher, Father du Lac. His career had been very different from Mercier's. A member of the Staff Corps from his first commission, he had met no difficulties, and his rise had not been slow: five years junior to Mercier, he had reached the rank of Divisional General only 15 months after his senior. His Russian contacts had given him a taste for politics, and he hoped that one day he would succeed to the Embassy at Saint Petersburg. As Chief of Staff in 1894, his work was devoted to the redrafting of the war plan as a result of the Russian military convention, and he left the current business of the War Office to his two assistant-chiefs, Generals Renouard and Gonse, the latter of whom had been attached to him at Nancy and was a lifelong friend.

3

In the eighteen-nineties the existence of the Army revolved round the assumption of a renewal at some date of war with Germany. In the early years of the Republic there had been constant fear of another invasion, and all plans had been de-voted to the defence of the new unfortified frontier of Alsace and Lorraine. But with the late eighties the possibility of at least a counter-offensive began to take shape. Between 1887 and 1892 five new plans had been drafted. On the signature of the convention with Russia yet another plan was undertaken, to come into force in the spring of 1895.

Now, in the early nineties, when new and improved weapons

[1] Félix Faure said of him, speaking to Cambon, that he was so diffident he feared to consult any brother officer on his defence plans.

were continually appearing, it was the duty of the Intelligence branches of all the War departments in Europe to keep abreast of what their potential enemies were preparing in the way of defences, weapons, explosives, tactics and mobilisation. To this end, spies were employed, while to defend themselves against the enemy's spies counter-espionage sections were formed. In the French War Office in the Rue Saint-Dominique such a section had been created about 1876 under the cover-name of the Statistical Section. It had no relationship and no communication with the formal Intelligence branch, the Second Bureau. Its officers were unidentifiable on the War Office list, and its head communicated only with the Chief of Staff, or with his assistants.

Spy stories woven by novelists have rarely reached the level of unreality that the espionage sections of the European War Ministries rose to during these years. The strange ruffians they employed were often drawing money from two or three sources. Many of them were on familiar terms, advising each other of jobs to be done, or if need be denouncing their own sub-agents. No spy was wholly trustworthy, and thus, in an attempt to confuse the demiurges they themselves had created, counter-espionage staffs began an elaborate industry in the fabrication of false reports and misleading plans to be deliberately sold to the enemy. By 1893, so involved had the practice become in the Statistical Section, that it is doubtful if its members knew what documents were secret, which were genuine and which of the low-lived creatures they paid were in their own service or that of the enemy. Moreover the whole security system in the War Office was laughable. There appears to have been no central registry and no record of the movement of papers. In evidence before the Criminal Appeal Court Lt.-Col. Cordier, late of the Statistical Section, stated that the Staff Warrant Officer in charge of the filing had sold an old strong-box in which the purchaser found a number of secret papers. Documents of vital importance were passed from hand to hand; no one knew who had read them. The Statistical Section had no certainty as to how or when, or whence, papers reached their office. In all branches officers had documents copied for their private use and put them in their private files. Photographs were taken in the Statistical Section, but no record was kept of how many prints had been made or how they had been distributed.

The head of this somewhat amateurish section was Colonel Jean-Conrad Sandherr, an Alsatian, the son of a convert from Protestantism to Catholicism who, like so many converts, had become the hater of all subscribers to a creed other than his own. The son, who had made France his home after the annexation of his native region, had brought with him from Alsace, the one area in France where Jews formed a fairly large group, a strong anti-semitism. He had been appointed to the Section in 1886. Between 1890 and 1892 a few trials and condemnations of minor officials spying on behalf of foreign countries had roused the Chamber to ask about the disappearance of secret papers. General Loizillon, War Minister in 1893, Mercier's predecessor, had assured the Deputies that the leakage had stopped; but, on his arrival at the Rue Saint-Dominique, Mercier was dismayed to hear from Sandherr that this was not the case. That such losses, apart from certain plans of fortresses, were of serious value is doubtful; but the weakness of security precautions meant that no one could be sure what had been stolen and what merely mislaid.

By 1894 Sandherr was already showing symptoms of the disease, creeping paralysis, which was to end his career in the following year, but he was still capable of working. His senior assistant, Lt.-Col. Albert Cordier, who had joined the Section at the same time as Sandherr, was a bluff, free-spoken soldier, and also an anti-semite. But he disliked the work and only stayed in the department from his affection for Sandherr. The rest of the staff consisted of Major Henry, Captain Lauth, Captain Matton, and the filing clerk and copyist, Gribelin.

Hubert-Joseph Henry, a man in his late forties, was the dominant figure in the office. He came from the small village of Pogny on the Marne canal, a few miles south of Châlons. A peasant, he had enlisted in the Army in 1865 and made it his career. He had been commissioned from the ranks and in 1877 had somehow attracted the notice of Miribel, who took him on his personal staff. In 1879 Miribel had had Henry seconded to the Statistical Section, but the officer then in charge disliked the ranker, and in 1880 had him returned to the infantry. Posted to the 2nd Zouaves at Oran, Henry distinguished himself in the South Oran campaign, during which he was wounded and decorated. From Algeria he was sent to Indo-China, where he showed himself to be a bold and resourceful leader in the never-ending guerrilla war against the Tonkinese. When, in 1890, he returned to France, he was promoted to Major in the 120th Infantry Regiment, and employed as Town Major at Peronne. Two years later he married the daughter of a small innkeeper in his native village.

Then in January 1893, apparently through his old patron Miribel, he was once again posted to the Statistical Section. Henry possessed both the virtues and the defects of the peasant. He was at once brave and astute, but with the simple cunning of the uneducated. His bravery often turned to audacity; he was the kind of man, someone said, who should have been employed in buying cattle, an opinion confirmed by his appearance. He was a big man, bullet-headed, with a low forehead and an upturned nose above a short, heavy moustache; his eyes were small and protruding. He was ambitious, but within the limits of his capabilities; that is to say, he hoped to reach a rank which would allow him to retire with a pension, small but wealth in the poor village of Pogny. (Boisdeffre at the Rennes trial said that Miribel, in the event of war, intended to make Henry camp-commandant of G.H.Q., a position far above his rank.) In Paris he and his wife lived modestly. Like all professional soldiers he had a high regard for the service, which was probably the lodestone of his life.

At the Statistical Section his chief duties were the provision of faked documents for the counter-spies to dispose of, and the examination and, where necessary, reconstruction of such papers as were brought in by the agents. His deficiency was a total ignorance of any language other than French. Thus the German documents had to be worked on by Captain Lauth, a cavalryman, much influenced by his senior, but, like Sandherr, an Alsatian, with therefore a ready command of German. The third officer, Captain P. E. Matton, the expert on Italian documents, was on the point in 1894 of being posted elsewhere: he disliked the work and was on cold terms with Sandherr. As for Gribelin, he was altogether in Henry's pocket. In the Section there was coolness, not to say dislike, between the two senior officers who disliked the dirty police work, and the junior group who had to deal with the lowly agents and suppliers of raw materials.

When Mercier took over the War Office in 1893 he was warned by Sandherr that, apart from organisations beyond the frontiers, there existed in Paris foreign secret-service groups, and that the centres of these were the military attachés of the Triple Alliance within the immunity of their respective Embassies. The two important ones were Colonel Max von Schwartzkoppen, the German, and the Italian, Colonel Alessandro Panizzardi. Their activities were concealed from their respective ambassadors; but since each attaché corresponded directly with his own War Office, there was no occasion for Münster or Ressman to know. Münster, indeed, had sacked Schwartzkoppen's predecessor for being involved in espionage by a French administrative officer, tried in 1890, and had at that time promised the Quai d'Orsay that in future there should be no attempts to seduce French military or civil officials. Panizzardi and Schwartzkoppen worked hand in hand, often employing the same agents or alternatively sharing the spoils they bought.

To counter their activities, Sandherr had bought the services of French domestics employed in the Embassies. Among these, in the German Embassy, was a housemaid named Marie Bastian who came to the Embassy daily. Her business was to collect all the fragments of writing from the wastepaper baskets and at intervals to hand them over to a French agent. This system was conventionally known as 'the ordinary route'. It is demonstrably false for Schwartzkoppen to deny, as he does, that all documents in the Embassy were either filed or effectively destroyed. Clearly quantities of letters were thrown aside. The existence of Bastian and her bags is enough to give the lie to Schwartzkoppen. But he could not admit to so much lack of security. Once or twice a month Henry met Bastian, usually after dark, probably at the church of Ste-Clotilde, and took from her the paper bags into which she had thrust, unsorted, the fragments of Embassy correspondence. On his return home, Henry examined the pieces, separating those in French from those in other languages. The former he kept for himself, the rest he handed over to Lauth next day. Usually little of interest emerged from the bags, though the writing of the military attachés became familiar, and much of their private lives. However, enough was obtained to establish that from December 1892 someone was selling to Schwartzkoppen large-scale plans of the fortifications of the eastern frontiers of France, and that those of the Alpine frontier were being passed on to Panizzardi. Among the intercepted letters was one which opened: 'Herewith twelve large-scale plans of Nice, which that lout (*canaille*) D. has handed to me for you'. The letter was signed 'Alexandrine'. (Both attachés often used the feminine form of their Christian names for their correspondence, some-times exchanging them).[1] The letter was undated, and, since the Section was extremely casual in its work, no record was made of the date it was received.[2]

Early in January 1894, however, a crumpled and torn ball of paper bearing some notes in Schwartzkoppen's handwriting did reveal that he was now in touch with a person of greater consequence than '*ce canaille de D.*' During the following March one of Henry's creatures, a shady police-informer named Guénée, had a conversation with a somewhat seedy but well-connected retired attaché of the Spanish Embassy named Val Carlos, who had once or twice passed on minor informa-tion to the Statistical Section. Val Carlos dropped a hint that someone whom he believed to be an officer in one of the War Office departments was handing documents to a foreign power: but he had not identified him. 'If I did, I would tell you'. A

[1] The Statistical Section consulted the Foreign Office experts as to the writer of the letter. Although the content showed it to be from Schwartzkoppen, the Foreign Office for some unexplained reason, assigned it to Panizzardi. It is odd that the handwriting was apparently unrecognised. The attachés used the names *Maximilienne* and *Alexandrine*: either writer might use either name. Both of them also added a number of words and phrases conveying a sexual allusion.

[2] At the trials in 1898–99 various dates were given by Cordier and Lauth. Cordier believed it dated from 1892, Lauth from December 1893. No photo-graph was taken of it until October 1894. In any case, other evidence tended to show that D. was not an officer: he was badly paid—no more than ten francs a sheet for the large-scale plans he purveyed.

month later he again spoke to Guénée: 'There is a wolf, perhaps more than one, in your sheepfold. Look for him'. Val Carlos was not at this time in the pay of the Statistical Section, though he received occasional sums of money: it may be he was trying to be placed on their regular pay-roll, as he was by the end of the year. Guénée reported these talks to Henry. In June, this time to Henry himself, Val Carlos said that an officer, either recently or now in the Second Bureau, was informing Schwartzkoppen and Panizzardi, but he did not know his name. However, during the rest of the summer nothing further was discovered.

4

According to his own narrative, on the afternoon of 20 July 1894, Colonel von Schwartzkoppen was told that a Frenchman had come to the Embassy about a passport for Alsace, which required the permit of the Governor of the Reichsland. Since these permits were frequently refused, French officers in the circumstances were used to claiming the help of the German military attaché. As Schwartzkoppen had guessed, the visitor proved to be a French army officer in mufti, a man in the middle forties, of medium height and slight build. 'He had a lined face, a crop of grey hair, a long greying moustache, and deep-set dark eyes'. In response to Schwartzkoppen's enquiry as to his business, he said that he was financially embarrassed owing to speculations which had gone wrong and to the serious illness of his wife. His choice lay between suicide and the offer of his services to Germany. He claimed to be able to give valuable information, since he had been a member of the Second Bureau and was friendly with Sandherr. He also claimed to be a friend of the well-known Deputy for Chambéry, Jules Roche, who had promised to make him Assistant Chief of Staff if he, Roche, became Minister of War. He was at the moment stationed outside Paris, but he expected an early transfer to the capital, when he would renew his connections with the War Office.

Schwartzkoppen indignantly repulsed the offer. Ready enough as he was to buy from the riff-raff, he was horrified that a commissioned officer should offer to sell his country. He sent the man away, but the latter, remarking that he was about to go to the artillery firing camp at Châlons for some trials, said he would call again. On the following day Schwartzkoppen received a note from his visitor, and wrote an account of the interview to his chief in Berlin. He was told to pursue the matter. The doubts and repugnance he felt for this task colour the notes he made for his personal guidance, torn up and rescued from his waste-paper basket by the indefatigable and never-detected Bastian.

On the evening of 27 July the visitor returned and introduced himself as Major Count Walsin-Esterhazy, commanding a battalion of the 74th Infantry Regiment, stationed at Rouen. In earnest of this, he produced the mobilisation orders of his regiment, and demanded a salary of two thousand francs a month. As before, the embarrassed attaché tried to dissuade the man, and, having failed to do so, suggested that he should deal directly with Berlin. Esterhazy replied that the only way of doing business of this nature was by personal contact, which was less dangerous, since many people came to 78 Rue de Lille. Once more Schwartzkoppen dismissed him, but he felt that he must have personal confirmation of his orders from Berlin. Consequently he went off to Germany, and on 4 August saw the head of the German Intelligence Branch, Müller, who reiterated the original order. On his return to Paris two days later, he found a letter from Esterhazy (who, by the way, was not a count) saying that he would leave Châlons on 10 August and go to his wife's house at Dommartin-la-Planchette until the 12th. At 10 p.m. on 13 August he appeared again and told the attaché that he could let him have the recently revised General Instruction for Artillery on Mobilisation. Two days later, the 15th, he brought the document. Schwartzkoppen weakened: the Instruction was a document asked for by Berlin. He gave some money to Esterhazy, who went off saying he would shortly bring other papers.

At 6.30 p.m. on 1 September, he reappeared, bringing (a) a list of covering troops for the frontier defences, (b) a description of the new short 120-millimetre gun, (c) the provisional 'Firing Manual of Artillery in the Field'. He said he had just come back from firing exercises at the Sissonne artillery range and would report what he had picked up. This he did on 5 September, and on the following day he handed in a note on the proposed Madagascar expedition.

What Schwartzkoppen did not know, and Esterhazy neglected to let fall, was that before going to Sissonne, he had left with the concierge at the German Embassy a letter containing a list of the papers he intended to hand over.

This letter, subsequently known as the *bordereau*, or list (it will be called the *bordereau* in this narrative), reached the Statistical Section at the War Office during the last week of September.

5

On the evening of 26 September Major Henry met Bastian and took from her the two paper bags containing the usual scraps and sweepings. On reaching home he began his normal sorting of the fragments. Mme Henry went to bed, but since her husband showed no signs of following her, came back and asked him: 'Why are you working so much later than usual?' To which he answered: 'I've found some interesting stuff which I must finish to-night'. He had in front of him a letter which he showed to her. It ran:

> Without news indicating that you wish to see me, nevertheless, Sir, I send you some interesting information:
> 1. A note on the hydraulic buffer of the 120 and the way in which this gun behaves (*s'est conduite*);
> 2. A note on the covering troops (some modifications will be made under the new plan);
> 3. A note on a modification to the artillery formations;
> 4. A note about Madagascar;
> 5. The preliminary Firing Manual of the Field Artillery (14 March 1894).
>
> The last document is extremely difficult to come by and I can only have it at my disposal for very few days. The War Office has sent a limited number to the Corps, and the Corps are responsible for them. Each officer holding one must return it after manoeuvres.

If therefore you wish to take from it what interests you and then keep it for me, I will fetch it. Unless you would like me to have it copied in extenso and only send you the copy.

I am just off to manoeuvres.[1]

This letter, the *bordereau*, was written on what is known as *papier-pelure*, or onion-skin semi-transparent paper. It was not in small fragments, or crumpled, but partly torn across twice. It was unsigned and undated, and the envelope was missing. Before going to bed, Henry repaired it with the gummed transparent paper he employed for this kind of work.

On the following morning, the 27th, instead of taking his normal ride, Henry went straight to the Rue Saint-Dominique. To Gribelin, the first to come in, he said: 'Here, see what's been given me. It's pretty strong and I only hope we catch him'. Lauth also was shown the paper on arrival. The three men discussed it for a few minutes and seem to have agreed that the writer must be on the staff and a gunner. During the morning the letter was taken to Sandherr. After showing it to Matton, the only artillery officer in the Section, who also thought that a gunner must have written it, he carried it to his immediate superior, General Gonse, the junior of the two Sub-Chiefs of Staff. Gonse in turn brought it to General Renouard, the other assistant Chief of Staff, who at the moment was acting for Boisdeffre, absent on leave. Renouard went with it to General Mercier. All the officers who saw the *bordereau* on the first day unanimously agreed that it was from an officer in the War Office itself, so much, according to Lt.-Col. Roget did it 'use the language of the house'.

It was now circulated confidentially to the chiefs of all the War Office departments: all replied that they did not recognise the hand. This took some time. On 4 October the letter was photographed and prints distributed to the departmental chiefs, with a request that they should compare the writing with that of the officers serving under them. By 6 October the heads of the First, Second and Third Bureaux, as well as the Director of Artillery, General Deloye, were convinced that the

---

[1] It is now seen that these manoeuvres were not the large scale manoeuvres round Paris, but garrison exercises for reservists near Rouen. (Thomas, *L'Affaire sans Dreyfus*, pp. 101-2).

bordereau was not the work of any of their subordinates. But on
that day there rejoined the Fourth Bureau from leave the sub-
chief, Lt.-Col. Albert d'Aboville. On being shown the print by
his chief, Colonel Fabre, Aboville said that it should be easy
to run down the writer if he were in the War Office. Because of
the technical notes, he must be a gunner: Aboville himself had
been at the Bourges Arsenal in the previous January and had
been refused all details of the new 120-millimetre gun. The
writer must also be highly qualified. Further, since staff learners
were the only officers to pass through all four bureaux, only a
staff learner could offer such a variety of information. Fabre
and Aboville then examined the writing of the four or five
artillery captains who were or who had recently been attached
to their Bureau. They hit on the name of Captain Alfred
Dreyfus, an Alsatian Jew, who had passed through the First,
Second and Fourth Bureau, and was now under Colonel
Boucher in the maneouvres section of the Third.

In the Fourth Bureau this officer had not been liked. Fabre's
report at the end of December 1893 had stated that while he
was gifted and intelligent, yet from the point of view of character, conscientiousness and obedience he was not ideally
fitted to be employed on the Staff; he was inclined to be critical
of his superiors and was not the pliant servant staff-duties
required. As he later admitted, the report was based on the
reports of Aboville's predecessor, Lt.-Col. Roget, and of the
head of the railway section, Major Bertin-Mourot, since Fabre
himself had only come to the Bureau in mid-November 1893,
towards the end of Dreyfus's attachment; but Aboville, who
had known Dreyfus for some three months, said he was secretive,
inquisitive and little liked by his brother-officers. Roget's sole
complaint had been that Dreyfus, having been given a fictitious
troop-movement exercise to do, had asked to be allowed to
carry it out with two existing corps and real transport. But
Bertin-Mourot, under whose eye Dreyfus had worked, had
said that after initial enthusiasm he had become indifferent to
the dull routine work of the department. Later, at Rennes,
Fabre added that Dreyfus had not the frankness of bearing to
which the staff was accustomed; he ferreted about in corners,
took an exaggerated interest in the important parts of the

railway network, especially those on the Est Railway, and showed little interest in day-to-day business. 'In his examination before the court-martial in 1894 it appears that he said he only sought to learn; he did indeed—even too much, but he did not do his duty'.

From the point of view of Fabre and Aboville, Dreyfus was thus not a good officer. He might be the man they were looking for, but a difficulty lay in the fact that the author of the *bordereau* had said that he was just off to manoeuvres. Now, by a circular of 17 May the second-year staff learners had been told that they would do their attachment to the troops from October to December, and thus would not attend manoeuvres, which took place between July and early October. Fabre turned this— it will be remembered that the *bordereau* was not dated—by pointing to a staff ride that had been held in June. On such frail reasoning the two went to the Third Bureau and got hold of a sample of Dreyfus's handwriting. In view of their expecta- tions, it is not surprising that their suspicions were confirmed. The writing, they were convinced, was identical with that of the *bordereau*. Fabre reported to Boisdeffre, who had now come back. He was instructed to discuss the matter in strict secrecy with Gonse. Gonse, keeping Fabre with him, sent for Dreyfus's chief, Colonel Boucher, Colonel Lefort of the First Bureau, and Sandherr. As soon as Dreyfus's name was mentioned, Sandherr slapped his forehead and exclaimed: 'I ought to have thought of it'. The five men examined the papers and concluded that there was sufficient similarity between the handwritings to warrant a searching enquiry. This was reported to Boisdeffre, who sought Mercier.

6

Had Sandherr been a competent intelligence officer, certain peculiarities about the *bordereau* should have struck him. First, only one of the items offered was a printed document, No. 5, and thus could possibly be identified. Had he verified this, he would have found that the title was not the 'Firing Manual of the Field Artillery', but the 'Firing Manual of Artillery in the Field', an error no gunner was likely to make. Further, far from being difficult to procure, some three thousand copies had been distributed to formations, that is down to at least section commanders; they were not 'confidential'; their return was not required, and in some units copies had been made and put on sale at twopence apiece. Again, had Sandherr enquired of a gunner about the hydraulic buffer, he would have learned that there were two 120-millimetre guns, of which the older, a siege-gun in service for some years, had a hydraulic buffer, but that the latest, a field-gun just coming forward, had a buffer known as 'hydro-pneumatic'. No gunner would have used the word 'hydraulic' about the new gun, and moreover, no gunner would have written '*s'est conduite*' which implies human behaviour, but '*s'est comportée*'.

As to the other three documents, a thorough consideration would have raised a nice crop of conundrums, turning on the date of the writing of the *bordereau* and what the 'notes' contained.

If, as at this time was assumed, the *bordereau* was of April or May, then the note on covering troops must refer to provisional dispositions taken on 1 March. If, on the other hand, it referred to further work undertaken in June-August which would not be made known to the corps commands until 1 October, then it must be at least of September.[1]

As regards the modification of artillery formations, this might refer to the transfer of the bridging trains from the artillery to the engineers, a subject which had been thoroughly discussed in Parliament and finally made official by the Law of 20 June. On the other hand, it might refer to the new and provisional artillery march formations, which were tried out at Chalons in August. As was to be known before the end of the trial from other documents secured from the German Embassy, the German War Office was asking for these regulations to be

---

[1] The date of April seems to have been adhered to throughout the trial of 1894. Although there was some argument between Demange and du Paty de Clam, Demange let the question drop (cf. his speech at Rennes). It was not until the end of 1897 that the mistake was seen and August substituted. But since Dreyfus had known by the circular of May 17 that he, with the other second-year staff learners, would not go on manoeuvres, and thus could not have written, 'I am just off, etc.', several officers were called at Rennes in 1899 to show that the possibility still existed up to the end of August.

procured. Last, the note on Madagascar equally presented a problem, since the only work done on Madagascar before August was a purely geographical study, in no way confidential. The work on the expedition had been carried out, not in the War Office, but by an inter-services committee formed of one representative from each of the four Ministries concerned—Foreign Affairs, Navy, Colonies and War—between 5 August and 22 August, and had not yet been seen by the chief of the Operations Bureau to which Dreyfus was attached.

Finally, to the Criminal Appeal Court and the court-martial at Rennes, General Sébert declared categorically that no officer who had passed through the Polytechnic could have written in the terms and language of the *bordereau*. None of these contradictions was resolved.

Reinach thinks that Sandherr, bent on finding the culprit, allowed his anti-semitism to get the better of his judgment—he had refused to allow Dreyfus to be attached to his section—and thus became obstinate in his pursuit of this officer. It may be so: but it must be remembered that the running down of the traitor, if, as was believed, he was a member of the War Office staff, was a matter of serious urgency in view of the current work now being done on Plan XIII.[1] This is quite sufficient to account for the precipitancy with which action was taken. The fundamental error lay in ascribing to the 'notes' a value far above their intrinsic worth, but this error is excusable in that no one could know—and in fact no one ever did know—what was contained in them.

7

The suspected man, Captain Alfred Dreyfus, came from a

---

[1] *Les armées françaises dans la Grande Guerre*, I, i, Ch. 1 (1922) gives the history of the series of war plans to 1914. The signing of the Russian Treaty in 1891 led to a revision of Plan XI. The new plan, XII, envisaged an immediate offensive against Germany. This came into force in February 1892. But the initialling of the military convention in December 1893–January 1894 called for further revision. A further plan, XIII, was put in hand, which was not ready until February 1895, but in the interval there was a reorganisation of the covering troops in March 1894, which seems to have been only partially carried out before September. It was no doubt to this that the writer of the *bordereau* was referring.

Jewish family long established in Alsace, that debatable land which the Germans had annexed in 1871. Under the Treaty of Frankfürt-am-Main, French nationals could, within 18 months of the ratification of the treaty, choose the country to which they would owe allegiance, but those who preferred to remain French citizens must cross the new frontier. The Dreyfus family owned a cotton-spinning mill at Mulhouse. Like many Alsatians and Lorrainers, whether Jew or Gentile, they were passionately French, and like many Jewish families of long residence they were more French than Jewish, completely assimilated. There were four Dreyfus brothers—Jacques, Mathieu, Alfred and Léon—and three sisters. In 1871 the whole family opted for French citizenship, except Jacques and Mathieu, who remained in Mulhouse to direct the factory: in 1897 Jacques moved part of the factory over the frontier into the Territory of Belfort.

Alfred Dreyfus had been born on 19 October 1859. In 1882 he had entered the Ecole Polytechnique and later had been commissioned in the artillery. Throughout his career, until he reached the War Office, the reports of his commanding officers had been uniformly excellent; their single unfavourable comment had been the tonelessness of his voice. He had entered the Ecole Supérieure at the end of 1890, sixty-seventh in the list, and had passed out nineteenth. He was then, in January 1893, seconded as a staff learner to the War Office. In 1890 he had married Lucie Hadamard, the daughter of a Paris diamond merchant, by whom he had two children. Some years earlier he had had a liaison with a young married woman, which he had broken off in response to an appeal by her parents. Beyond this, it seems, he had two brief liaisons of no serious character in 1893 and 1894. Moreover, he was rich. At this date he had a private income of 25–30,000 francs and could look forward to inheriting at least 50,000 francs a year. Everything in his existence cried out against the probability of his being in the pay of Germany.

At the War Office he had passed his first six months in the First Bureau, his second in the Fourth, his third in the Second, and at this date he was attached to the Third. During the staff ride in June, with the other officers he had dined in Boisdeffre's mess on the last evening. Something having arisen about the new guns, Dreyfus described some recent trials at Bourges and Calais so effectively that Boisdeffre after dinner spent an hour walking up and down the Moselle bridge at Charmes in conversation with him. Dreyfus believed that he had made a friend of the Chief of Staff. As has been seen, his report from the Fourth Bureau stated that he was unsuited to staff employment. The report from the First Bureau stressed his intelligence and width of knowledge and ended: 'Desires to and should succeed'. From the Second Bureau (Intelligence) Colonel de Sancy, while praising his intellect and adaptability to the work, thought him possibly a little too sure of himself. In this Bureau, however, Sandherr had specially requested that he should not be attached to the Statistical Section. The report from the Third Bureau was not due until December, but Major Picquart, ordered to post the staff learners, had not put him in the Operations Section dealing with secret and confidential matters, but in that of manoeuvres.

Generally, it emerges from the testimony given by his brother-officers that Dreyfus was not liked. He was admitted to have an excellent brain, but he was inclined to boast. 'I thought his manners', wrote Major de Pimodan, a contemporary in the Rue Saint-Dominique, 'not very agreeable, and altogether hardly suited to our society, although I attached no importance to it'. Other officers with whom he served said he put his nose into matters which did not concern him, especially mobilisation plans, and talked about them too much. It certainly appears that Dreyfus had an extremely limited range of interests. He was ambitious and a passionate student of military affairs. He seems to have had few interests outside his family; neither literature, music, art nor sport made any appeal. His *Lettres d'un Innocent*, written from his confinement on The Devil's Island, even allowing for the exigencies of censorship, show a man of commonplace, even narrow imagination. It would seem that Dreyfus, with his ambition and self-sufficiency, possessed a simple vanity which made him show off his professional knowledge; this was in itself harmless, but, since talking shop was regarded with disfavour in the Army, it was enough to chill less ambitious men. G. W. Steevens, the English journalist who covered the Rennes trial for the *Daily Mail*, considered he had been 'bumptious'. Thus when those who had served with him were asked to give evidence, they recalled these trifles, which, in their cumulation, weighed with the judges.

Moreover, one officer (Duchâtelet, at Rennes), to whom Dreyfus had been attached for a short time, stated on oath that the accused man had suggested that they should call on a *poule de luxe*, in whose house he said he had lost a large sum of money. Another, (Lemonnier, also at Rennes), testified that Dreyfus had boasted to him of being present at German army manoeuvres in Alsace. Dreyfus denied the fact of both these things, but Jean France, a Sûreté agent present at the Rennes trial, was certain that both officers were speaking the truth, in so far that Dreyfus had made the statements. This somewhat foolish boasting by a young man, of things he had not done, took its revenge. Dreyfus was vain. He liked to display his capacity, his wide knowledge of secret and confidential topics. He talked ostentatiously of his wealth, perhaps of women. At Rennes an officer, Maistre, compared him with another, Captain Junck, 'a very unpretentious lad, very sound, who is counted one of our best. He has a family to support and a sister to coach for her degree. Obviously, compared with him, Dreyfus was on velvet'.

Reinach put this hostile evidence down to anti-semitism: that, in fact, is the theme of his history. But there is little evidence to support this thesis. Anti-semitism no doubt existed, but it cannot be shown to have played a dominant part in the arrest and trial of Dreyfus. As General Lebelin de Dionne, Commandant of the Ecole de Guerre when Dreyfus was a student, said at the Rennes trial, he did not wish the school to be a place of religious persecution, and a Christian would be sent back to his regiment for faults which in a Jew were passed over. So far as the War Office was concerned, apart from Sandherr the only two identifiable anti-semites were Major Picquart of the Third Bureau[1] and Major Cordier of the Statistical Section, both of whom were to struggle on behalf of Dreyfus. Picquart said that anti-semitism was rife in the War

---

[1] When Gallet, one of the judges, remarked that he could find no motive for the crime, Picquart replied, 'Ah! but you don't know these Mulhouse Jews'.

Office and that in consequence he had taken care to put Dreyfus in a section where he would have an unprejudiced chief,
Lt.-Col. Mercier-Milon, and also would not have to deal with
security matters. On the other hand, Leblois, the Alsatian
lawyer, and confidant of Picquart, himself as deeply involved
in the case as Picquart, remarks: 'The case appears essentially to
have been an army mistake . . . We doubt that anti-semitism
should be made responsible for the opening of the case, though
it seems likely that, at the War Office, an appeal was made to it
from the beginning, and it is certain that the case then at once
found powerful reinforcement'.

Dreyfus in his *Souvenirs et Correspondance* quotes 'one of my
comrades' on the War Office staff in 1894. 'When the Sub-
chief of staff called us in to tell us that you were guilty and that
they had certain proofs, we accepted this assurance without
discussion since we were informed by a senior officer. Thence-
forward we forgot all the qualities, the friendly relations we had
had with you, to concentrate our minds on whatever might
corroborate the certainty which had been given us'.

The darker anti-semitic shadows on the case came not from
the Army, but from the press.

Chapter Two

The Arrest

1

On 8 October Boisdeffre laid the case before Mercier. All Mercier seems to have said was that, since neither Fabre nor Aboville was a graphologist, someone competent to pronounce on the papers should be found. Boisdeffre passed this on to General Gonse, who sent for Major the Marquis du Paty de Clam of the Operations branch, said to have some technical knowledge. Du Paty was not a fool: he had passed second out of Saint-Cyr and second from the Ecole de Guerre. He was looked on as one of the brilliant officers on the Staff: recently he had been the War Office representative on the joint committee planning the Madagascar expedition. But he had a frivolous and romantic mind. A tall man, with an upturned nose, a sprouting moustache, an eyeglass, and going bald, he looked like a figure from a Viennese musical comedy. He had some taste for literature and thought the world of himself. On seeing the documents, he at once jumped to the conclusion that the hands were identical. But when Gonse warned him that the matter was one of treason he asked to be allowed to make a thorough study. Major Picquart, who was in the same branch and had had Dreyfus in his sub-section, was told to provide du Paty with all the Dreyfus handwriting he could find. On looking at the *bordereau*, Picquart remarked that the divergences between the two hands were so numerous that one could not be sure. Du Paty thought otherwise, and in his report, delivered within the next twenty-four hours, he reaffirmed his first impressions.[1]

[1] Picquart asked du Paty how Dreyfus had been paid for his treachery. Du Paty said that the Dreyfus family had been paid in the form of insurance money for a site at one of their factories in Alsace. This was later shown to be nonsense. Picquart commented that he then formed a poor opinion of du Paty's understanding, and from that moment distrusted his judgement.

Boisdeffre and Mercier were easily convinced. On this day therefore, the 9th, Mercier, at a meeting of the Cabinet, asked Guérin, Minister of Justice, if he knew a handwiriting expert. Guérin suggested the Bank of France's man, Gobert. On the 10th Mercier told the President that a letter to the German Embassy had been discovered which demonstrated the treason of a member of the War Office staff, but that the documents which had been handed to the Germans were of little moment. From the Elysée Palace Mercier then sought Dupuy at the Ministry of the Interior in the Place Beauveau. Dupuy saw at once that more was involved than the misconduct of a single officer and recommended the utmost discretion: he summoned a meeting of the four Ministers who might be concerned: those of Justice (Guérin), Interior (himself), War (Mercier) and Foreign Affairs (Hanotaux). They met on Thursday, the 11th, at the Place Beauveau. Mercier told them that the *bordereau* had been found in the wastepaper basket of the German military attaché and had been reconstituted at the War Office; he was led to believe that a Staff Officer was the culprit. But he withheld the name and merely asked for advice.

Hanotaux was never more than a second-rate Minister, a civil servant translated into politics; but his spirit of routine and his lack of character had not yet been perceived. However, he was at least conscious of the diplomatic complications which would follow the public accusation of a French officer trafficking with the German military attaché. He insisted that, without better evidence, it was impossible to open a prosecution, and anyhow it was not in the national interest to proceed: even an official investigation would be an error. Neither Dupuy nor Guérin appears to have offered opinions. Eventually Hanotaux wrung from Mercier an agreement to do nothing unless more weighty evidence was forthcoming.

At this juncture Mercier was pressed for time. During the next two days he must be at Limoges on army manoeuvres; he must then return to Paris and go off at once on other manoeuvres round Amiens on the 16th and 17th. He had Gobert, the expert, sent for, and at the same time despatched Sandherr and du Paty to the Sûreté-Générale to obtain the co-operation of the police. When Gobert arrived he was handed over to Gonse, Sandherr, Lefort, Fabre and Henry, who all drew his attention to the similarity of the handwritings in the documents. Unimpressed, he asked a few questions and made a request for a photograph of the *bordereau*. Gonse, although he knew prints had been distributed among the departments a week earlier, refused, on the ground that if the War Office produced a photograph it would be all over Paris the next day. Gobert then asked that Alphonse Bertillon, of the Préfecture of Police, should be allowed to take one. To this Gonse agreed, thus unfortunately bringing Bertillon into the enquiry.

That evening Hanotaux, who had become uneasy, called on Mercier after dinner and once more tried to persuade him to drop the enquiry. Although Mercier admitted that the most experienced and senior officer in the Army, General Saussier, Military Governor of Paris and Vice-President of the Conseil Superieur de la Guerre, was also against prosecution ('No publicity', Saussier had said: 'send him off to the colonial frontiers and see he doesn't come back'), he refused, on the ground that the treason was by now too widely known, and that 'we'—the Cabinet—'would be accused of making a pact with espionage'.

However, he left Hanotaux with the impression that nothing more than a search of the traitor's home, which had been agreed to by Dupuy, was intended. He did not reveal that he had already seen a *commissaire* from the Sûreté and had arranged for his presence at the arrest of the still unnamed accused on his return from Limoges.

With Mercier and Boisdeffre at Limoges, the enquiry was left to Gonse. He tried to hurry Gobert. Gobert asked for the name of the officer involved; the law required it. Gonse refused; but Gobert found enough evidence in du Paty's file to identify Dreyfus from the Army List. On the morning of Sunday the 14th he sent in his report. Gonse, certain in his own mind that Dreyfus was the culprit, had already arranged with du Paty to recall Dreyfus on Monday from the regiment in Paris to which he was temporarily attached, and that he should come in civilian clothes, be given a handwriting test by du Paty and, if necessary, arrested. To his chagrin, Gobert's report was negative: 'the anonymous letter could well be from some other person than the suspect'. Gobert stuck to his opinion. But in the meantime du Paty had hurriedly sent over to the Police Préfecture to ask for the assistance of Bertillon. By now all the officers who had taken part in the investigations found their own reputations involved: should Dreyfus be proved innocent, what would Boisdeffre, what would Mercier, say?

The file was hurried over to Bertillon. Bertillon was not a handwriting expert, but head of the anthropometric department for the identification of criminals. Furthermore, from what had been let fall, he believed that other evidence against Dreyfus was available. He therefore set to work under the impression that he was dealing with secondary and supporting material. Nevertheless he, like Gobert, was uncertain, and reported to this effect during the afternoon, adding, however, that the *bordereau* might be a forgery.

Mercier got back to Paris on Sunday, and in the evening saw Boisdeffre, Gonse, Sandherr, du Paty and Cochefert of the Sûreté. It was arranged that after the dictation and the subsequent arrest Dreyfus should be handed over to Major Henry to be taken to the military prison in the Rue de Cherche-Midi, and that his house would be searched. So besotted were the group that they expected an immediate confession of guilt from the prisoner, in which case he would be invited to commit suicide. However, should he not do so, Mercier planned to go forward, in spite of his promises of three days back to Dupuy, Hanotaux and Guérin. Remembering that Saussier, who also had preached discretion, was, as Military Governor of Paris, the commander of the Cherche-Midi, Mercier decided to avoid the chain of command by sending a message direct to the prison governor, Lt.-Col. Forzinetti, to the effect that a senior officer would communicate with him on the next day, and he gave orders to Aboville to instruct Forzinetti to hold the prisoner in complete secrecy but not to inform Saussier.

It may be that Mercier accepted the opinions of the seven or eight officers he had heard a great deal too readily. In any case, in view of his conversations with Hanotaux and Saussier, he acted with immense recklessness: for if the case against Dreyfus broke down—and the evidence was extremely dubious his own situation would not be improved. The Chambers would re-open on 23 October; he well knew that many members, especially those of the Army Commission, would be sharpening their knives for him, and that Dupuy would not hesitate to drop him. No doubt the conviction of a traitor would give him some kudos, but scarcely enough to weigh against his mishandling of the Army in August. In any case, the trial of the prisoner was not likely to take place before he was interpellated. He had told Hanotaux, on the evening of 11 October, that the name of the traitor was known to practically every officer in the War Office and that this would undoubtedly leak out.

Did he fear the press, which had had no mercy on him in August? Certainly his actions lend some colour to the supposition. Yet Mercier was a man of cold, almost insolent courage, who never feared to stand alone: years later he is to be found treating the press of both sides with equal disdain. From what he said to General André on the eve of the Zola trial in 1898, it is clear that at the time he was convinced of Dreyfus's guilt, although he had not himself examined the *bordereau*.

2

At the beginning of October Dreyfus had left the War Office to do his period of attachment to a regiment stationed in Paris. In accordance with the orders he had received from du Paty, he reported at 9 a.m. on 15 October to Major Picquart at the Rue Saint-Dominique.

Dreyfus was a man of medium height with broad, high shoulders. He had a prominent jaw, but except in profile his features were not Jewish. He had light hair and a light brown moustache and wore pince-nez over closely set eyes. His voice was reedy and weak.

Picquart showed him into Boisdeffre's room, where he found du Paty and three men in civilian clothes: Cochefert and his secretary and Gribelin, the archivist of the Statistical Section. Du Paty, saying Boisdeffre would come later, asked him to take down a letter for Boisdeffre's signature: du Paty had his hand bound up to demonstrate that he could not write. He then dictated to Dreyfus a letter based on the wording of the *bordereau*. After Dreyfus had written about ten lines, du Paty sharply exclaimed: 'What's the matter with you, Captain? You're trembling'. 'Not at all', Dreyfus calmly replied: 'my fingers are cold'. The dictation continued, and Dreyfus imperturbably took down the words. Again du Paty tried to provoke some evidence of disquiet, but without effect. The letter finished, du Paty rose, placed his hand on Dreyfus's shoulder and in a loud voice said: 'Captain Dreyfus, in the name of the law I arrest you; you are accused of high treason'. The victim of this masquerade stammered some words of protest. Du Paty then sat down again and, taking up the Code of Military Law, read out the article on espionage; in doing so, he deliberately uncovered beneath a file on the table a revolver. Dreyfus shouted: 'I am innocent: kill me if you want to'. Du Paty answered: 'It is not our business to do the executioner's work; it is yours'. To which Dreyfus returned: 'I shall not. I am innocent'. Cochefert and his aide then searched the prisoner. 'Take my keys', said Dreyfus: 'open everything in my house. I am innocent'. He now broke out into loud protests, claiming that he, an Alsatian, married, wealthy, could not be guilty of such a crime. He said he would have compensation for the insult, that he was the victim of a plot. Du Paty attempted to open an interrogation: 'What have you to say?' Dreyfus asked of what he was accused, and du Paty said nothing. Nor did he produce either original or print of the *bordereau*.

The interrogation was short. Du Paty hinted that there were documents, whereas there was only one, of which he refused to speak.

'Have you been on a staff ride, and when?'

'In the second fortnight of June'.

Dreyfus was then asked what documents he had had in his hands on the covering troops, Madagascar etc. He answered that the only secret document he had handled was one on covering troops. 'Have you had any contact with the artillery technical section?' 'Yes, twice'. Cochefert now took a hand, but all he got was: 'If the facts alleged against me were established, I should be a villain and a coward. I wish to live to confirm my innocence'. On this du Paty called Henry, who was waiting outside. 'Major, you have nothing to do but escort Captain Dreyfus to the Cherche-Midi'.

In the carriage on their way to the Cherche-Midi, Henry and Dreyfus talked. Dreyfus said he was accused of treason. 'The devil! Why?' 'I have no idea. I'm going mad. I'd rather put a bullet in my head. I'm not guilty. This accusation is the end of my life'. Henry comforted him. 'If you are not guilty, don't lose your head. An innocent man is always strong. You will get justice'. Dreyfus went on: 'Major du Paty told me I am accused of handing documents to a foreign power'.

'Do you know what the documents are?'

'No. Major du Paty spoke of secret and confidential documents without saying which'.

Henry expressed astonishment and suggested that Dreyfus might have enemies who had forged them. Dreyfus replied that he had no enemies capable of such hatred.

After handing the prisoner over, Henry returned to the War Office, where he wrote out a report of the dialogue, adding from his imagination that Dreyfus was making a wilfully lying statement, since from the next room he had heard du Paty mention three of the documents in the *bordereau*. (It is possible that he had mistaken the documents mentioned in the dictation for part of the charge.) The statement went unchallenged. Next day Bertin-Mourot told du Paty that in the Fourth Bureau Dreyfus had shown particular interest in the plans for mobilisation on the eastern frontier, and that in consequence, after his departure, the doors of the Bureau had been closed to him.

Immediately after the handing over of Dreyfus to Henry, du Paty, Cochefert and Gribelin went to Dreyfus's house in the Avenue du Trocadéro. They informed his wife of the arrest, but refused all information as to his whereabouts or the charge. Lucie Dreyfus wanted to telegraph for Mathieu Dreyfus. Again du Paty refused. 'A word, one single word, from you will bring about his certain ruin. The only means of saving him is silence'. The three men searched the house. They found nothing, not even a sheet of paper resembling the *papier pelure* of the *bordereau*. Everything, even his accounts, were in perfect order, and his bank-book showed a balance of four hundred thousand francs. They took away a number of papers.

When questioned by Mercier, Cochefert said his personal impression of Dreyfus's behaviour was one of guilt: this derived only from the fact that he had been told that the *bordereau* was undoubtedly Dreyfus's work, and that there was other supporting evidence. But he was shaken by the accused's refusal to use the revolver and the fact that the search of the house had revealed nothing.

Du Paty was told to prepare the War Office brief against Dreyfus. On 16 and 17 October he and Cochefert went over the 22 bundles of papers they had taken from the house in the presence of Mme Dreyfus and her mother, Mme Hadamard. Not a thing to rouse suspicion was discovered. Next day, on Mercier's orders, du Paty went to the Cherche-Midi.

Having been kept in solitary confinement for three days without any communication with the outer world, Dreyfus was on the verge of a breakdown. Forzinetti, alarmed at his condition, broke Mercier's injunction and informed his chief. Saussier told Forzinetti that but for their being old friends he would have punished him. To Mercier he repeated his earlier recommendation to hush the matter up and deal with Dreyfus on the frontiers of the Empire: a trial would only let loose the press.

Du Paty's proceedings during the examination of Dreyfus need not be examined in detail. Dreyfus was shown by faint lamplight one line of a photograph of the *bordereau*, which he failed to recognise. He was interrogated in involved sentences, of which he could no more than guess the meaning. On some days he was left in solitude, while du Paty attempted to draw evidence from Lucie Dreyfus. From neither did he secure one admission that could help the prosecution.

In the meantime Bertillon had been set to work. As he understood the case, there were other proofs against Dreyfus besides the *bordereau*. A couple of years earlier a spectacular case of forgery of a will had been cleared up after the handwriting experts had been proved wholly wrong'. With this in mind, he did not reject the theory of a plot. The handwriting of the *bordereau* and Dreyfus's were both of that commonplace sloping character which all French children were taught, but the writing of the *bordereau* was irregular. He therefore reached the conclusion that Dreyfus had produced a forgery of his own hand. This was on 20 October. Three more experts were now obtained from the Préfet of Police and were given prints of the *bordereau*. One, Pelletier, refused to talk with Bertillon, and on 25 October rejected any connection between Dreyfus's hand and the writing of the *bordereau*. The other two, Charavay and Teysonnières, were persuaded by Bertillon to accept his conclusions, though Charavay did so with considerable hesitation. These reports came in on 29 October.

By Saturday 27 October Dreyfus was so ill that Forzinetti feared for his sanity. He reported to Mercier and was summoned to the War Office, where, Mercier being busy, he was seen by Boisdeffre. Boisdeffre asked him his opinion of Dreyfus, to which Forzinetti replied that he was as innocent as himself. Boisdeffre, saying that Mercier had to be away until Monday, asked Forzinetti to do his best to keep Dreyfus going till then, when the Minister would 'get himself out of his Dreyfus case', thereby implying that he himself did not approve of what was going on. He allowed Forzinetti to send the prison doctor to Dreyfus under the seal of secrecy. That evening Mercier left Paris for Pau.

Du Paty was feeling frustrated. Turn where he might he could find no evidence. On the 27th he had been told by Boisdeffre that all he had produced amounted to nothing. He must obtain a confession by Dreyfus, otherwise Saussier might well refuse to order a prosecution. In desperation he dared to advise dropping the whole case. On Monday 29th Boisdeffre sent for him. 'Are you mad?' he said, 'Dreyfus is *canaille* and ought to be shot. It is I, your superior officer, the Chief of Staff, who tells you this. Take away this rubbish, and forward march, trot, and don't play the fool'.

On this same Monday, the *Libre Parole*, the violently anti-semitic daily edited by Drumont, ran a note: 'Is it true that a highly important arrest has been made by order of the military authorities? The person arrested seems to be accused of espionage. If the information is true, why do the military authorities maintain complete silence?' In the War Office there was consternation. Who had disobeyed Mercier's instructions?

The journalists who hurried to the Rue Saint-Dominique got the uniform reply: nothing was known.

3

If up to this point there had been hesitations as to whether the hitherto fruitless examinations of Dreyfus should continue, those hesitations were brushed aside. That evening du Paty showed the prisoner a print of the *bordereau* for the first time, and invited him to own himself the writer. Dreyfus indignantly replied: 'I never wrote this infamous letter. Some of the words are like my handwriting, but it is not mine. The letter as a whole is not like my writing; they have not even tried to imitate it'. Du Paty made him copy the *bordereau*, and the difference was so great that he did not even submit this copy to the experts.

Up to the morning of 29 October no hint of the arrest had been given to the general public. Outside the War Office and those investigating the case, it was known only to the President, Dupuy, Hanotaux and Guérin. It is unlikely that any one of the four except Hanotaux had realised what might arise out of the case. Casimir-Perier and Dupuy had both prescribed discretion to Mercier and relied on him to follow their advice. Hanotaux had also wrested a promise from the War Minister. To each of these, involved as they were in immediate and pressing problems of their own, the case was a minor matter.

Casimir-Perier had now been in office for four months. As Prime Minister he had enjoyed authority and respect. At the Elysée he was alone and found himself powerless. Ever since his election he had been attacked by the Socialist press in language as violent as that employed by Drumont against the Jews. In September Gérault-Richard had printed in the *Chambard* an article headed 'Down with Casimir!' and was now awaiting trial. From the Ministers he received little support. Hanotaux's impudence in refusing to show him Foreign Office papers was infectious. Mercier's failure to inform him before producing the blundering decree of 1 August, Dupuy's resentful neglect of him, were similar pieces of insolence. Casimir-Perier had not desired the Presidency; he had only yielded to the pressure of the conservative Republicans, and these now failed him. The fact was that he was not and had never been a Chamber politician. As President he was isolated and distressed.

Du Paty's report, handed in on 31 October, while suggesting that Dreyfus's guilt was established, left the decision as to proceedings to Mercier. The account of what had been said by the prisoner during the examinations, if not completely falsified, was sufficiently distorted to make it appear that a case could be built up. It attributed to Dreyfus a hatred of Christians. It implied that he had bought his accelerated promotion. It gave him mistresses, including a rich middle-aged Austrian. But in spite of this loading, the case was transparently thin. The central, indeed the only solid fact was the *bordereau;* here du Paty cast doubts on the credentials of the two experts who had refused to ascribe it to Dreyfus. But on the evidence which du Paty had collected, no court could convict. Mercier hesitated.

That morning the *Eclair* (of which the political editor was an ex-Communard turned Nationalist, Alphonse Humbert), had said that the man in Cherche-Midi was not a high-ranking officer and that his examination had just been completed, while in the *Patrie* Millevoye, the Boulangist, said that the traitor was a Jewish officer attached to the War Office, who had tried to sell confidential papers to Italy. Both alleged he had confessed. Mercier contented himself with sending out through Havas, the official news agency, a note to the effect that an officer was under provisional arrest, that the documents, though confidential, had little importance, and that the case would soon be cleared up—a note scarcely calculated to damp down inquisitive journalists: moreover, it was issued too late. For next day, 1 November, the *Libre Parole* headline ran: 'High Treason. Arrest of the Jewish Officer, A. Dreyfus'. The follow-up article asserted that the traitor had made a full confession, that there was ample proof he had sold 'our secrets' to Germany, that he was in the Cherche-Midi under another name. 'But the case will be hushed up because the officer is a Jew. . . . He will be allowed to find a shelter at Mulhouse, where his family resides'. At once the rest of the press was in the hunt: *Matin, Journal,*

Petit Journal and others, all had versions of the *Libre Parole* statements. The *Figaro* contented itself with suppressing the traitor's name and saying the charge was not yet clearly proved. Alone, the violent Bonapartist polemist, Paul Granier de Cassagnac, owner and editor of *L'Autorité* refused to follow Drumont's lead. 'The arrest of a French officer on the charge of high treason without serious proof would be a crime as abominable as treason itself'.

Only the four Ministers who might be officially interested in the case had heard of Dreyfus. The first intimation the other seven received was from the newspapers of 1 November. Poincaré telephoned to Dupuy, who, although it was All Saints' Day, hastily collected those members of the Cabinet he could reach. Félix Faure, Viger and Lourtice were not present. There arrived at the Place Beauveau eight irritated and perhaps alarmed men, four of whom knew nothing whatever of the case—Poincaré, Barthou, Leygues and Delcassé. They complained that they had not been informed. Hanotaux defended Dupuy on the ground of international relations. But the nub of the matter was what should be done. Like the others, Mercier had seen the *Libre Parole* and knew he must take decisive action one way or the other. He had brought to the Place Beauveau a print of the *bordereau*. This he laid before his colleagues and explained its significance, or rather the significance dictated to him by his own interpretation. He told them that Dreyfus was undoubtedly the writer, that he alone could have had access to the five documents, that only he could have taken them, and that therefore only he could have sold them. He went on to say that the dictation test supported this view, and that at it Dreyfus had shown his feelings. The motive was disappointed ambition. He offered no other document than the *bordereau*.

There was no reason for the Ministers to suspect Mercier's good faith. Thus deceived by the unambiguity of his statement, they unanimously voted that the prosecution should be undertaken; even Hanotaux, who had foreseen the diplomatic consequences. Dupuy took Mercier over to the Elysée to explain the case to Casimir-Perier, who had no *locus standi* at an informal Cabinet meeting. The case was then sent to Saussier, as Military Governor of Paris, the executive authority, who in turn communicated the matter to the *rapporteur* of the First (standing) Court-Martial of the Paris garrison, Major Bexon d'Ormeschville (3 November).

4

On 31 October du Paty had at last granted Mme Dreyfus's plea to be allowed to inform her brother-in-law at Mulhouse. Mathieu Dreyfus, though ignorant of what had happened, arrived the next day. Naturally he was overwhelmed, indignant and full of misgivings that a great error had been made. He arranged for du Paty to meet him at Alfred's house. Du Paty appears to have indulged his mania for pompous dramatics. Mathieu asked that he might be permitted to see his brother on any conditions: 'If in a moment of madness he has committed an imprudence, he will tell me all, and I will put the pistol into his hand'. Du Paty cried: 'Never, never, never. One single word, and it would be war, a European war'. So Alfred Dreyfus was left in solitary confinement.

During November the press raged. The most fantastic stories were built up by the imaginations of journalists, particularly in the *Libre Parole, l'Intransigeant*, by Judet in the *Petit Journal*, by Barrès in the *Cocarde*, and by the Augustin Fathers of the Assumption in their organ *La Croix*[1]. Quite false but fully detailed accounts were given of the papers the traitor had sold: the Alpine fortifications, the complete mobilisation scheme. Every possible reason was found for his action: he hated France; he was not really rich, but took money either from Germany or else from wealthy Jews like the Rothschilds who wanted the ruin of France. It would be tedious to enlarge on these fantasies. But one note was struck again and again by Drumont—the note for Mercier to hear: again and again it was hinted that Mercier was sold to the Jews and that the case would be hushed up. And

---

The Assumptionists 'were: scarcely intellectuals of the calibre of the Dominicans or Jesuits, having been recruited in the main from the sons of peasants, but they understood what they were about. *La Croix* was orthodox, clerical, narrow, suspicious, exaggerated and violent: but its conscienceless brutality was effective'. (R.P. Lecanuet: *L'Eglise de France sous la Troisième République*). Their paper had an enormous circulation in the provinces.

lest he should seek the support of the Right in the Chamber and
Senate, they too were threatened, particularly those on the
boards of companies.

5

As the news leaked out and the uproar of the press rose,
Schwartzkoppen was at first alarmed, but the headlines of the
Libre Parole on 1 November, naming Dreyfus, relieved him of
anxiety; he was, however, puzzled by the press statement that
the accused had made a full confession. So, too, was Panizzardi,
since the majority of the newspapers said that Dreyfus was in
the pay of Italy. Both attachés took it that Dreyfus had been in
direct touch with their own War Offices. Panizzardi wrote to
Rome assuring the Italian military authorities that neither he
nor his German colleague knew anything of the prisoner. On
2 November he telegraphed in cipher: 'If Captain Dreyfus has
not had relations with you, it would be well to order the Ambassador to publish an official denial, in order to avoid press
comment'. The Italian War Office replied on the same day that
it had had neither direct nor indirect contact with Dreyfus. At
the same time the German War Office circulated an enquiry
among its military attachés, all of whom replied that hitherto
they had never heard of Dreyfus. Both War Offices were bewildered by the allegations. Schwartzkoppen and Panizzardi,
with perfect honesty, assured their ambassadors of their
ignorance of the prisoner.

The Panizzardi telegram of 2 November was intercepted
by the French Post Office, and a copy sent to the Foreign Office.
The cipher, a new one, had to be broken down. At the first trial
the only certain word was 'Dreyfus'. Eventually the first part
of the text was unravelled, but for the phrase 'to avoid press
comment' the Foreign Office version read 'our messenger
warned'; the decipherer admitted that this reading was doubtful, and Sandherr, who apparently was waiting eagerly beside
the decipherer, was expressly cautioned. He took this version
away to show Mercier, Gonse and Boisdeffre, to whom, according to Boisdeffre, he said: 'Well, General, here's another proof
of Dreyfus's guilt'. Before returning them to the Foreign Office,

Sandherr made Henry take copies of the telegram in cipher and of the doubtful translation. Within a week the correct reading was discovered, and handed to Sandherr. He ignored it. Hanotaux also saw the final text, though he naturally attached no significance to it.

The German Ambassador, Graf von Münster, an old-fashioned aristrocrat, who had not feared Bismarck, and who hated spying, soon saw that some of the press were now claiming Germany as the traitor's paymaster. On 10 November he published an official denial in the *Figaro*, stating categorically that Schwartzkoppen had never had relations with Dreyfus, nor had ever received a letter from him. Two days later the Italians published a similar denial, as did the Austrians. The journalists treated the denials as lies. From Berlin the Chancellor Hohenlohe ordered Münster to repeat the denial to Hanotaux. Münster obeyed, once during an informal conversation, once officially. As Reinach says, 'A more intelligent man than Hanotaux, one less exclusively preoccupied with himself, knowing as he did the fragility of the proofs against Dreyfus, Dreyfus's protests, and the impossibility of discovering a motive for the crime, would have seen light in the darkness'. But Hanotaux was not acute and was obsessed with form. The case was one for justice, and therefore, as a politician, remembering the doctrine of the separation of powers between the judiciary and the executive, he forbore to pry into the evidence. The file of evidence was never brought before the Cabinet, and he never asked to see it. With perhaps even greater nonchalance, he no more mentioned Münster's *démarche* to Casimir-Perier, who constitutionally and by long custom should have been informed of what Münster had said. Nevertheless he told his fellow-Ministers, but they wholly failed to appreciate the denials of the ambassador. They believed that, if he were not lying, the relations between Schwartzkoppen and Dreyfus were simply unknown to him.

Behind the scenes, the officers working on the case in the Rue Saint-Dominique had seen more clearly than the Minister of War that the prosecution's case, based solely on the *bordereau*, would be torn in shreds by a competent lawyer, and that further evidence must be found. Moreover the complete absence of motive must somehow be explained. Du Paty took it on himself to guide the *rapporteur*,[1] Bexon d'Ormeschville, and influence his presentation. Henry set on his agent Guénée to build up evidence of the prisoner's bad character. Guénée, recklessly seeking the very common name of Dreyfus among the low haunts of Paris, soon returned with information of a Dreyfus, an habitué of gambling dens, a pursuer of women of the *demi-monde*. The Préfet of Police, Lépine, who had also set enquiries on foot, at once recognised a confusion of identity, and officially informed Henry that Dreyfus neither gambled nor whored. Lépine's notes were not put into the record; Guénée's were.

Ormeschville, faced by the blank denials of Dreyfus, turned to his brother-officers for evidence of character. Even this was unsatisfactory. While Fabre, Aboville, Bertin and others gave more or less hostile evidence, a number of officers from other departments testified in his favour, or at least declared that nothing about him would lead them to foresee treason. All that remained were the contradictory reports of the handwriting experts, and Henry's tale of what he had heard through the door. By 12 November the case for the prosecution was crumbling. Sandherr ordered Henry to go through the Section's files and bring him such documents as might bear on the case. Henry found what he could—eight or nine pieces, he said later. Sandherr and Cordier went over them. There was the *canaille de D* letter of January, which Cordier believed to be 'an antique'; it amounted to very little, but since there was an initial, it might as well go in. The rest offered even less: 'All the dead heads in the files', said Cordier. They eventually made up weight with a letter from Panizzardi, warning Schwartzkoppen not to let Colonel Davignon, the War Office spokesman, know that the two attachés had any connection; 'one must never let it be seen that one agent deals with another'. There was a

---

[1] The *rapporteur* of a military court-martial had the equivalent function of the *juge d'instruction*, the examining magistrate, in civil criminal trials. Up to the Law of 8 December 1897 (i.e. three years later) the suspect was without legal assistance, nor could he even be present at the hearing of witnesses. The task of the magistrate was to build up the case, and this he often carried out to the prejudice of the prisoner.

report from Henry of his conversation with Val Carlos in June. There were the remains of a torn and crumpled ball of paper from Schwartzkoppen's wastepaper basket with notes for a letter. This last, which was in German, ran: 'Doubt—Proofs—Authority. Dangerous situation for me, relations with a French officer. To bring what he has. Absolute (word partly missing) Bureau de Renseignements [in French]. No relation with the troops. Importance only in coming from the Ministry. Already somewhere else'. This note had reached the War Office in late December or early January. Dreyfus had only come to the Second Bureau on 1 January.

On 6 November Mercier's troubles with the Chamber began. The Chamber Army Commission unanimously found that he had acted unwisely, and by a majority that he had exceeded his powers. In the full Chamber he underwent bitter criticism from Le Herissé, deputy for Rennes, a retired officer. Mercier's reply was heard in silence, and Dupuy, to save his Minister, accepted a 'pure and simple' passage to the order of the day.

A week later, on 13 November, Boisdeffre left Paris to represent France in Russia at the funeral of Alexander III and to be present at the marriage of his successor, Nicholas II. He did not return until 30 November.

6

Ormeschville's interrogatory went slowly on. Prompted by du Paty, he accepted every witness he could find: the evidence of those against Dreyfus he included, that of those who spoke in his favour, so far as he could, he omitted. But the slowness of the proceedings irked the journalists. Cassagnac, for all his anti-semitism, dared to say that the evidence rested on a single contested document, and that he was not happy to see the shooting of a French officer on the word of actors professing to be experts in handwriting. Mercier felt he must reply. On 28 November an interview with the War Minister was printed in *Figaro*, in which he asserted that from the first day there were crying proofs against Dreyfus: that it was neither Italy nor Austria to whom the papers had been offered; and that the only missing piece in the puzzle was whether Dreyfus had been paid. A few deputies, a few editors, voiced their astonishment that Mercier should dare to publicise his views before the trial. Dupuy was even roused to tackle him. Mercier blandly denied that he had given the interview. The correspondent of *Figaro* was content to reaffirm all he had printed and to say that the General had said a good deal more. Five years later Mercier admitted the interview.

Münster read the interview and saw that by implication his own Embassy was the one involved, and that a responsible Minister had made the accusation. He once more protested to Hanotaux, who tried to placate him by sending a note to Havas that no foreign Embassy or Legation was involved. The War Office, knowing that the *bordereau* had in fact come from the German Embassy, were convinced the Ambassador was either lying or being deceived. The quicker journalists replied that of course Dreyfus's correspondent was the German military attaché in Brussels. William II, irritated that the good faith of his Minister was questioned, ordered Münster to protest more strongly. Münster, sick in bed, asked Hanotaux to call. Drumont at once pounced on Hanotaux as the lackey of Germany and said that the case would be hushed up. Barrès went so far as to say that Dreyfus would be decorated—he would be, but not for many years. The German press retorted acidly on the French idea of diplomatic conventions. The *Libre Parole* stated that one letter had been found among the papers of a military attaché of the Triple Alliance which overwhelmed Dreyfus, but it was so important that it would be suppressed. It followed this by claiming that the letter had indeed been suppressed, but that Mercier had a photograph of it.

This romance went on for several days and included an allegation that two vital letters had been returned to the Ambassador. (In these fantasies are to be observed the embryo of the story that the Kaiser had written to Münster about Dreyfus, and that Dreyfus had been writing directly to the Emperor.) Hanotaux, seeing his worst forebodings fulfilled, protested to Dupuy. Dupuy said that he found the Minister of War highly elusive and could never get to the bottom of things. On 13 December Hanotaux took to his bed, leaving another note for Havas to the effect that no documents had been handed back to the German Ambassador, and that Münster had done no more than protest against the allegations involving his Embassy.

7

Meanwhile du Paty, instructed by Sandherr, had been working on the documents Sandherr had selected from the Section files. After long study he presented a commentary intended to show the connection between three of the documents and the *bordereau*. In this he identified Schwartzkoppen as the purchaser of the plans from the *canaille de D*. He interpreted Panizzardi's letter to Schwartzkoppen about Davignon as showing that the German had a friend in the War Office who was also his agent. He interpreted the Schwartzkoppen fragment 'Doubt, Proofs' to mean that the German attaché had become involved in January with an officer who was important because he belonged to the Intelligence Bureau. This commentary he gave to Sandherr, who had a fair copy made.

The commentary was in fact a feat of wilful romancing, a highly ingenious, almost unintelligible rigmarole, though it is fair to say that du Paty never committed himself to the statement that Dreyfus was D, or that he was the traitor; he merely said that he could be. Sandherr obviously saw that in this form the commentary was useless, since none of the judges would be able to understand it. As Davignon, by then a general, exclaimed on being shown it during the final revision of 1904: 'I can't make head or tail of this nonsense; it's so complex and complicated that it's beyond my understanding'. Sandherr decided to discard it, and handed back to du Paty his original telling him to keep it; he might one day need it as protection.

Someone, almost certainly Sandherr himself—who else could it have been?—then set to work to produce a group of documents of sufficient weight to convince the judges. It was in two parts: one, several original documents; the other, a biographical notice giving an account of all Dreyfus's treasonable activities. What we know of the contents of this file comes from the evidence of Captain Freystaetter, one of the judges at the court-martial of 1894, which he gave at the Rennes court-martial of 1899. It contained, he said, the *canaille de D*, and

Davignon letters, and a biographical notice. He also remembered reading the words 'Dreyfus arrested, our messenger warned', and possibly also 'precautions taken'. The biographical notice appears to have stated that Dreyfus began his career as a spy at the Explosives School at Bourges in 1890. While he was there, a charred paper was found of instructions on the filling of shells with melinite; only two hundred copies had been issued. Dreyfus was alleged to have been copying it but failed to get rid of the original. Then, in 1894, the Statistical Section had got hold of part of the Ecole de Guerre course on the defences of Lyon copied out in the hand of a supernumerary attaché at the German Embassy. Dreyfus had been at the school from 1890 to 1892. The date was unimportant; Dreyfus had sold the information.

Freystaetter's memory in 1899 was not perfect; he was not sure as to the identity of the documents, but he was certain as to the allegations against Dreyfus. Until 1898 he had wholly believed in the guilt of Dreyfus. A highly honourable man, he had certainly not been prompted by anyone: he had no interest in falsifying his testimony and he could not have known any of of these points except from the file submitted to the judges of 1894.

Sandherr had the biographical notice copied out and the file put together. At the Rennes trial Mercier said that he saw and approved the biographical notice, which he had had made for his personal use. It was agreed at Rennes by three other of the first court-martial judges that the *canaille de D* letter was also with it, probably the Davignon letter. As for the Panizzardi telegram, either the first erroneous version (with the invented addition: 'precautions taken') was included in the file, or its content was written into the biographical notice. Mercier at Rennes denied this, but Freystaetter was immovable that somewhere during the court-martial he had read the words 'Dreyfus arrested'.

It seems that Mercier took this new file into his private keeping and put it in the safe of his private office, where it remained until it was brought out on 22 December. The contents then, in the presence of Mercier and Boisdeffre, were put by Sandherr into an envelope, which was sealed and given to du Paty to carry to the president of the court-martial.

That Sandherr was the author of the biographical notice seems incontestable. Mercier had obviously neither the knowledge nor the time to compile it. It is unlikely that it was Henry, as yet a minor figure in the case. It was certainly not du Paty, who did not see the document until 1897. Except for Henry, Sandherr alone knew all the papers. Furthermore, leaving aside both his anti-semitism and the fact that his professional *amour-propre* as head of the Section required the conviction of the prisoner, there is that cry uttered when Fabre first suggested Dreyfus by name: 'I ought to have thought of it'. More weighty are two further facts. First: he had handed back to du Paty the draft commentary with the hint that he should keep it as 'protection', a hint repeated in January that he, du Paty, might have to suffer heavy attacks. The second, after the verdict he did not obey Mercier's order to break up the file and return each piece to its original folder; he did not, as he knew Mercier had done, destroy his own copy of the biographical notice. This disobedience by a senior officer suggests that he, too, felt that he might later need 'protection'.[1]

[1] The various files should be distinguished. First, there is the judicial file, containing only Ormeschville's report and the original of the *bordereau*, which was sealed up in December 1894. Next there is the Secret or Little File, which contained the biographical notice and its accompanying documents in one part, and various other unused pieces, e.g. the Schwartz-koppen memo ('Doubt, Proofs') and photographs of the *bordereau* in another. Thirdly there is the Ultra-secret File referred to by Henry at the Zola trial, which nobody ever saw, which was supposed to hold the letter from Alsace identifying Dreyfus as the spy, and possibly the mythical letters from the Kaiser. This file probably never existed. The Secret or Little File was intact when Picquart saw it in August 1896. Thereafter it seems to have been monkeyed about with by a number of people, Henry, Gonse, Roget, Cuignet until it was swollen to nearly four hundred exhibits.

Chapter Three

The Verdict and Sentence

1

Bexon d'Ormeschville completed his report on 3 December. He identified all the papers on the *bordereau* as being secret or confidential documents, which must have been known to Dreyfus, while the evidence of his colleagues, coupled with his knowledge of several languages, 'notably German', showed him to be of the spy type: everything pointed to his guilt. Prompted by du Paty, he omitted everything favourable to the prisoner. He threw doubt on Gobert's motives and on Pelletier's capacity. This report he presented to General Saussier, and next day the military Governor issued orders for the summoning of a court-martial.

Mathieu Dreyfus had hitherto been able to do litle. He, asked the most eminent barrister in Paris, Waldeck-Rtousseau to undertake the defence. Waldeck had given up criminal practice; his last appearance of this kind had been in defence of Eiffel in the Panama Company proceedings early in 1893. He recommended Edgar Demange, a barrister of fifty-three, bred in the highest traditions of the law, a believing and practising Catholic, who had behind him a long series of brilliant defences in criminal actions. Demange agreed to undertake the defence if, after seeing Dreyfus and reading the indictment, he believed him innocent. On 5 December he saw Dreyfus and went over the documents. They were not many: a *copy* (*not* a photograph) of the *bordereau*, the reports of the experts, of du Paty and Ormeschville, with the statements of the witnesses. He at once perceived the hollowness of the case. He also saw no less clearly the odium and insults he would incur for his boldness in defending a Jewish traitor. He accepted the brief.

On 13 December Mathieu and Léon Dreyfus at last obtained

an interview with Sandherr. The conversation displayed Sandherr as determined to do nothing whatever to assist the defence.
He wilfully misunderstood what Mathieu said, or replied that
he did not know the answer. They asked him about the trial
in camera. Sandherr said that it was a matter for the court only.
Du Paty, said Mathieu, was treating Alfred abominably;
Sandherr rejoined that he knew no more honourable officer.
When Mathieu said that they would do everything to discover
the real traitor, and that their fortune was at Sandherr's
disposal if he was able to help them, Sandherr took them up
sharply and insinuated that they were trying to bribe him. And
when finally they said: 'We will find the traitor. Can you help
us?' Sandherr coldly answered: 'I can do nothing, and I do not
see how you could find this, according to you, other traitor.
Believe me, if your brother has been arrested, it is because a
long and serious investigation was made before a decision was
reached. And then, to carry out your vindication, you would
have to be installed in the War Office, have the Minister and all
the officers at your disposal etc. That does not seem to me very
practical'. Fortunately for Mathieu, Sandherr wrote down the
gist of the conversation that day, guaranteeing its exactitude;
but talking to friends during the next months, he left them with
the impression that Mathieu had attempted to bribe him.

Reinach alleges that Mercier did not dare allow a public
trial, since the emptiness of Ormeschville's report would cry
aloud. But, since some of the documents on the *bordereau* dealt
with secret matters, which must be explained to the court—for
example, that on covering troops—normal security reasons are
equally probable, so that as in all spy cases the trial would be
held *in camera*. Mercier could not order a secret trial: that was
the prerogative of the judges. Nevertheless, the knowledge that
the Minister desired a closed hearing would, if conveyed to the
president of the court, be tantamount to an order. The Dreyfus
family were aware of the danger. Demange asked Waldeck-
Rousseau to approach Casimir-Perier.

Joseph Reinach was the most prominent Jew in the Chamber.
He had been the head of Gambetta's secretariat, and for a time
owner and director of the Gambettist *République Française*, which
had now been acquired by Méline. He had the misfortune to be

the nephew and son-in-law of the luckless crook, the Baron de Reinach of Panama notoriety. 'He [Joseph] was a blatant, domineering, loud-voiced French Jew, yet with the accent on the French. . . . The Reinachs, though very Jewish, were even more French: and Frenchmen, notwithstanding their dislike of Jewishness *per se*, recognised in Joseph Reinach a devotion to France equal to their own. This was the secret of his personal influence. For him the Affair was not solely or even primarily a Jewish concern: it was a fight for principles he believed essential to save Republican, Revolutionary, Democratic France from the clutches of Reaction.' (So Wickham Steed to the author.) And a further point, Dreyfus was the first Jew ever to have been admitted to the War Office, and was therefore, for his co-religionists, an important figure in the fight against Drumont's anti-semitism.[1] Reinach himself had a deep interest in military matters; as a reserve officer he had served on the staff of Galliffet, perhaps the best senior officer in the Army in the nineties, and a thorough Republican.

From the abnormal volatility of the anti-semitic press he had guessed that the evidence against Dreyfus was doubtful. He, too, feared a trial *in camera*, and also sought Casimir-Perier. To him and to Demange the President said he would pass on their appeal, but that he himself was constitutionally powerless. Reinach also appealed to Mercier, who coldly refused him. The press broke out into a confused and virulent debate: on the one side, those who feared involving Germany and increasing the risk of war, on the other those who knew Mercier wanted the trial to be secret. The Cabinet stood aside and let Mercier have his way.

2

The trial opened on 19 December in an old building across the street from the Cherche-Midi. After the announcement that it was almost certain there would be no public audience, there were few sightseers. The judges were Colonel Maurel, Lt.-Col. Echemann, Majors Gallet, Florentin and Patron, Captains

[1] On 6 November the *Libre Parole* stated that Joseph Reinach had, through Freycinet, forced Dreyfus on the War Office.

Roche and Freystaetter; all, except Gallet, who was a cavalryman, were infantry officers, Freystaetter of the Marines. There
was no gunner member.

As soon as the accused had answered to his name, the military
prosecutor, Major Brisset, asked the case to be held *in camera* on
the grounds of public policy. Demange protested that since the
case rested on a single document . . . He was cut short by Maurel
who requested him not to speak of a single document, and continued to prevent him from stating his argument. 'The interests
of the defence . . .' said Demange. 'There are other interests than
those of the defence and the accusation laid in this case', returned Maurel. Demange's mouth was closed. The judges
retired, read his written submission against the closed court
and rejected it. The court was closed: there remained only the
judges and the three judges in waiting, the military prosecutor,
the prisoner and his counsel, Lépine, Préfet of Police, and Major
Picquart of the Third Bureau, detailed by Boisdeffre to report
to him on the progress of the trial.

The Ormeschville report was gone over and Dreyfus replied
in his usual toneless voice to the questions, with all the respect
that an officer should show to his seniors. He protested against
the charge of treason. His denials of precise statements were
heard with indifference: if the statement was inaccurate, Major
Brisset might nonchalantly suggest that its accuracy was
unimportant: when he denied possessing any knowledge of
changes in artillery formations the president rejoined that a
gunner could not help but be interested. The examination was
short. During the rest of the day and on the next two the witnesses were heard: Gonse, Henry, du Paty, with seventeen
officers called by the prosecution, Cochefert and the handwriting experts. For Dreyfus, the Chief Rabbi of Paris, a few
friends and half a dozen officers, honourably risking their
reputations, took the stand. One witness—Lt.-Col. Jeannel, who
had lent Dreyfus the artillery manual—was not called, in spite
of the prisoner's request.

Gonse in evidence did his utmost to discredit the good faith
of Gobert, who had refused to identify the writing of Dreyfus
with that of the *bordereau*. It was pointed out that information
about the covering troops was known to the copying clerks in

the Ministry as well as to the officers: the point made no impression. Henry gave his version of the dictation scene and the subsequent interchanges. Du Paty gave his own account of the day of the arrest, asserting once more that Dreyfus had trembled when he heard the phrase about the hydraulic buffer. Demange offered him the piece of writing, and du Paty had to admit that it showed no signs of agitation: but of course Dreyfus had been warned. By whom? He did not know. He was again confounded over the question of the date of the *bordereau*: if it was of April, as was alleged, then Dreyfus could not have had information available only in July, while if the *bordereau* was after July, then he could not, in view of the 17 May circular, have written that he was just going on manoeuvres.

At the end of the second day the judges were shaken in their original belief in the prisoner's guilt. While they had been told that Mercier and Boisdeffre were convinced, the evidence was thin; it proved nothing. Picquart, reporting to Boisdeffre, said that if he did not know of the Secret File he would be very doubtful. Lépine thought acquittal probable. So too did Henry.

Henry had no illusions. Headquarters needed the conviction of a spy; so did the Statistical Section. In his thirty years' service he had seen much of the peculiarities of military justice. It was no matter to him who was condemned, so long as some-one was. He was unscrupulous, and he was bold. He asked to be recalled.

In the box he told the judges that long before the arrival of the *bordereau* the Section had suspected a traitor in the War Office. They had had warnings from a man of honour as early as February. This man repeated his warnings in March that the traitor was a member of the Second Bureau. 'And there is the traitor!' Dreyfus and Demange both loudly demanded the name of this informant, that he might be called. Henry replied brutally: 'There are secrets in an officer's head which even his cap mustn't know'. Maurel weakly intervened: 'You are not asked the name, but tell us on your honour whether this individual told you that the officer-betrayer was in the Second Bureau and was Captain Dreyfus'. Henry raised his hand and in a loud voice cried: 'I swear it'.

Four experts were heard on the second day, two for, two

against; on the third morning, Bertillon. He had evolved a system largely based on his own method of measuring the heads of criminals. It was complex and needed a lot of explanation with the aid of diagrams and blackboards. The court heard him through for an hour, stunned by his unintelligible verbosity. All they understood was that Bertillon believed that Dreyfus had forged the *bordereau* in a mixture of his own hand and those of his wife and brother.

By the end of the third morning the opinions of the judges were still wavering. Henry had made an impression, yet the material proofs were still absent, and no one had been able to divine any motive for the crime.

After lunch the prosecutor made a laconic speech, which Lépine thought empty of facts. Demange for the defence spoke for three hours, attacking the only substantial evidence he knew of, the *bordereau*. His policy as he saw it was to raise doubts in the minds of the court, and these doubts were already there. But, as someone in the court said, 'He had not the trick of courts-martial'; he talked to them as he would to High Court judges. Brisset in his reply abandoned all attempts to show motive and relied solely on the single document.

At the luncheon interval du Paty approached Maurel and handed him the sealed envelope he had received from Sandherr. At the conclusion of the speeches the court retired. Maurel, who was a sick man—it is said he was suffering from piles—produced the envelope he had been given by du Paty and broke the seals. The members of the court were not versed in procedure; they did not know that the production of documents not shown to the defence was irregular and illegal in both civil and military law: they relied on their president, who himself relied on the Minister of War. The first document was the biographical notice of Dreyfus. Maurel discussed this, and then, feeling very ill, contented himself with passing round the other papers. The officers examined them and were convinced that they had before them an arch-spy. Although hitherto they had believed that only Germany was involved, now they saw that Italy too was in the game. They saw that the War Office believed in the prisoner's guilt, and they saw too that these documents could not have been shown in public. On the question of motive they were still bewildered; but Henry's evidence and the *canaille de D* letter seemed overwhelming in the light of the biography dating back four years. Each member voted Guilty. Neither president nor judges were required to support their verdict by a reasoned judgement. The death penalty for political crimes had been abolished by Article 5 of the Constitution of 1848. They therefore sentenced Dreyfus to deportation for life to a fortified place, to forfeiture of his rank and to degradation. It was the heaviest sentence they could give.

According to military law, Dreyfus was not present at the delivery of the verdict and sentence. Demange when he heard it burst into tears. He at once went to the room where the prisoner was kept and still weeping embraced him, unable to speak. A few minutes later the prosecutor appeared and read the sentence, adding that the prisoner had twenty-four hours to lodge an appeal if he desired. On his return to his cell Dreyfus gave himself up to despair, and tried to beat his brains out against the wall. He begged Forzinetti to give him a revolver that he might commit suicide. Forzinetti, still believing in his prisoner's innocence, refused. That night he came to Dreyfus again and again, telling him that it was cowardice to accept defeat and that suicide would only confirm the verdict. His reward was a promise to survive and wait for justice to be done.

3

When the court rose, Picquart reported to Mercier and Boisdeffre. Mercier made no comment: Boisdeffre remarked that he would dine more peacefully. Before he left the courtroom, Maurel had put the documents back in the envelope and handed it to du Paty to take to Sandherr.

The press, whether for or against the trial *in camera*, welcomed the verdict. The unanimity of the judges swept away all doubts: no one imagined the possibility of the illegality of the proceedings. Liberal public opinion was reassured. The Socialists joined in the chorus of approval. Even the most bitter critics of Mercier were convinced: a volley of insult was fired at the traitor. The anti-semites shouted for the expulsion of the Jews. Mercier's reputation was no longer in danger; he had saved

France from betrayal. The single regret was that the traitor could not be shot.

On 24 December Mercier tabled a bill to re-establish the death penalty for treason and espionage; included in the text was an article which made it practically impossible for the press to discuss Army affairs. The restoration of the death penalty was at least equitable since a mutinous, even an insubordinate, soldier could in certain circumstances be shot in peacetime: a conscript had recently suffered the extreme penalty for throwing a button from his tunic at the president of a court-martial.

On 31 December the revising court rejected Dreyfus's appeal. Since they could not deal with matters of fact, only with matters of law, which so far as was known had not been mishandled, there was no case. By now Dreyfus had recovered his strength of mind: he wrote to his wife that he would face punishment with the dignity of a clear and calm conscience. He had other trials to endure. On the same day, Mercier, knowing how near-run the verdict had been, sent du Paty to offer him certain alleviations: a choice of prison, the presence of his wife and children, if he would confess, confess almost anything in confirmation of the verdict. The conversation between the two men was peculiar: du Paty, shaken by Dreyfus's unfailing denials of guilt, but holding to what he had taken to be circumstantial evidence, appears to have tried to make the prisoner admit that he had handed over important documents to Schwartzkoppen to get in return information useful to France. Dreyfus stubbornly maintained that the traitor was another man, and that it was the duty of the War Office to discover him. At the end he told du Paty that it was his duty to pursue the investigations. 'If you are innocent', cried du Paty, 'you are the greatest martyr in history'. 'Yes, I am a martyr, and I hope the future will prove it. Search'.

Du Paty regretfully reported to Mercier that the prisoner was adamant. His report was left in the Minister's private office: in due course it vanished, to be replaced by a more politic account written in September 1897. Dreyfus wrote a full account of the meeting for Demange. On the same day he wrote to Mercier that he did not ask for mercy, but that in the name of his honour he begged that investigations into the identity of the culprit should be pursued. Mercier, enraged, persuaded the Cabinet that the hardened traitor should be sent, not to the Ducos peninsula in New Caledonia but to The Devil's Island, a leper settlement which was just being cleared to accommodate criminals, off the Guiana coast.

On 2 January Lucie Dreyfus was at last permitted to see her husband at the Cherche-Midi behind a double grill. The interview so harrowed Forzinetti that he persuaded Saussier to allow them to meet in his private office. They saw each other again two days later, and so far as they could comforted each other. 'For you and the children', he said, 'I shall submit to to-morrow's Calvary'—the public degradation.

4

Mercier had desired that the degradation should take place at Vincennes or Longchamps, in order to bring together as many people as possible: the Cabinet, not wishing a mob demonstration, decided for one of the courts of the Ecole Militaire. Though crowds gathered in the streets, only a few favoured journalists were given permission to watch the spectacle.

Dreyfus was brought from the Cherche-Midi, handcuffed, in the charge of Captain Charles Lebrun-Renaud of the Republican Guard. At the School he was put into a small room and kept waiting for an hour. Asked by Lebrun-Renaud why he had not committed suicide, he told the whole story so far as he knew it, and added that the Minister of War knew he was innocent; he had even sent Major du Paty de Clam to him in prison to ask if he had not handed over an unimportant paper in order to obtain others in exchange. At length his escort came. The courtyard into which he was marched was filled with detachments from each of the regiments of the Paris garrison. The parade was brought to attention; the drums rolled. Dreyfus was led before General Darras, commanding the parade. The sentence was read. At its conclusion Darras shouted: 'Alfred Dreyfus, you are unworthy to bear arms. In the name of the French people we degrade you!' Immediately, in a loud voice Dreyfus shouted: 'Soldiers! An innocent man is being degraded! Soldiers! An innocent is dishonoured! Long live France! Long live the Army!' The crowd beyond the walls hearing his voice broke into howls and whistles. A warrant-officer stripped him of his badges and buttons, and drawing Dreyfus's sabre from its scabbard, snapped it across his knee.[1] The condemned man was then marched round the courtyard, still proclaiming his innocence. The soldiers were silent, but the pressmen and reserve-officers who had been admitted to the atrocious ceremony shouted abuse at him. Outside the walls the mob howled '*A mort*'. When he had completed the circuit his wrists were tied, he was thrust into a police-van and taken first to the Depot and then to the Santé.

5

Dreyfus had scarcely reached the Santé when rumours began to circulate that he had confessed. Their originator was Lebrun-Renaud, the dull heavy escort, who, in the few minutes between the time when he had handed Dreyfus over and the beginning of the parade, had joined a group of officers and given them a hurried garbled account of what the prisoner had said. As he was later to admit, there was nothing amounting to a confession, but he let fall apparently a version, omitting du Paty's name, of Dreyfus's account of Mercier's offer of better treatment in return for a confession. This version ran: 'The Minister knows that if I handed over documents, it was to get more important ones'. At this moment he certainly had not taken Dreyfus's words as amounting to an admission, since he did not report them to General Darras, nor did he enter anything about his conversation with Dreyfus on the formal report he put in after the parade to Military Government Headquarters. Neverthe-less, a story of a confession remained in the minds of those who had heard him and, from this, rumours began to circulate: by evening the newspapers were printing as a fact that Dreyfus had

[1] Reinach records that Picquart, at the scene of the degradation, replying to a neighbour who had remarked on Dreyfus's impassivity as the gold braid was stripped from his arms, said: 'He's a Jew, don't forget that, he is thinking of the weight of the braid, so many ounces at so much.' Reinach: *Histoire de l'Affaire Dreyfus* (IV, 248).

2 *Alfred Dreyfus, c. 1894*

3 *General Auguste Mercier*

confessed.[1] The rumours reached the ears of Picquart, who had been present at the parade as the representative of the Minister of War. Believing that he had missed a matter which he should have reported, he sought confirmation of Military Government Headquarters. Colonel Guérin told him that he too had heard the rumours, but that nothing of the kind was stated on Lebrun-Renaud's report. Picquart brought this news to Boisdeffre, who took him to Mercier. The two generals, after a private word, dismissed Picquart, who, it being Saturday night, went off to his mother's house at Versailles.

At this point the complications foreseen by the now bed-ridden Hanotaux materialised. The diplomatic aspects of the case, which had hitherto scarcely impressed the public, but which had a little disturbed the Cabinet, began to assume threatening colours. Hanotaux's *démenti* of 30 November through Havas, that no foreign Embassy was involved, had not silenced Drumont or Rochefort. Mercier's *Figaro* interview of 27 November had clearly impeached Germany, while stories of documents filched from the German Embassy had wide currency. On 26 December Münster, once more through *Figaro*, issued a denial: 'The German Embassy has never had the slightest contact, direct or indirect, with Captain Dreyfus; no approach has been made for a trial *in camera*'. Since Dreyfus had been convicted three days earlier, Drumont, Barrès and Rochefort replied with a volley of anti-German invective.

That day Hanotaux took himself and his troubles off to the south. He was perhaps really ill with anxiety over the crisis he had so signally failed to contain: it seems clear that he guessed Mercier had made an unforgivable error. In his absence, Dupuy took over the Foreign Office; even less than Hanotaux did he dare withstand the press. On the day of Dreyfus's degradation, 5 January, Münster visited Dupuy and presented an official note:

His Majesty the Emperor, with complete confidence in the honour of the President and Government of the Republic, requests your Excellency to tell M. Casimir-Perier that

[1] The statement appeared in *Le Temps* dated the 6th, in fact issued at 5 p.m. on the 5th.

C

should it be proved that the German Embassy has never been implicated in the Dreyfus case, His Majesty hopes that the Government of the Republic will not hesitate to make the the declaration.

Without a formal declaration, the legends that the press continues to foster concerning the German Embassy may persist and compromise the Emperor's representative.

Hohenlohe

The note was stiff. Dupuy, perturbed, hurried over to the Elysée and asked Casimir-Perier to see Münster. Hitherto the President had been held at a distance by Hanotaux, and though he had been informed of earlier conversations between the Foreign Minister and the Ambassador, knew nothing of their substance. He agreed to talk to Münster, but before inviting him, required to know what had been said at the previous exchanges. He sent over to the Foreign and War Offices for the relevant files.

His request had just reached Mercier when Boisdeffre arrived, bringing news of the rumoured confession of Dreyfus. Mercier was embarrassed. An avowal extracted by du Paty could have been couched in suitably vague terms and officially made public, whereas if Dreyfus had talked freely to Lebrun-Renaud he might well have given away the fact that the Statistical Section had an agent in the German Embassy who had stolen the *bordereau*. He told Boisdeffre to bring Lebrun-Renaud, whose name neither had yet heard, to his office early the next morning. Considerable difficulty was met in running the officer down. Finding himself the centre of interest, he had spread his story round his mess, and now between 10 and 11 p.m. was doing the same at the Moulin-Rouge. Boisdeffre laid it on Gonse to discover the Republican Guard captain, and to bring him to the War Office early next day. Gonse rose early on the Sunday morning and with some trouble got hold of Lebrun-Renaud and took him to Mercier's room.

To Mercier and Gonse, Lebrun-Renaud denied that any confession had been made. His questioners, very impatient, were severe. He then told them, so far as he recalled, exactly what Dreyfus had said, including a version of the interview with du Paty. Nothing, however, amounted to an avowal of guilt. Lebrun-Renaud was told very sharply to say nothing about du Paty's visit to the prisoner, and nothing of any theft from the German Embassy; in short, to hold his tongue, hard.

None of the three men knew that this morning's *Figaro* carried a version of Lebrun-Renaud's talk at the Moulin-Rouge, picked up from his lips by an enterprising journalist. The story as printed said nothing about a confession, though it repeated Dreyfus's protests of innocence, but it stated that the main piece of evidence was a paper stolen from a wastepaper basket in the German Embassy. This item had already come to the eyes of Casimir-Perier and enraged him. He spoke to Dupuy, who in turn telephoned to Mercier. Mercier at once sent the thoroughly scared Lebrun-Renaud to the Elysée.

After a long wait, he was taken by Dupuy to the President. Casimir-Perier questioned him closely as to what he had let fall about the paper stolen from the German Embassy: but Casimir-Perier apparently had not seen the note in the *Temps* and, since the *Figaro* had said nothing about a confession, asked him nothing more on this score. Finally the unhappy officer was sent off, having been told for the future to be silent. Dupuy then, with the aid of Mercier, concocted a message for Havas, to the effect that Lebrun-Renaud had certified that he had given no information to any newspaper or journalist. It was hoped that this would evade any fresh trouble with Münster.

For all his dislike of his office, Casimir-Perier was a cool and capable man. Now given the opportunity of action, which he had missed for the last six months, he did what Hanotaux had had neither the wit nor the firmness to do. He had only looked looked through the files on the previous evening. Out of the few pieces in the War Office file, which did not, of course, contain the Secret File, he concocted yet another version of what had happened. Although it was not in the file, he remembered the *canaille de D* letter and linked it with the *bordereau*. There was no reason why he should not believe that the *bordereau* had reached the German Embassy and been read. He believed that Schwartzkoppen was deceiving Münster—as indeed he was, but not about Dreyfus. He invited Münster to visit him during the afternoon.

Münster and Caismir-Perier were old acquaintances. From the moment the Ambassador was seated, the President led the conversation. Pointing out that he was constitutionally without responsibility, he said he would have left the matter to the Prime Minister, but since he was mentioned in Hohenhloe's despatch, he took this to be in a way a private conversation between the heads of two sovereign states, the Emperor and the President; the matter was therefore personal and not diplomatic.

Having thus made his position clear, he took up the German despatch. He stressed the word 'implicated', and said that nothing of what he was about to say *implicated* the German Embassy. Dreyfus had been the object of suspicion for some time and had been watched. In course of time the Cabinet had been informed of an anonymous letter, coming, they were assured, from the German Embassy. Münster interrupted him by saying that he had made full enquiries: the Embassy received many letters, but it was impossible that an important document could be stolen. Caismir-Perier rejoined that it was possible that the letter from Dreyfus had been thought unimportant and thrown away. Whatever its value, it was enough to establish Dreyfus's guilt, but its receipt by the Embassy in no way made them responsible for it. All that was required was to have the traitor sentenced without involving the innocent Embassy staff. Hence the trial *in camera*. Münster naturally accepted Caismir-Perier's version. It remained to find a formula which would satisfy the Kaiser and not raise trouble in France. After some argument they agreed that a note through Havas clearing all the foreign Embassies of any connection with the traitor would be most sensible. On the Monday (7 January) Dupuy, with the agreement of the President and Münster, drafted a soothing communication, which, after it had been approved by Berlin, was sent out by Havas. The slight diplomatic tension, which was known only to a few highly-placed men, was at once relaxed.

The matter would be of no importance but for the fact that, on the basis of the intervention of the President, Mercier was to build up a legend of the night of 5 January (or 6—he was never sure of the date) when he and Boisdeffre stayed at the War Office, expecting each moment to be told that war was imminent and that mobilisation orders should be sent out. On the other hand, he had said nothing either to Dupuy or to Casimir-Perier of Dreyfus's alleged confession to Lebrun-Renaud, nor did he take any steps to go behind the message he and Dupuy had drafted together for Havas denying Lebrun-Renaud's story.

Gradually the fury of the gutter press over Dreyfus died away. The victim's protests of innocence were played down. But Demange said openly that while he submitted to the findings of the court, he remained at heart convinced of his client's innocence. The press told him to be silent; by talking he proclaimed himself an accomplice.

6

Casimir-Perier had had enough of the position of President. He had been considering resignation since early in October. He was tired of the threats and abuse of the press, of his treatment by his Ministers, of being no more than a rubber stamp. The death of his intimate friend Burdeau in December had deprived him of the moral support he needed. His suggestion of Félix Faure as President of the Chamber in succession to Burdeau had been vetoed by Dupuy; the Radical Brisson had been elected over the Republican Méline. In the New Year a further demonstration against him was staged, when Gérault-Richard who in November had been sentenced to a year's imprisonment for insults to the President, was put up as the Socialist candidate at a by-election in the XIIIe arrondissement of Paris, and on 6 January, the very day when Casimir-Perier was smoothing out the German difficulty, was elected. The Chamber, waiving an old privilege, rejected a motion from the Extreme Left to have Gérault-Richard's sentence suspended, but the motion was defeated only by 300 to 218; the Radicals joined with the extremists, their leaders—Léon Bourgeois, Sarrien, Doumer and Lockroy—voting with the Socialists.

Within the next week the country faced a political crisis

irrelevant to Dreyfus, a conflict between the railway companies, the Minister of Public Works and the Conseil d'Etat, in the middle of which Dupuy asked for a vote of confidence, which the Chamber, playing the old game of what is so delightfully called 'pure politics' refused him. Casimir-Perier, seeing in these manoeuvres another personal attack on himself, sent Dupuy away. He saw a few individuals to explain his action and then sent his resignation to the Presidents of the two Chambers. The message stated that he found he was deprived of the means of action and control. In spite of twenty years' service to the Republic, Republicans distrusted him. He had been the victim of a campaign of obloquy against the Army, the judicature and himself personally. He believed that reform could be carried out only by a strong executive resolved to secure respect for the laws and to command the obedience of its subordinates. Hence he resigned.

The message and the action were received by Parliament and the press with condemnation. Abroad the reaction to the message was one of shocked amazement. Yet those who knew the President well were not surprised. 'Casimir adores clear-cut situations', wrote his old friend Paul Cambon from Constantinople: 'now, in politics situations are never so . . . And Casimir has never understood the divine aspects of politics, as one talks of the divine "aspects" of war. . . . He has never looked on politics as the art of guiding men . . . and forms of government as essentially transitory. . . . He thumbed the Constitution instead of manipulating ministers'.

The two Chambers were summoned to meet in National Assembly at Versailles on 17 January. The Left put up inevitably the Radical Henri Brisson: it was the fourth time he had stood. The Republicans of the Chamber were for Félix Faure, but those of the Senate wanted Waldeck-Rousseau, who had recently shown a reviving interest in politics. The Monarchists had no candidate: but the Duc d'Orléans, who, owing to the recent death of his father the Comte de Paris, was now the Bourbon representative, remembered that in 1886 Faure had spoken against the expulsion from France of the claimants to the throne and their families, and told his followers to support him. Privately General Mercier allowed it to be known that

he too was a candidate; he circulated an advertisement com-
mending himself as the saviour of the Republic, and accusing
Casimir-Perier of meditating a *coup d'état*.

At the first poll Brisson led by 338 to 244 for Faure, and 184
for Waldeck: Mercier secured 3. On this Waldeck withdrew,
and at the second poll Faure was given an absolute majority
over Brisson, 430 to 361. The declaration was greeted by
the now usual hullabaloo from the Extreme Left, the Socialists and Socialist Radicals, in which accusations of bribery and
threats to force the new President from office were mingled.

The career of Francis Félix Faure had been unspectacular
but solid. The son of the owner of a tannery at Le Havre, he
had, it was said, worked in it as a manual labourer in his youth.
He had later turned to shipping. In 1881 he was elected for one
of the constituencies in this most republican and bourgeois city,
whose interests he firmly defended in the Chamber. He had
been Minister of Marine in Dupuy's Cabinet. He was tall and
handsome. With his eyeglass, his well-cut coats, check trousers,
gleaming waistcoats, four-in-hand ties and shining white spats,
he was said to be 'rotten smart'. He was conservative, something
of a snob, and though now on the edge of fifty-four, he liked it
to be known that he had preserved all the vigour of his youth,
in the saddle and in other less public activities. Naturally he
leant towards the Army. His election produced caustic shafts
from all sides. 'Laid by Aynard, hatched by Léon Say', wrote
Clemenceau. 'The poor gentleman is not a president', said
Millerand, 'but a ballet dancer'. Jules Delahaye, the Nationalist, said: 'He owes his election to the affability of his approach,
his incontrovertible mediocrity and his tailor, much appreciated
by the Parliamentary Right'.

On his arrival at the Elysée, Faure at once called on Léon
Bourgeois, whose Radical group had been the biggest in the
majority against Dupuy, to form a Government. To the general
surprise Bourgeois, who was believed to have a Cabinet ready
to take office, failed to secure enough support in the Chamber.
Ribot, summoned in his place, had no difficulty. A conservative
Republican, thoroughly hostile to the Left, Ribot had already
twice presided over the Cabinet, and had steered the Chamber
through the last months of the Panama scandals with some

success. In his team he retained Hanotaux at the Foreign
Office, moved Leygues from Public Instruction to the Interior,
and Poincaré to Public Instruction from Finance, which he
took over himself. A Senator, the worthy Trarieux, became
Minister of Justice, André Lebon Minister of Commerce, and
a mild Radical, Alphonse Chautemps, Minister of Colonies.
Mercier was dropped: his administrative errors had been too
gross and his attemps to exploit the Dreyfus case so indiscreet
that he could no longer be borne. He was given command of
IV Corps at Le Mans. His place as War Minister was taken by
General Zurlinden. 'Thus', wrote the Nationalist, Millevoye,
'Dreyfus is avenged'.

7

Dreyfus was held in the Santé from 5 to 18 January. During that
time he was allowed to see his wife twice. On the night of 18
January he was awakened and taken to a train for La Rochelle,
in freezing cold, with irons on his wrists and ankles. At La
Rochelle his presence was betrayed. A mob gathered and it was
only with difficulty that he was saved from its blood-lust. He
was taken to the Ile de Ré, where he was treated with brutal
savagery by the head of the prison. He was not allowed to
speak to his jailers; his letters to his wife were deliberately
delayed. He wrote one petition to the Minister of the Interior,
begging him to continue investigations to establish his innocence. The letter was not answered. Yet he continued to believe
that the truth would one day be known.

In February Lucie Dreyfus received permission to visit him:
but her visits were limited to half an hour, during which she
stood out of reach, with the chief warder between them. She
saw him for the last time on 21 February, but she was permitted
neither to kiss him nor to take his hand. Though she had guessed
from the sight of the ship lying in the harbour that this was
their final meeting, she was told nothing. That evening he was
once more stripped and searched—the daily routine since he
had reached the island—by special order of the Ministers of
Marine and Colonies. He was then taken on board the convict
ship and put into his cell. A hammock was thrown to him. He

was left without food. *La Ville de Saint-Nazaire* raised anchor and set sail for Cayenne.

8

With the end of the trial, Mercier began to take his precautions against the future. On 8 January he informed General Saussier that contrary to the usual practice, he was keeping the file of the trial in the War Office and not handing it back to the Paris Garrison Headquarters.

Nine days later, when Dupuy was on the point of resignation, he took the secret dossier from Sandherr and burned du Paty's commentary on the ground that it was his, Mercier's, personal property and that it was no longer needed. He handed back to Sandherr the other documents and told him to return each to the original folder from which it had come. Sandherr however was not prepared to leave himself without protection should the case be revived. He kept the file to which he added a few photographs of the *bordereau* and, unknown to both Mercier and Boisdeffre, handed it over to Henry who put the papers in an envelope, wrote on it 'Dossier secret D', added his own initials 'J. H.' and, with Gribelin standing by, locked it in the office safe at the Statistical Section.

During these days of political crisis, it seems that Mercier took the further precaution of requiring from his subordinates, Boisdeffre, Gonse, Sandherr, du Paty and Henry, an oath that they would never reveal anything of the proceedings before and during the trial of Dreyfus.

Chapter Four

Picquart

1

Dreyfus had been sentenced to deportation to a fortified area. By a special law passed on 9 February 1895, on the motion of Delcassé, without discussion, the Îles de Salut, off the coast of Guiana some thirty miles from Cayenne, were added to the usual Ducos peninsula in New Caledonia as places of detention for political prisoners. These were three islands, on one of which were already incarcerated the most desperate convicts, and on another the permanently sick, mostly criminal lunatics; the third, The Devil's Island, was a leper colony. It was now hurriedly cleared for Dreyfus. On this burning and desolate lump of rock, four hundred yards wide, two miles long, a small stone hut was built with a tiny yard in front, to accommodate him and the jailer on duty. The chief warder had received instructions to shoot the prisoner down at the slightest movement to escape. He was permitted to exercise only on a narrow path some two hundred yards in length. He was not allowed to communicate with the jailers. His food was scarcely adequate; he must prepare it himself; he was not allowed wine. A lamp burned all night in his room, in which clustered a myriad insects. He was eventually permitted to write and receive a limited number of letters, strictly censored at the Ministries of War and the Colonies. Always he hoped to have news that the real traitor had been found. He heard nothing, and his appeals to the President, to Boisdeffre, to du Paty, went unanswered. Yet he refused to give in. On a number of occasions he was ill, either from the intolerable heat and the insects, or mentally. He suffered and he aged. Neglecting his appearance, he let his beard grow; it turned white. Except for his career and his family he had had no interests. Without them he had no resource. His existence was death in life. Except by his jailers and his family, he was forgotten.

In Paris Mathieu Dreyfus had begun his task. Conscious as he was that anti-semitism had grown fiercer with the trial, he moved very cautiously. Some men knew or guessed that his brother had been condemned on documents not shown to the defence; few of them, even Ministers, seemed to be aware that the communication to the court was illegal. Indeed, had they known, it would not have weighed with them: at the Zola trial, Trarieux, Ribot's Minister of Justice, in 1898 a leading Dreyfusist, admitted that, had Dreyfus really been a traitor, he himself would not have had the courage to raise any questions about illegality in the form of the trial. A few Alsatian friends, a few editors, encouraged Mathieu. Whatever scent he followed, it ended in air. He had copies of some of the trial documents, parts of Ormeschville's report: he kept them hidden lest the police-agents who watched him should raid his sister-in-law's house.

Lucie Dreyfus petitioned the Government to be allowed, as was her right under a law of 1873, to join her husband. Her petition was twice rejected without explanation. On the third occasion, Guieysse, Minister of Colonies, saw her and told her that it was, in the circumstances, impossible.

2

Ribot's Government did not have an easy life. Having in his policy speech to the Chamber stressed the need for pacification and understanding, he showed almost at once that he meant peace with a difference. To please the Radicals he proposed to fill the gap in the budget by squeezing the religious Orders. As it in fact worked out, the Orders were a match for the Treasury; little more than a third of the expected sum came in after five years of law-suits. Ribot had however exasperated the Ralliés (the Catholic politicians who followed Leo xiii's policy of accepting and collaborating with the Republic), the bishops and the Vatican, who saw that the Pope's advance was not being met halfway by the Republicans. Leo xiii made no public protest, but he let it be known that he was deeply wounded by the Government's ingratitude. The clerical press rushed into action. *Croix*, *Vérité*, *Univers*, *Libre Parole*, Cassagnac's *Autorité*, abused Ribot with all the venom and disrespect at their command.

On top of all this, although they were not responsible, the Government had to meet bitter criticism of the casualness with which the expeditionary force for the conquest of Madagascar had been prepared by Mercier. No French transports had been available, and the Republic had had to hire ships from British companies; the sanitary and medical preparations had been abominable; 500 men had died on the voyage, and 3,000 more within a few months of landing.

Finally on 28 October Ribot was defeated on the question of the change of judges in the middle of a trial. 'M. Ribot's Cabinet, say his adversaries, fell on a question of morality. The only morality which can possibly be extracted from the debate is the incoherence of Parliament', was the bitter comment of a political editor.

Félix Faure summoned Léon Bourgeois as the leader of the main group in the hostile vote. Bourgeois produced the first wholly Radical Cabinet, with a civilian, Cavaignac, at the War Office. Hanotaux declined to serve, and the Foreign Office was taken over by Marcellin Berthelot, a distinguished chemist, who knew nothing about diplomacy.

The new Ministry was received with enthusiasm by the Left, with chilly courtesy by the Republicans, and with hostility by the Liberals and Conservatives. The remaining Boulangists at this point tried to concentrate their forces by forming a parliamentary group under the name of Nationalists.

Léon Bourgeois had made his career up the ladder of the Ministry of the Interior, prefecture by prefecture. He was notorious for promoting his friends: 'He is the leader not so much of a party as of a clientèle', someone had said. Naturally he himself took over the Interior. It was too late in the year to offer much of a programme, since the Budget of 1896 still had to be passed. On many of the Radical reforms demanded in opposition he was silent, but the mention of a further discussion of income-tax, coupled with the presence of Doumer, its chief enthusiast, at the Ministry of Finance, augured a stormy existence, while the inclusion in the Cabinet of nine Freemasons, one of them Emile Combes, a renegade seminarist, at the Ministries of Public Instruction and Public Worship, warned the Catholic members that they would have to fight for their beliefs. In one direction Bourgeois was successful. Adopting the financial proposals of the Ribot Government, he pushed the Budget through both Chambers by the end of the year, a feat which had not been accomplished since 1890.

The year 1895 ended in a dust-storm of scandals, dying storms raised by the widespread activities of the late Baron Reinach. In January Doumer spoke of his intention to reduce indirect taxation and compensate the losses by a progressive income-tax: 'a Republican Budget would replace a Monarchical one'. The Senate became restive. In February a Senator accused the Minister of Justice of illegal interference in a case, and on the debate the Ministry was defeated. In the Chamber the Ministry maintained that the Senate were in error and secured a vote of confidence. The Senate riposted by confirming their original vote. Bourgeois refused to acknowledge the right of the Upper Chamber to press his resignation. Three of the four Republican groups in the Senate at once issued a declaration maintaining the Senate's equal rights with the Chamber in the matter of Cabinet responsibility. At the end of February the Chamber Finance Commission rejected Doumer's income-tax proposal by an overwhelming majority. In March Doumer brought the proposal before the Chamber. In a series of complex debates Bourgeois four times in five days had to request a vote of confidence. His majorities were tiny, between seven and sixteen. In the provinces over 80 per cent of the departmental councils declared their opposition to the tax proposals. Clearly the Bourgeois Cabinet was not going to survive long. The Senate felt strengthened. On 22 April a vote of credit for the Madagascar operations came to it from the Chamber. The Senate decided to adjourn the vote 'until it finds before it a constitutional Ministry possessing the confidence of both Chambers'. After some hesitation Bourgeois resigned. At once the Senate passed the vote of credit.

Félix Faure asked a Radical, Sarrien, to replace Bourgeois, but Sarrien could get no support. Faure then sent for Jules Méline. He was an old Republican, an old Gambettist from the days of the National Assembly, a frontiersman from the Vosges. He had once been Minister of Agriculture and had been the proponent of the tariff laws of 1891 with their heavy duties: 'His heart', said an irreverent journalist, 'beats only for cereals'. But he was an old parliamentary hand. First he tried to get a Cabinet of concentration by the union of the Centres, that elusive dream which every Prime Minister had pursued in vain. His advances were repulsed by the Radicals. He fell back on the Government Republicans. On 29 April he met the Chambers, with Hanotaux once more at the Foreign Office, Barthou at the Interior, Cochery at Finance and General Billot at the War Office. The survival of his Ministry seemed problematical. Bourgeois, in defiance of tradition, attacked him, asserting that the crisis had arisen solely out of the conflict with the Senate, and that constitutional revision to eliminate the Upper Chamber was the only remedy. Méline got his vote of confidence by no more than thirty-four, not a strong majority. Yet the Cabinet was to live for more than two years. Whatever conflicts of doctrine might exist between the Right and the Republicans, they could always be relied on to unite to prevent the return of a Ministry dedicated to the imposition of income-tax. Méline's fall was eventually to come through unforeseen and mysterious events revolving round the case of the forgotten prisoner on The Devil's Island.

3

In October 1895, among other letters, Dreyfus received one, as usual passed by the Director of Prison Administration, Guégen, signed: 'Your old cousin, L. Blenheim'. The name was unknown to him; the letter of no importance; he threw it into the drawer in which he kept his papers. He did not discover until after his return to France in 1899 that between the lines, written in an invisible ink which would become opaque only by the application of heat or by gradual discoloration, was a cryptic message. This ran: 'Thread broken. Try to re-knot. Our two attempts have failed. We are forced to be very careful. Everything nearly discovered. Let me know where 2249 was. The Jura business 34 is known'.

It is evident that the writer counted on the message becoming visible to the censor, and thus another nail would be firmly driven into Dreyfus's coffin. Who was the writer? Only someone whose interest it was *at this time* to produce further proofs of guilt. Since Sandherr was already as good as dead, since Esterhazy as yet had no knowledge that he was involved, since du Paty was back in the Third Bureau and was no longer in touch, the only probable author is Henry, who knew that not only was the evidence of the prisoner's guilt dubious, but that the Chief of Staff had desired that the case should be strengthened by the discovery of a motive.

4

Neither Schwartzkoppen nor Esterhazy had an inkling that it had been their relationship which had led to the arrest of Dreyfus. During 1895 Esterhazy appears to have passed to the German attaché, at ever-increasing intervals, papers of less and less value to the Germans. He had in fact no serious knowledge of guns or gunnery, and, as came out later, he drew the attention of Captain Le Rond, the officer in charge of the visitors to the Châlons exercises in 1894 and 1895, by asking questions which demonstrated his basic ignorance. By the beginning of 1896 Schwartzkoppen was considering dismissing this useless and exigent agent. In March he broke with him.

Before this time, changes had occurred in the Statistical Section. During the spring of 1895 Sandherr's disease had suddenly worsened and in June he was stricken with paralysis. His second-in-command, Cordier, had no desire to remain in the office he detested; he was posted to an infantry regiment. Sandherr's place was taken by Major Picquart of the Third Bureau, the War Office representative at Dreyfus's trial.

Marie-Georges Picquart was, like Sandherr, an Alsatian. Born in Strasbourg in 1854, he was sixteen when Alsace was annexed. At Colmar, under the eyes of the Germans, he studied for the French Army. He left Saint-Cyr fifth in his class, and joined the 4th Zouaves, with whom he fought in Algeria in 1878. He then entered the Ecole Supérieure de Guerre, from which he went as Intelligence Officer to Galliffet's staff. In

1893 he was seconded to the Third Bureau (Operations and Training) at the War Office. His chiefs throughout had had a high opinion of his abilities. As a Strasbourger he was bilingual in French and German, and he possessed a knowledge of other languages. He was good-looking, quiet, cultivated, thoughtful and reserved.[1] He was unmarried and lived in modest lodgings near the Etoile. Boisdeffre, as he said at the Rennes trial, thought that he had too good an opinion of himself; nevertheless he could not disregard the strong recommendations of Miribel, Galliffet and Millet, the Director of Infantry, under whom Picquart had served. Picquart, though not a violent anti-semite, had like other Alsatians prejudices against the Jews. At the trial he had been unmoved by Dreyfus's protestations of innocence.

He took over the Section on 12 July, with the rank of Lieutenant-Colonel. Sandherr, whose mind had not yet wholly given way (he died in May 1897), saw him a couple of times and handed over the secret funds. He warned him that Boisdeffre was still worrying about the Dreyfus case, but that he himself thought the less it was looked into the better: Picquart would find the file which had been communicated to the judges, with its convincing proofs of guilt, in Henry's hands.

On taking over, Picquart was seen by Boisdeffre, whose uneasiness seems to have derived from a recognition that, even with the secret documents, the case against Dreyfus was inconclusive. He told Picquart to follow up the case: it was absolutely necessary to discover the motive for the crime.

Whether, as has been alleged, Henry was disappointed at being passed over for a younger man, even though his senior in rank, is impossible to verify. Picquart at least had no doubts about Henry's loyalty. For light on Dreyfus's private life, Henry recommended the ex-policeman, Guénée. Picquart soon found that Guénée was incompetent: he could fish up

---

[1] He also had his peculiarities. It is related that he took some interest in spiritualism. He went to a séance to see what he could make of it. Suspecting the medium of some trickery with a hat which was used, he insisted on the use of his own. 'And', he reported, 'they not only caused my hat to rotate on the table, but they imparted to it such an impetus of rotation that it continued to rotate upon my head all the time I was walking home'.

nothing better than gossip from door-porters of gambling-houses. At the same time Picquart had the correspondence of the Dreyfus family intercepted and read, as well as the letters to and from Dreyfus on The Devil's Island. Again nothing emerged: he had read unmoved Dreyfus's continued protestations to his wife and brother of his innocence. Gradually he discovered that every seedy rogue of the underworld was ready to sell information about the prisoner and that all of it was worthless. Fragments delivered by Bastian were either unintelligible or trivial. Moreover, it was certain that staff papers were still being filched. He was severely shaken at being offered by an Englishman at an enormous price a copy of the mobilisation positions opposite the German frontier, accompanied by a threat that if he did not pay, the document would go to Germany. Knowing that the seller would keep a copy anyhow, he refused, and, after enquiries of the Bureau from which it had come, found that it had been in so many hands that no hypothesis could be formed as to who had lost or sold it. Thus during eight months nothing came to light to stiffen the case against Dreyfus. Nevertheless, Picquart's work more than satisfied both the Chief of Staff and the successive War Ministers, Zurlinden, Cavaignac and Billot. In April 1896 his temporary rank of Lieutenant-Colonel was confirmed.

In March of that year Henry, still the recipient of Bastian's waste-paper, was much absent from Paris, partly employed on a treason trial at Nancy, partly visiting his mother, who was dying at Pogny. However, he succeeded in making a rendezvous with Bastian between two trains, about 15 March, and took from her two bags of torn paper from Schwartzkoppen's waste-paper basket. It was a big delivery, which he had just time to hand over to Picquart. Picquart locked the bags in his cupboard and next day gave them to Lauth to sort out and reconstitute. In a few days Lauth came to his chief with a reconstructed *petit bleu* (a special-delivery letter resembling a letter-card on thin blue paper, for local use in Paris), and laid it before him, saying: 'It's frightening. Is this another of them?'

The *petit bleu* had been reconstructed from a great number of tiny fragments, none of them bigger than a little fingernail. It ran:

Sir, Before all I await a more detailed explanation than you gave me the other day on the question in suspense. Will you therefore be good enough to let me have it in writing to enable me to decide whether I can continue my relations with the firm of R- or not. C.

It was addressed to Monsieur le Commandant Esterhazy, 27 Rue de la Bienfaisance, Paris.[1]

5

Marie-Charles-Ferdinand Walsin-Esterhazy was the son of a French general of an illegitimate branch of the Hungarian Esterhazys, who had died in 1857. Although later some stress was laid on Esterhazy's origin, with the implication that he was a foreigner, he was by blood almost wholly French. Stories that he entered Saint-Cyr but failed his examinations, that he later entered the Austrian Army and in 1866 fought at Custozza, appear to have no foundation. In 1869, at the age of twenty-two he joined Lamoricière's Roman Legion, and in 1870 secured a commission in the French Foreign Legion, from which, during the Franco-Prussian War, he had been transferred to the 2nd Zouaves. After various re-postings, among which he was, for a year or so, Orderly Officer to General Grenier, he was sent to the Statistical Section in 1878, where he stayed until 1881, thus getting to know Sandherr and Henry. By this time he had reached the rank of Captain. From July 1881 to 1884 he was in Tunisia, during which time he claimed, quite falsely, to have been decorated. Returning to France in 1884, he married two years later Anne-Marie de Nettancourt, younger daughter of the Marquis de Nettancourt-Vaubecourt with a dowry of two hundred thousand francs, and a little later bought with his wife's money a country house at Dommartin-la-Planchette, near Sainte-Menehould. From 1889 he was stationed in or near Paris, running after women, speculating on the Bourse and losing.

[1] Fragments of a second letter preserved in the dossier of the case in the Archives Nationales, were examined much later by M. Marcel Thomas. They convey a more elaborate refusal to continue relations with Esterhazy, and like the first letter, this one was never sent to him.

By the close of 1893, perhaps earlier, he had reached the end of his resources. In 1892 he had been promoted to Major, but ordered to a regiment garrisoning Dunkirk. He had made such a fuss about this exile that in the end the War Office transferred him to the 74th Infantry Regiment at Rouen, at this date within two hours of Paris by train.

Esterhazy was an adventurer, but without purpose. He took little interest in his battalion, spent as much time as he could in Paris, leading a debauched but apparently unhappy existence, always short of money, in debt to his tradesmen and borrowing where he could. On the other hand, he was far better read than the average army officer, and the master of a ready pen. Although remaining anonymous, he assisted in the writing of various columns in the newspapers dealing with military matters, in particular the articles by Commander Biot in the *Libre Parole*. He was possessed of a fantastic and sardonic humour. Moreover, he was an impressive figure. Corporal Julien Benda, no respecter of persons, when he was doing his military service at Courbevoie in 1892, watched him one evening strolling to and fro in front of the officers' quarters: 'tall, thin, a little bent, the face sallow, bony and lined . . . a careworn air. He might have been an elegant and treacherous gipsy, or, better, a great wild beast, alert and sure of itself. Charmed by his distinction, I could not take my eyes from him'.

This was the man who had boldly offered himself to Schwartzkoppen on 20 July 1894, and to whom the *petit bleu* picked up in the German Embassy was addressed.

6

The *petit bleu*, as Lauth pointed out to Picquart, had no postage stamp: thus it had been torn up before despatch: it could therefore not be used to incriminate the intended recipient, i.e. Esterhazy. The writing was not that of Schwartzkoppen.[1]

Picquart naturally jumped to the same conclusion as Lauth, that here was possibly another traitor. However, remembering

[1] Some writers have stated that it was written by Schwartzkoppen's mistress, the wife of the counsellor of the Netherlands ministry in Paris. This has no foundation. The writer of the *petit bleu* is unknown.

the difficulties caused by leakages from the War Office in 1894 and the consequent press campaign, he decided to make no report until he had more solid information.

The 74th had been transferred from the Rouen area to Paris in October 1894. Finding that among the officers of the regiment was an old friend, Major Curé, he invited him to call and asked his opinion of Esterhazy. Curé replied that Esterhazy was a thoroughly bad officer, dissolute, a stock-market gambler; on the one hand paying little attention to his duties, on the other always trying to obtain confidential information on guns and gunnery, adding that he had twice gone to firing-practices, and a third time at his own expense, and finally that he employed soldiers in his battalion to copy documents. Curé, however, refused to help Picquart to procure a sample of Esterhazy's writing. At the same time he warned Picquart that Esterhazy was cleverer than he was.

Picquart consulted Henry, who admitted having known Esterhazy in the Statistical Section fifteen years earlier, but said he had lost sight of him. They arranged to have him shadowed by one of the special police attached to the War Office, Desvernine. He discovered Esterhazy's financial troubles and also that, in the Rue de Douai, he kept a young woman, Marie, called Marguérite, Pays, a registered prostitute, known as Four-Fingered Margaret, whom he had picked up at the Moulin-Rouge. Desvernine twice saw his quarry visit the German Embassy in broad daylight, but Picquart was warned by Curé that Esterhazy had probably gone there on legitimate business. The shadowing continued during April, May, June and most of July without result, and in the meantime no further fragment of interest came from the German Embassy by 'the ordinary route'. The *petit bleu* was photographed by Lauth and Junck, still another Alsatian, who had joined the Section late in 1895.

During part of this period Picquart was away from the Section, owing partly to the illness of his mother, partly to his accompanying Boisdeffre on a staff tour. During this tour Boisdeffre's Orderly Officer, Pauffin de Saint-Morel, told him that the French military attaché in Berlin, Colonel Foucault, had written to him saying that a renegade German agent, one

Richard Cuers, had confided in Foucault information which Picquart ought to know. On his return to Paris Picquart saw Foucault. Cuers, he was told, had said that the German War Office staff had never themselves employed Dreyfus, nor had they found a single military attaché in any capital who had ever heard of him before the trial. The only agent believed by them to be a French officer was a senior officer, a battalion commander, aged about forty-five, said to be decorated, who had given Schwartzkoppen information about artillery, much of it of little value, and had recently given notes on various technical details from the gunnery school at Châlons.

Picquart, knowing from Curé that Esterhazy had borrowed from the colonel of his regiment and had copied some of the Châlons papers, was roused. He arranged with Foucault to send Cuers to Bâle, where he would be interviewed. He told Lauth and Henry to meet and examine Cuers, and sent with them two agents from the Sûreté. On 5 August Cuers was met. Tomps, one of the Sûreté men, knew him by sight, but he was questioned by Henry, who knew no German, and Lauth; Cuers's French was poor. The interview was a failure. The only serious information they got was, (a) that four documents had been received by Berlin, reports on a new file, on the quick-firing gun,[1] on the entrenched camp at Toul, and on the Nancy fortifications, but Cuers could give no date of delivery; and (b) that the German General Staff suspected that the French officer was a counter-spy and in October 1895 had told Schwartzkoppen to break off relations. The man, said Cuers, was undoubtedly a 'senior officer', but he refused to name him.

On the day that Lauth and Henry set out for Bâle, Picquart reported to Boisdeffre that he feared they had discovered another traitor, Major Walsin-Esterhazy.

Boisdeffre commended the discretion with which Picquart had acted, and approved his proposal that for the present the information should be given only to the War Minister, General Billot, and not to Gonse, the Assistant Chief of Staff. Gonse later complained of this short circuiting. Billot, after

[1] This might be the 75 mm quick-firing gun for which a large subsidy was voted by the Chamber in 1897.

hearing Picquart, also commended his prudence, but refused to allow him to ask Esterhazy's colonel for a specimen of his writing. A little later Boisdeffre, while showing no signs of a desire to shield Esterhazy, said: 'I don't want another Dreyfus case. He'll be put on retired pay and sent about his business. He must be got rid of without any scandal'.

In the same month, Esterhazy, no longer on Schwartz-koppen's pay-roll, conceived the audacious scheme of getting himself seconded to the War Office. To further this, he applied to an old friend, who had been in the Statistical Section about 1879, Weil. Maurice Weil, an officer on the retired list, was now employed as Orderly Officer to General Saussier, the Military Governor of Paris. His wife was Austrian and said to be Saussier's mistress, for which there is no serious evidence. A pleasant little Jew, his main business in life was to run errands for his elderly General and to have a wide circle of useful connections. He had, however, had the misfortune as a Jew to have been denounced as a traitor in the *Libre Parole*. There was nothing tangible to support the accusation, but as always, the smell of the mud which had been thrown remained. Weil wrote a personal recommendation of Esterhazy to Calmon, Billot's chief private secretary. Esterhazy also approached several Deputies, among them Adrien de Montebello and Jules Roche. In spite of their support nothing happened. He continued to press Roche, and also secured the help of a couple of generals. He followed this up by writing, on 25 August, directly to Calmon.

A day or two later, when Picquart was reporting to Billot, Calmon told him of Weil's recommendation. Picquart told Boisdeffre, who laughed at the impudence, and Billot, who said he was being inundated with letters from deputies and generals. Picquart spoke of his suspicions of Weil, to whose door Desvernine frequently tracked Esterhazy, whereupon Billot, reversing his earlier orders, told Calmon to give the correspondence from Weil and Esterhazy to the head of the Statistical Section. On 27 August Picquart received two Esterhazy letters. As soon as he saw them, he perceived that the writing was already known to him. He compared it with one of the prints of the *bordereau;* he hands were identical.

Since his talk with Foucault, it had once or twice crossed his mind that Dreyfus might be innocent but, having been present at the court-martial, he had dismissed the idea. Now he was converted. However, he took care. He covered up the dates, the signature and one or two revealing phrases in the Ester-hazy letters, and had Lauth photograph them. He showed the prints to du Paty, who had believed that the Dreyfus brothers had collaborated in the writing of the *bordereau*. Du Paty at once exclaimed: 'Mathieu Dreyfus!' Bertillon, to whom he also showed the prints, said: 'Ah, the handwriting of the *bordereau*. So the Jews have been training someone for a year to imitate the writing'.

For the moment, bewildered, Picquart believed that Esterhazy and Dreyfus were accomplices: but since the writing of the *bordereau* was Esterhazy's, on what evidence had Dreyfus been found guilty? Henry was on leave, and on either 27 or 28 August Picquart told Gribelin to get him the Secret File which had been shown to the judges, and sought in it the crushing proofs of which Sandherr had talked. Not one of the few documents showed a trace of Dreyfus, though the Schwartzkoppen scribble, 'Doubt, Proofs, Authority' might refer to Esterhazy. The only other piece was a commentary in what Picquart believed to be du Paty's hand. To the Criminal Appeal Court Picquart said: 'I broke off relations with him but without a row'.

On 1 September Picquart set out a full written report, sustained by the documents, added a request for an enquiry, and submitted it to Boisdeffre. Boisdeffre heard him in silence until he produced the Secret File, when he exclaimed: 'Why wasn't it burnt as was arranged?' Picquart, who knew nothing of this order, was astonished. Otherwise Boisdeffre made no comment, merely told him to see Gonse, then on leave in the country, and take his opinion. Picquart visited Gonse two days later.

Gonse, but for his thirty years' friendship with Boisdeffre, seems to have had no qualities. He looked like a battered Napoleon iii, and had the reputation of being a gasbag. He was without decision or moral courage. After Picquart had made his explanation, Gonse merely grimaced and said: 'So it looks as if a mistake has been made'. On being asked for instructions, he replied: 'Separate the two cases, Dreyfus's and Esterhazy's'.

Picquart thought this absurd, since the *bordereau* belonged to both. In 1898, at Rennes, Gonse claimed that, being incompetent to judge handwriting, he had told Picquart that the *bordereau* was Dreyfus's, and the charge against Esterhazy should be based on the *petit bleu* and any other exhibit that could be found. Otherwise he in no way contested Picquart's argument.

Picquart saw Boisdeffre again: Boisdeffre showed only indifference, and told him to wait before reporting to Billot.

7

On the same day (1 September) on which Picquart saw Gonse, the London *Daily Chronicle*, quoting the *South Wales Argus*, announced that Dreyfus had escaped. When the report reached Paris, Andre Lebon, the Colonial Minister, cabled to Cayenne and on the following day received a denial of the story. The false news had in fact been 'placed' by Mathieu Dreyfus. All his efforts to find evidence to refute the accusation against his brother had failed. Realising that by now Alfred was nearly forgotten, he conceived the idea of reawakening interest by publicising news of his escape. It was a singularly unhappy stratagem, which was to add to his brother's sufferings. In spite of the wholly reassuring reports from Cayenne, Lebon feared the attitude of the press. He cabled to the Governor to build round Dreyfus's hut a double palisade, and until that was completed, to put Dreyfus in irons each night. Thus for four and forty nights of insupportable heat the wretched prisoner was clamped immovably on his bed. The fetters cut into his shins, and although his warders tried to ease the pain by winding rags round his legs, his flesh was cut and bruised. Furthermore, they were no longer allowed to speak to him, he could not understand this new torture: he thought he was going mad. But on the second day Bravard, the commandant of the islands, visited him and explained these new security measures. When at last he was freed, he found that one of his few consolations, the sea, was hidden from him by the eight-foot palisades within which alone he was permitted to take exercise. Lebon, both ashamed and afraid, did not disclose to his colleagues what he had ordered. Bravard appears to have protested to the Governor of Guiana, who tried to reassure the timorous Minister. Lebon replied by recalling Bravard and sending from France a prison officer, a pitiless sadist called Deniel.

Lebon's fears had also been increased by a further mystery. Within a day or so of the *Daily Chronicle* alarm, a letter was addressed to Dreyfus through the Colonial Ministry. It was ostensibly written by a Jew calling himself Weill or Weyler. Commonplace in content, between the lines were written in bad sympathetic ink words which, when the letter was treated, conveyed a cryptic message that implied a regular secret correspondence with the prisoner concerning documents. Lebon and Picquart were bewildered. Picquart thought it genuine, that it emanated from the Dreyfus clan, whose recent letters had indicated a hope that they were approaching a solution of the judicial error.

Mathieu Dreyfus's aim had been achieved. The prisoner was remembered by the journalists. The anti-semitic papers announced that the vast Jewish international 'Syndicate' was going to buy off the warders. On the other hand, Gaston Calmette, one day to perish at the hands of Mme Caillaux, published in *Figaro* a sympathetic article describing Dreyfus's existence and miseries on The Devil's Island, while Cassagnac once more forcibly expressed his doubts about the trial: military judges were 'no more infallible, no more enlightened and no more honourable than their brothers, cousins and friends, the jurymen who are so often mistaken'.

On 9 September, the *Eclair* published a measured attack on the handling of the case, in which it proposed putting an end to the accusations of the Dreyfus clan by insisting that certain evidence in the War Office should be made public. To those who knew, it seemed that the *Eclair* was asking for the revelation of the secret dossier of 1894. Picquart had already feared that the Dreyfus family would find some clue to the truth and that the deplorable nature of the case would be revealed to the humiliation of the officers concerned. He learned that Sabatier, the editor of the *Eclair*, was a friend of the Nationalist deputy for the Aisne, Castelin, who was thought to be in touch with Mathieu Dreyfus. Hence, when on 11 September, Castelin, in an open letter to the Prime Minister, announced that, on the

re-opening of Parliament, he would raise the question of the
indifference of the Government towards the activities of Dreyfus and his friends, Picquart, deceived as to the Deputy's
motives, came to the conclusion that revelations damaging to
the War Office were about to be made. If this was so, it would
be the wisest course to admit at once that an error had been
made, to prosecute Esterhazy and release Dreyfus. He now,
after several applications, obtained Boisdeffre's permission to
lay the whole case before Billot.

As to what was said at this interview, the testimonies of
Billot and Picquart before the Cour de Cassation in 1898
conflict. Picquart said that at this moment Billot was persuaded
of Dreyfus's innocence, but subsequently swung back to the
opinion that both Dreyfus and Esterhazy were guilty. Billot
replied that he warned Picquart that the guilt of Esterhazy did
not in itself absolve Dreyfus, and that he inclined to think, since
spies do not work alone, that other men were involved besides
Dreyfus and Esterhazy: he had seen the writing of two who
should be looked into. He did not name them, but one was
certainly Maurice Weil.

At this interview he directed that enquiries should be pursued
and better evidence procured: above all, in view of the
approaching visit of the Tsar in October, rumours must be
prevented.

Billot, a tubby, white-moustached old gentleman nearing
seventy, had been a political general for the last 25 years. He
had been elected to the National Assembly in February 1871,
one of the three soldiers who voted against the acceptance of the
German peace terms, and one of the few Republican army
officers. He had taken a big share in the debates on the reconstruction of the Army in 1875, and had been elected a life-
senator. Once before, in the early eighties, he had been Minister
of War. It is argued that had Billot been a strong man, had he
at this point sent for Boisdeffre and taxed him with having left
him, the Minister, in the dark for ten days over this judicial
error, had he then faced the Cabinet and the Chambers, none
of whose members knew more than did the general public about
the original trial, he would have carried the revision through,
to his own undying glory. It may be so, but it is doubtful, since

even Picquart at this date had not really got to the bottom of the case.

On the 14th a second more detailed article, openly hostile to Dreyfus, appeared in the *Eclair*. It revealed that in September 1894 a letter from the German to the Italian embassy had been seized in transit and photographed before being sent on. It was in the German cipher: it concerned the spy service in Paris and contained the phrase: '*Decidedly this Dreyfus animal is becoming too demanding.*' In view of its importance it could be shown, in secret, only to the judges of the court-martial in the absence of the accused. A few days later there had come into the possession of the War Office another unsigned letter intended for the German embassy, containing a list (*bordereau*) of the information that had been delivered to Germany: this was quoted, and apart from a few minor errors of detail gave accurately enough the contents of the original *bordereau* of 1894, including General Renouard's plan for the invasion of Madagascar. There followed an account of the arrest, and du Paty, Henry, Forzinetti, Gonse and several others were named as having been present.

Whatever disturbance the publication caused in the War Office, it had no effect on the public at large. The only effect of any importance concerned the relations of Picquart and General Gonse. Picquart had been told by Boisdeffre to put himself for the future under the direction of Gonse. When he saw the *Eclair* article, he at once wrote to the Assistant-Chief: 'I told you we were going to have heavy troubles on our shoulders if we did not take the initiative'. He would try to discover who had so cleverly prepared this bombshell,[1] but first action must be taken. 'If we still hesitate, we shall be overrun, cornered in an inextricable position, and we shall no longer be in a position to defend ourselves or establish the real truth'. Seeing Gonse next

[1] The author or inspirer of the article has never been identified. The matter was revived before the Cour de Cassation in 1899. Henry was then dead; Guénée, who died before the Rennes trial, took refuge behind 'professional secrecy'. Various names have been suggested, including Forzinetti and one of the judges, Florentin. It could have come from Henry, but there is no proof that it did. Picquart believed du Paty responsible, which was unlikely since he was on manoeuvres. But Picquart throughout displayed a kindness for Henry and a loathing of du Paty.

day, he suggested that steps be taken against the *Eclair*. Gonse declined to move; it was outside his competence; they must wait for the return of Billot and Boisdeffre, now at the manoeuvres in Charente. He went on: 'Why do you make such a point of Dreyfus leaving the Devil's Island?' Picquart answered: 'But General, he's innocent'. Gonse returned: 'The case can't be re-opened. General Mercier, General Saussier, are involved in it', 'But since he is innocent!' 'That is unimportant; that is not a consideration which should be brought into the reckoning'. Trying another line, Picquart said: 'You are well aware that the Dreyfus family are at this very moment at work. . . . Well, if they succeed in finding the real culprit, what will our situation be?' To which Gonse: 'If you say nothing, no one will know'.

'I confess', said Picquart at Rennes, 'that I was completely floored, and I said to him: "What you are saying is abominable, General. I will not carry this secret to my grave", and I left the room'.

Boisdeffre waited to see whether any controversy would follow the *Eclair* article, and as none did, he left the paper alone. Picquart perceived that he was not going to be allowed to follow up the Dreyfus side of the affair.

He had already been forbidden on the grounds of security and prudence to place the *bordereau* and Esterhazy's letters before the graphologists. Now on 16 September Gonse asked him how he proposed to deal with Esterhazy. Picquart suggested arrest. Gonse thought this too elementary: there was no evidence, he said, except the *petit bleu*, which, since it had not been through the post, was valueless. Picquart then proposed to send Esterhazy a telegram, ostensibly from Schwartzkoppen, inviting Esterhazy to call. Gonse said he would consult Boisdeffre. Boisdeffre sent Picquart on to Billot. Billot refused to have Esterhazy arrested. 'I won't be a sub-Mercier'. He tentatively approved the bogus telegram, but on Picquart asking for a written order, refused to give it. At Rennes Billot sketched a noble portrait of himself repulsing temptation. Yet he was probably wise to refuse. If Esterhazy had read the *Eclair* article, he might have recognised the *bordereau* and would have taken precautions. Yet Schwartzkoppen, who did not know the *bordereau*, never having received it, but had received some of the papers listed in it, failed to identify them from the article.

Immediately after the *Eclair* publication, Lucie Dreyfus, observing no *dementi* from the War Office as to the revelation of documents withheld from the defence, addressed a petition to the Chamber. A few journals noticed it, but for most it was obscured by the preparations for the reception of the Tsar.

Left by his chiefs with his hands half-bound, Picquart interviewed one of Esterhazy's former copyists and also Le Rond, the officer in charge of the firing practice at Châlons in 1894. But since he had been warned to be prudent, he was unable to push his enquiries to more than superficial corroboration. Esterhazy was still being shadowed. At the end of September, when his regiment was sent back to the Rouen area, he left 27 Rue de la Bienfaisance. His repeated applications through deputies and generals had become a nuisance to Billot. He told Picquart to search Esterhazy's recent lodgings. Nothing was found except a couple of cards with cordially worded messages from Drumont, which at least showed Esterhazy to be linked with the *Libre Parole*. About the same time Picquart heard from Cavard of the Sûreté that the 'Weyler' letter which had so much disturbed Lebon and himself was not, as they had supposed, from the Dreyfus family, but probably a forgery, designed to strengthen the evidence against the prisoner.

8

During the summer Henry had been on the best of terms with his chief, but he had been first irritated, and then alarmed at Picquart's fixation on Esterhazy, his 'marotte'. There is no vestige of evidence, either direct or indirect, to show a connection between Henry and Esterhazy at this period. Henry was neither more nor less than an experienced professional soldier, loyal to his country, to the service and to his chiefs, though he knew enough about these not to trust them too absolutely. He seems to have had quite a high opinion of Picquart, but he was growing to look on him as a menace to the service. A reopening of the case of 1894 would be disastrous, to the senior officers, to the Statistical Section and to himself, who had made so vehement a declaration at the trial on no basis whatever. He was perfectly conscious of the weakness of the evidence: he probably knew, from either Sandherr or Picquart, that Boisdeffre was uneasy. He had (no one else can have done it) concocted the Blenheim letter to Dreyfus in October 1895, and it is not less credible that he was the author of the Weyler letter: both designed, if read by the Director of Prison Administration, to create a presumption of the prisoner's guilt. Watching Picquart slowly weaving the case against Esterhazy, whose arrest and trial might lead to the release of Dreyfus, he began a more constructive foundation of the case against the prisoner, and since solid materials were not available, he turned to manufacturing them.

He had for a long time had connections with the reporters of the popular press. That he provided the writer in the *Eclair* with the materials for the articles of 10 and 14 September cannot be proved; but though a dozen officers could have given the information to the *Eclair*, only du Paty, who was on manoeuvres, had an equal interest in preventing the re-opening of the court-martial, and du Paty knew nothing about Esterhazy. That Henry was the source of the articles is supported by the fact that in this same month of September he began his career of falsification and forgery, an undertaking in which he more and more deeply entangled Boisdeffre, Gonse, Picquart, and du Paty, tying a net from which they could not free themselves, while he himself, cunning but neither subtle nor far-seeing, was driven to strengthen his earlier experiments with further fabrications, until the day when the truth burst through the web he had created.

The first act of tampering with a document which can be definitely assigned to him appears to have occurred in this month, September 1896. It was an old note of March 1894, from Panizzardi to Schwartzkoppen, which had reached the Section by the 'ordinary route'. It ran: 'Finally, yesterday evening I had to send for the doctor, who has forbidden me to go out. Since I cannot come to you, will you please come to me to-morrow morning, for P has brought me a number of interesting things and the work must be shared as we have only ten days left'. Henry rubbed out the P and substituted a D, while, since the letter, in accordance with the usual negligence of the office, bore no date of receipt, he added 'March 1894' in his own hand, a date which, as was discovered later, happened to be correct. This he carried to Gonse, without informing Picquart. Gonse, as he had been with Picquart, was hesitating and indecisive. Failing to make an impression here, Henry then approached Boisdeffre, who roughly told him that he was uninterested and threw him out. Henry then went back to Gonse, a far more malleable subject, and confidentially suggested that while Picquart was an upright and intelligent man, he was distracted, and neglecting the work of the Section in favour of the Dreyfus-Esterhazy problem.

It was untrue. Picquart, left without orders either to drop the case or to continue, had turned back to his ordinary work, the study of foreign armies. But when talked to by the two Generals about the case, he invariably showed that he could not be dissuaded from his belief that Dreyfus was wrongly convicted. In consequence, Boisdeffre and Gonse came to think that Henry was wholly right in his criticism of Picquart, and decided that he must be removed from the head of the Section. Boisdeffre proposed to Billot that he should be posted to Indo-China, but Billot considered that this would be a bad mark against a good officer. He thought of sending him on a special mission to organise the intelligence section along the frontier, while, to avoid comment, Gonse should take provisional charge of the Statistical Section. Picquart was told of the decision, which was to take effect at the end of October.

Picquart, in evidence, said that he had never yet spoken to any member of his staff about the connection between the Dreyfus and Esterhazy cases, though they must have guessed it after the interview with Cuers at Bâle. Now for the first time Picquart took Henry into his confidence and laid the matter before him. The ex-ranker replied: 'When I was in the Zouaves, some fellow, son of a colonel, got involved in theft. His officer wanted him charged. The seniors thought differently. The officer was broken and the culprit set free'. Henry knew his army on a different level from Picquart's: he knew that one doesn't make oneself a nuisance to one's superiors. 'Your words are golden', answered Picquart, 'but this is a case of conscience. I can't say the opposite of what I think'. This exchange no doubt wiped away whatever hesitations Henry may have had: Picquart was becoming a serious danger. He began planning a decisive stroke.

The extraordinary autumn session of Parliament opened on 27 October, with the Castelin interpellation still pending. Billot and his staff had been perplexed. They had believed that Castelin, in spite of being a Nationalist, was in the pay of the Dreyfus family, and that a highly compromising situation might arise.[1] Billot, on the point of sending Picquart off, postponed his tour. At the same time Gonse took the Secret File into his own keeping.

On All Saints' Day, a holiday, Henry set to work with the aid of papers selected from the various files. He had taken two of no importance, letters to Schwartzkoppen from Panizzardi, signed with the conventional 'Alexandrine'. From each he removed the top and bottom of the page which had not been written on. On one he wrote in pencil, imitating Panizzardi's writing:

> I have read that a deputy is going to interpellate about Dreyfus. If new explanations are needed at Rome, I shall say I have never had relations with this Jew. You understand. If you are asked, say the same thing, for no one must ever know what happened with him.[2]

On the second he wrote:

> Here is the manual; I have paid as arranged (180) on your account. It is agreed for Wednesday. 8. p.m. at Laurent's. I have invited three from the embassy, but only one is a Jew. Don't fail.

To each of these Henry attached one of the headings and one of the signatures with the usual gummed paper. To the first he added in his own hand 'Sept., 1896'; to the second trivial

[1] In fact, Castelin's only interest was to bolster up the circulation of the *Eclair*, in which he was financially involved. All he succeeded in doing was to alarm the War Office.

[2] Henry indulged in a number of forgeries and improvements of documents, but this one is the central piece, and is known throughout the subsequent proceedings as the 'faux Henry'. In order to distinguish it from the other fakes, I shall refer to it in future by that name.

4 (top) *Waldeck-Rousseau*
5 (above) *Casimir-Perier*

6 *Picquart*

7 (top)   *Esterhazy*
8 (above)   *Zola*

9 (top)   *Henry*
10 (above)   *du Paty de Clam*

letter—put in to show that the handwriting of both pieces was the same—'14 June, 1894'. The first, if accepted, would blow Picquart's circumstantial evidence into thin air; it was the ace of trumps.

But though he knew it not, there were two fatal flaws. First, while in 1896 there were indeed three Italians of Jewish stock at the Italian embassy, in 1894 there was none. In the second place, the papers on which the original letters had been written, although to a casual eye identical, were in fact different. On one the feint lines were blue-grey, on the other grey-claret. Not observing this, Henry stuck the blue-grey head and tail on to the grey-claret body and the grey-claret head and tail on to the blue-grey body.

The work was slow and unsatisfactory. Mme Henry, who was at his side, several times advised him to start again because the second piece did not resemble the first faithfully enough.

These pieces he took to the War Office on the next day and showed them to Boisdeffre and Gonse. They were not shown to Picquart since, according to Boisdeffre, Billot had decided that Picquart should not be shown any more of the Dreyfus papers in view of his attitude to the case.

Boisdeffre lapped up the forgery with no other comment than that its resemblance to the writing on the other piece seemed 'perfect, too perfect'. So too did Gonse. Henry now had Gribelin copy the new false Panizzardi letter. He also asked Lauth, who was on long leave at Senlis, to come back to Paris. On Lauth's arrival, he had the copy of the forgery and an appropriate envelope formally attested by Gribelin, Lauth, Gonse and himself: 'the undersigned certify that the present conforms to the original of the letter and its envelope'. It was then photographed by Lauth. Thus should the original be 'mislaid', there would be the photograph (perhaps not too clear a negative) vouched for by four members of War Office staff. It is to be noted that although Junck was in the office, it was Lauth who was brought back to Paris, although the former was a perfectly competent photographer.

Yet in spite of all these elaborate precautions, there were errors. According to Henry, the *faux Henry* had come by the 'ordinary way' on 31 October. He offered no explanation as to

D

how it was that this document came apparently alone, and not as part of the usual delivery? He could not have done so, since the previous full delivery had taken place on 8 August and the next one would be in a week's time on 7 November. (Gribelin, who drew the money for Bastian, did so for 7 November, but not for 31 October). Not surprisingly, no one later would remember exactly how this key document arrived and when. At the final revision Lauth even stated that he had not seen it until six or seven months after its arrival when, he said, he had been told to photograph it.[1]

On the day Henry showed him the forgery, Boisdeffre, before handing it back to Henry, showed it to Billot, who was delighted that Picquart's suspicions could no longer be justified. He decided that the officer had acted too precipitately and indiscreetly and agreed to his departure from Paris as soon as the Castelin interpellation was out of the way.

9

Meanwhile Mathieu Dreyfus believed that he had prepared the ground for the revision of the case. Some time earlier he had been approached by a young Zionist Jew, Bernard Lazare—something of a saint—who believed that an error had been made at the court-martial. Lazare had prepared and had printed in Brussels a pamphlet which showed the contradictions between such facts as had leaked out. The *Eclair* divulgations gave him a great deal more matter. On 6 November *La Verité sur l'Affaire Dreyfus* was published and copies sent to deputies and other prominent men. It made little stir. Jaurès was cold. Clemenceau would not read it. Rodays of the *Figaro*, though believing in Dreyfus's innocence, shrank from action.

On 10 November the *Matin* published a reproduction of the *bordereau*. Although the photographs distributed to the various individuals working on the case had been withdrawn by the Statistical Section, no check had been carried out: Teyson-nières, one of the graphologists of 1894, had made a somewhat

---

[1] The details of the *faux Henry* in all their mistaken elaborations occupy twenty pages of exposition by M. Marcel Thomas (*L'Affaire sans Dreyfus*, Part II, Ch. VI, pp. 325–45).

coarse engraving of the document and sold it to the *Matin*. The publication excited a good deal of comment. Schwartzkoppen, though he had never seen the document, recognised the traitor's hand, and at once informed Panizzardi, from whom he had concealed Esterhazy's identity. No Frenchman came forward to identify the writer.

On 12 November Billot told Picquart that he now had in his hands a document completely establishing Dreyfus's guilt, and read out to him Henry's forgery. Surprised that such a paper should not have passed through his Section, Picquart expressed some doubt as to its authenticity, but Billot would not discuss it, and dismissed him.

On the following morning Maurice Weil found among his letters an anonymous note in a hand he did not recognise, to the effect that he and Esterhazy would be accused by Castelin of complicity with Dreyfus. Much alarmed, he sent for Esterhazy, and after discussing what to do, Weil asked Adrien de Montebello, one of his friends in the Chamber, to hand the letter to Billot.

It would seem that the information contained in this letter must already have been given by someone to Boisdeffre: for, accidentally meeting Picquart that morning, the Chief of Staff, visibly in a state of irritation, cried: 'Ah, Lieutenant-Colonel Picquart, they're regular wrong'uns, your Weil and your Esterhazy, and this looks like the moment to catch them redhanded'. He swept on, leaving Picquart speechless.

Henry had now been working on the pliable Gonse for some time. He had told him that Picquart was responsible for the article in the *Eclair* and for the facsimile *bordereau* in the *Matin*, and that he was no doubt also the prompter of Castelin, the confidant of the Dreyfus family. Only some such intervention can account for the fact that the normally deferential and hesitant Assistant-Chief went that afternoon to the Minister himself, and in the presence of Boisdeffre told him that either Picquart must go or he would resign. Billot at once agreed.

In consequence, on 14 November the three generals had Picquart before them. Billot reproached him with lack of discretion in handling Esterhazy's case and read out the letter which Weil had received. He asked how another letter from

Weil to Esterhazy had reached Picquart's hands. Picquart said that it had been seized in the post, the normal practice of the Section over years. Billot played the noble Roman over these police practices, and declared that Picquart would not only find himself in jail, but would compromise his Minister. He would not, however, punish him for indiscipline, but he must leave the Section for the time being. He was to set off at once on the mission they had already discussed. Realising that he was being got rid of without being allowed to defend himself, the disciplined and obedient soldier made no protest. Next day he handed over the Section to Gonse, and to Henry confided the *petit bleu*. 'You'll see us again at Christmas', said Gonse. On 16 November Picquart reported to Corps Headquarters at Châlons-sur-Marne.

10

Superficially it would appear that Picquart had been sent away because he wished to re-open the case of Alfred Dreyfus, and this superficial aspect has passed into legend. But there is a case for Picquart's superiors, and their problem deserves examination. Dreyfus had been condemned, if not legally, at least in their minds justly. That the condemnation was based on error seemed to them improbable. As regards Esterhazy, he might well be a traitor, but there was no evidence against him that would carry conviction to a court-martial. He might be a loose fish, but that was not enough. The *petit bleu* in fact contained no more than the fact that he might be in correspondence with some unidentified member of the German Embassy, not necessarily the military attaché. Therefore, real evidence must be found before steps against him could be taken. Picquart had found none—nor, as is known today, was he likely to, since Schwartzkoppen had broken with Esterhazy before the *petit bleu* was written. Six fruitless months had passed, and his persistence was becoming a nuisance: Alsatians had the reputation of being obstinate. His obvious preoccupation with the case meant that he was becoming less useful as head of the Section, and, worse, his conduct was bordering on indiscipline. Hence, he must be removed.

There is no doubt that Picquart had an unshakeably high opinion of his own intelligence and a profound contempt for points of view he could not share.

It is said that his superiors ought to have suspected the *faux Henry*, as Picquart had. But only those who had examined the documents in full and over many months read the interchanges between Schwartzkoppen and Panizzardi could have done so. The senior officers relied, as all senior officers do, on the technical skill of their subordinates. They had no reason to consider Henry other than honest. They were in fact grossly misled.

Chapter Five

The Beginning of the Crisis

1

On 18 November Castelin's dreaded interpellation came before the Chamber. Billot, sustained by Henry's forgery, took, the wind out of Castelin's sails by mounting the tribune at the opening of the session. In grave tones he told the members that both justice and State security were involved, and that everything from the preliminary investigation to the final rejection of Dreyfus's appeal had been carried out in conformity with the rules of military procedure. 'The case is therefore *res judicata* and no one has the right to re-open it'. He added that the higher considerations which had necessitated the hearing *in camera* in 1894 had lost none of their validity, and he appealed to the patriotism of the Chamber to cut short a dangerous debate. Since not even his colleagues knew what lay behind his words, he was applauded. Castelin could do no more than take up the crimes of the Dreyfusists, make charges of attempts to bribe officers, etc., and leave the stand, shouting, '*Vive la France! Vive la République!*' As usual with these frivolous interpellations, there was much confusion as to what motion should be put forward. Méline, bored with the whole thing, accepted Castelin's motion of confidence which enjoined the Government to investigate the Dreyfusists: it was passed after a show of hands. Experienced political commentators regarded the whole thing as one more example of the incurable levity and lack of discipline of the deputies. Méline, with no reason to doubt Dreyfus's guilt, and preferring to let sleeping dogs lie, prevented the Minister of Justice, Darlan, from ordering the prosecution of Lazare.

On 3 December the Chamber Commission of Petitions rejected Mme Dreyfus's appeal on the grounds of *res judicata*.

2

Henry recognised that by the forgery of the letter from Panizz-ardi he had put himself in jeopardy, if Picquart should bring about the unmasking of Esterhazy, and Picquart might well be brought back. Therefore his best security was to blacken irremediably his late chief's reputation. Picquart's correspond-ence was still coming to the War Office. Henry proceeded to open it and take copies. Picquart had a small circle of friends, who met at the house of the Comtesse Blanche de Comminges, a middle-aged cousin of his. They often wrote to each other using a slang of their own and imaginary names. From these letters Henry began to forge others in the same style, which implied that Picquart was involved in a conspiracy, and for the first of these he chose a code signature, *Speranza*. Beyond this he opened a file on Picquart for future use, into which he put the *Speranza* letter.

During 1895–96 Picquart had on several occasions consulted a lawyer friend of his, Louis Leblois, on legal points connected with the registration of carrier-pigeons and with the case of a minor German agent. Henry persuaded Gribelin that Picquart had shown secret documents to Leblois, including letters in the Dreyfus file. Further, he attempted to make Commissioner Tomps of the Sûreté produce a report indicating that Picquart had given the photograph of the *bordereau* to the *Matin*. Tomps refused, and thereby earned the distrust and enmity of the Section. Next, taking the *petit bleu*, Henry first scratched out Esterhazy's name on the outside, then re-wrote it, with the intention of making it appear that another name had originally been there, thus suggesting that Picquart had attempted to fix another man's crime on to Esterhazy (but he forgot to look for and destroy the plate and prints of the *petit bleu* made by Lauth in March 1896). In addition, seeing in a newspaper in January 1897 an announcement of the death of Esterhazy's father-in-law, the Marquis de Nettancourt, he cut it out and dated it January 1896, intending by this to show that Picquart had already decided to fasten the *bordereau* on to Esterhazy two months before the arrival of the *petit bleu*. Finally, he took a letter from Panizzardi, dated 28 March 1895, in which the attaché said that he was on the point of receiving the French railway mobilisation plan, and dated it 1894: again he omitted to find out whether copies of the letter had been made, as indeed they had. All this ingenious work could succeed only if the Dreyfus file never left the War Office, never came before a civil court or went to the Sûreté. And this depended on his ability to persuade his chiefs to hold to the *res judicata*, and on the unlikelihood of the Dreyfus family finding a new fact which might lead to the re-opening of the case. These conditions were precarious.

In the meantime Gonse had thoroughly entered into the spirit of the game of making intolerable the life of an officer rash enough to become a nuisance to his superiors. He sent Picquart from corps to corps, writing to him continually, requiring daily reports of his activities. Finally, having driven him from Châlons to Marseilles, he despatched him to organise the intelligence service in Tunisia, attaching him to the 4th Tirailleurs (29 December). All his letters were friendly; Picquart's pay and allowances were handsomely raised; he was given to understand that his somewhat fatuous mission was highly secret and demanded the utmost prudence. Picquart was not deceived and felt that his career was finished. He asked for a transfer to a regiment; he was told to wait. In between times he exchanged friendly letters with Henry, and admitted to him his depression, to which the astute soldier answered: 'I should tell you frankly, and as man to man, that you should have listened to me on the day you said my words were golden. . . . Now I can do nothing and I am profoundly sorry for it' (4 December). Indeed, Picquart's situation was unbearable. He had lost the confidence of his seniors, he had perhaps ruined his career, and he had not quietened his conscience. In early April he wrote out a long statement of the case, saying where the documents were to be found, and addressed it to the President of the Republic, to be handed to him in the event of his, Picquart's, death.

During the spring, since they had not been informed of his absence, agents continued to write to him at the War Office. At length, on 1 May, he wrote a sharp personal note to Henry, asking him to tell the agents something of the truth—he was tired of 'the lies and mysteries' raised by his mission. Henry, against the advice of Gonse, drafted a bold answer, which he despatched on 3 June, but dated 31 May. He wrote that, as a result of Picquart's reference to 'lies and mysteries', an enquiry had been held in the War Office into the fact that he had suggested to two members of the Section that they should testify that a paper filed in the office had been seized in the post and had come from an identified individual, and that he had opened a Secret File and examined its documents, which had led to indiscretions. He added that there were material proofs of these actions, while as for the word 'lies', the enquiry had not discerned when, how and to whom this word should be applied.

It was not the letter a junior officer writes to his senior unless he has powerful backing. Picquart saw that Henry too had turned against him: what was worse, he knew from the Dreyfus trial what 'material proofs' could mean. He replied on 10 June in a brief note protesting against the insinuations. He applied for leave to go to Paris. Arriving on 20 June, he at once saw Leblois and gave him a general sketch of his situation, without, however, mentioning the *petit bleu*; but he showed him 14 letters from Gonse. To all the courts before which he was to appear in the future, he claimed that he was merely taking steps to defend his personal honour. Leblois, however, saw that the fate of Picquart was now inextricably bound up with that of Dreyfus, and urged him to pursue both ends. Picquart hesitated. He was still a soldier subject to military discipline, which he respected. He was still anxious to pursue his chosen career. The argument lasted a week. Then, while giving Leblois general powers for his defence and leaving with him the Gonse letters, he forbade him to communicate with either Mathieu Dreyfus or Demange. Of two other generals whom he approached, one did not see him and the other advised him to 'sham dead'. On 29 June he went back to Sousse. There can be no doubt that he was watched during his visit and that Henry knew he had seen Leblois frequently.

3

Although Mathieu Dreyfus had found sympathy among some unprejudiced men, he was no nearer the truth. Among the politicians and journalists the only champions he had found were Arthur Ranc and Joseph Reinach. Ranc had had a stormy career. A Republican journalist, he had been Gambetta's director of Sûreté at Tours in 1870–71. Later he had been the victim of Right-wing hatred, had been condemned as a Communard and had spent several years in exile. He had been one of the most formidable opponents of Boulanger and had thus earned the hatred of the Nationalists. He was now one of the Senators for Seine and a power in the Radical party.

Both Ranc and Reinach had been convinced early in the Affair that there was something fishy about it. They had met the Dreyfus family and been moved by the letters which the prisoner wrote from his ghastly cell. They realised that they needed powerful support. They therefore approached the much-respected Alsatian patriot, Scheurer-Kestner, vice-president of the Senate. From now onwards what became known as the Syndicate of Dreyfusists began to form.

Scheurer-Kestner had been a manufacturer of explosives in Thann. After 1871 he had crossed the new frontier into France, and in the National Assembly was the embodiment of the lost provinces. A founding father of the Republic, he had been a close friend and associate of Gambetta and had succeeded him as the editor of the *République Française*. Early in 1895 he had met Mathieu Dreyfus and been, if not convinced, shaken by what he had to say. He took up the matter with various prominent politicians, among them Billot. Billot warned him in veiled terms not to meddle in the case. Freycinet and Berthelot also cautioned him in vague phrases. Dissatisfied, he began his own enquiries, but except for the unsupported opinions of his friends in Mulhouse, he made no progress. In the spring of 1897, again adjured by his Alsatian friends, he once more embarked on an examination of the case. He found little. He read Lazare's memoir, but he confessed he was not capable of judging between the handwritings. Among the Senators he found one sympathetic ear, that of Trarieux, Minister of Justice in Ribot's Government, who also thought an error had been made. Nor could Demange help him. Yet again Scheurer-Kestner approached Billot, but, now armed with Henry's forgery, Billot affirmed that the evidence was overwhelming. He went so far as to give his interlocutor a brief version of the *faux Henry*. Scheurer at once suspected a forgery and said as much, but Billot was not to be persuaded.

Scheurer was on the point of giving up, when his nephew happened to meet Leblois at a dinner of Alsatians. Leblois asked for an appointment with Scheurer, and on 13 July told him in confidence Picquart's story. Scheurer-Kestner, who, like many others, romantically believed Army officers to be the pattern of honour, was horrified on reading Gonse's letters: but he perceived that if he approached Billot the ruin of Picquart would follow. Nevertheless, on the following day, at the Longchamps review, he told a number of Senators that he was now convinced of Dreyfus's innocence. Waldeck-Rousseau, having picked up some of Scheurer's remarks and himself having private suspicions of the conduct of the case, begged Méline to look into it, as the matter might have serious consequences; but Méline, after a talk with Billot, refused to move. Scheurer's difficulty remained: how to bring up the case without un-uncovering Picquart. Leblois suggested securing some of Esterhazy's handwriting; but though he obtained several letters and convinced himself that Esterhazy was the author of the *bordereau*, Scheurer realised it was only his word against those of Bertillon and the other experts. Further proof was needed.

4

When nothing followed the *Matin* publication of the *bordereau*, Esterhazy's fears gradually faded. He appears once more to have applied to Schwartzkoppen, but the attaché refused him. He set about a further siege of his political acquaintances to procure himself a staff appointment. No one in the War Office would touch him. Henry promised one of his friends to help him, but in fact did nothing: Esterhazy wrote a scathing letter about Henry to Jules Roche, in which he claimed that Henry was his debtor since 1876—an improbable statement. On a direct approach, Billot told Jules Roche that Esterhazy was a rogue and a bandit and that he lay under the worst suspicion that a Frenchman could lie under. Esterhazy's friends dropped him; he turned to the gutter press. In March 1897 he dashed off a series of articles for the *Libre Parole* and the *Intransigeant*, attacking Billot and drawing attention to the fact that the head of the Intelligence Section, Henry, did not know a word of German. As for Boisdeffre, he was 'lazy and ignorant as a carp, glib, self-assured and full of effrontery'.

During the spring, however, he found temporary relief. He had got in touch with a young cousin, Christian Esterhazy, whose mother had been lately widowed. These Esterhazys, though not wealthy, had in the Gironde some property which had recently been sold. Esterhazy, saying that he was a friend of the Rothschilds, offered to re-invest the money, and managed to get hold of some 33,000 francs. In June Billot, tired of this vagabond parasite and possible traitor, told Boisdeffre to get rid of him. Boisdeffre had him put on half-pay for 'temporary infirmities', and Esterhazy, perhaps realising that he had done himself harm, submitted and retired temporarily to Dommartin-la-Planchette.

5

Scheurer-Kestner's confident statements on 14 July had disturbed Billot. Although the War Office possessed Henry's forgery, in the genuineness of which Billot believed, his doubts of Esterhazy were still not allayed; he was almost persuaded that the ruffian was Dreyfus's accomplice. Moreover, in replying to Castelin's motion of the previous November he had committed himself to the treatment of the Dreyfus verdict as *res judicata*. Even if, in defiance of Hanotaux's refusal to involve the foreign Embassies, he should dare to produce the *faux Henry*, he would be retreating from the impregnable position of the Dreyfus case. Since Mercier, his predecessor, must be sheltered (there is, by the way, no indication of how much Billot knew of the proceedings of 1894), the re-opening of the case was out of the question. But Scheurer-Kestner might become a nuisance. In September Billot sent Bertin-Mourot, now his orderly officer, to find out from the Senator what evidence he had. Scheurer refused to say. Therefore, on Bertin's report, Billot sent a message to Scheurer begging him to do nothing until they had met. Scheurer consented, but Billot, not satisfied, tried through other emissaries to discover what lay behind Scheurer's confidence in Dreyfus's innocence.

He failed, and in mid-October spoke to Boisdeffre of his uneasiness. Boisdeffre was even more perturbed and consulted Gonse, who saw it was now vital to put some stuffing into Billot. On 15 October, he indited a long report in which he cited all the earlier arguments, recalled all the earlier documents, including the *faux Henry*. Not content with this he summoned the essential scapegoat to his side. Du Paty had had nothing whatever to do with the case since 1894. He had heard nothing about Esterhazy, whom he had met twice in Tunisia seventeen years earlier, and nothing of the *petit bleu*. Gonse and Henry now revealed to him the existence of the campaign to substitute Esterhazy for Dreyfus; Esterhazy's wild life, his debts, his *bizarrerie*, were obvious weaknesses for the 'Syndicate' to seize on, though he was in truth merely a sick and embittered man: they feared that if he were denounced, he would either commit suicide or jump the frontier, which would be taken as tantamount to a confession. There would follow terrible complications, in which the generals (not to mention du Paty himself) would be involved: there might even be an international incident. The romantic du Paty swallowed every word of it. One thing Gonse refrained from speaking of was the *petit bleu*. At this meeting du Paty suggested that Esterhazy should be sent for and told to keep quiet. This did not suit Gonse, who had other plans in mind, but he said nothing.

Gonse, Henry and du Paty now considered warning Esterhazy and the last prepared a letter, re-edited by Henry, but Billot, shown it by Gonse, refused to allow its despatch since it would involve him. Gonse went back to du Paty and explained the situation as he saw it. 'You see? that is where we are'. (Gonse later denied having said anything of the sort.)

Left alone with du Paty, Henry said, 'You know what words mean? The general couldn't be clearer. It was not for nothing you've been brought in: it is to warn Esterhazy. You must devote yourself to it. We of the Section can't do it, it would be too indecent. Besides, if they are obliged to disavow whatever officer does the job, he will be sent back to his regiment. We have nothing but our pay, and relegation to the provinces would be hard to bear, with the loss of the Paris allowances, the cost of the move and all the rest . . . but you?'

Du Paty, filled with the spirit of duty and comradeship, replied without thinking, 'I'm ready from the moment the general and you tell me that the man is innocent and the victim of an abominable plot'. Henry at once gave him his word, and when Gonse came in, told him that all was arranged without saying how. Gonse did not enquire. 'Good!' he merely said, smiling; 'go ahead, go ahead!' 'I understand, sir', answered du Paty. As M. Thomas comments, 'by those words, unaware, he smashed a career which might have been among the most successful'.

Hence on 16 or 17 October a letter went off to Esterhazy at Dommartin signed 'Espérance', a reminiscence of the forgery signed '*Speranza*' placed earlier in the year in Picquart's dossier. In this it was stated that the Dreffus (*sic*) family had procured through Picart (*sic*) letters from Esterhazy and was about to denounce him as the author of the *bordereau*. The letter reached Esterhazy on the 19th. Panic-stricken, he hastened back to Paris to his rue de Douai apartment, whither he summoned Marguérite Pays to join him. For the moment he was in despair and spoke wildly of suicide. He was talked out of this by the sensible Pays who pointed out that the flat was in his name and on his death would be sealed up by the police, which would be awkward for her. On the next day he had the lease transferred to her.

Henry had already made a serious blunder in his fabrication of the Panizzardi letter (the *faux Henry*), but so long as the forgery remained invisible in the War Office, it could not harm him. His new move—the drawing into his web of Esterhazy—was infinitely graver, an error of tactics. For, by indicating the existence of Picquart to Esterhazy, he was ensuring the re-opening of the Dreyfus trial. From the moment Esterhazy revealed Picquart's name, Picquart must be called in evidence, and thus the documents could no longer remain hidden in the Rue Saint-Dominique. Boisdeffre and Gonse had in fact seen far deeper than Henry when, in 1896, they had ordered Picquart to separate the Dreyfus case from that of Esterhazy.

If Picquart could have secured the conviction of Esterhazy on other evidence than that of the identity of his writing with that of the bordereau, then there would never have been any need to re-examine that fatal document, or recall the court-martial of 1894. Henry, clumsy and with short views, was now, by his very audacity, to become the author of the revision he was so actively trying to prevent. At the same time, it is another proof of Gonse's stupidity that he allowed himself under the persuasion of Henry to fall into the error he had so carefully avoided a year earlier. True, Henry acted without his knowledge, but there was still time to suppress Esterhazy.

On 19 October Billot received a letter written in a form much akin to that of the 'Weyler' letter, summoning him to take action against Scheurer-Kestner and Picquart, who were trying to substitute Esterhazy for Dreyfus. The letter was passed to Gonse, who on 20 October again consulted with du Paty and Henry. Various methods of warning Esterhazy were mooted, for one an anonymous letter. Drafted by du Paty, it was shown by Gonse to Billot, who forbade its transmission. On his return to the Section, Henry added the initials 'P. D. C.' (Paty du Clam) and filed it, thus beginning to enmesh du Paty. On the same day Gonse sent for Lebrun-Renaud, Dreyfus's unwise escort on the morning of the degradation, and under his and Henry's eye got him to write out and sign a declaration that Dreyfus had then said: 'I am innocent; in three years my innocence will be proved: the Minister knows that if I handed over unimportant documents, it was to obtain serious ones from the Germans', thus once again travestying Dreyfus's account of what had passed between him and du Paty on 31 December 1894.

Still in his vein of *roman policier*, Henry sent Staff Sergeant Gribelin, equipped with dark glasses, to call at Esterhazy's apartment. He was out and Gribelin called again on the following day (28th) leaving a note telling him to be outside the Montsouris Park that afternoon between four and five.

On that afternoon Esterhazy was shadowed by the police as he went from lunch to the Crédit Lyonnais, to his hairdresser's, to the flat of a senator interested in Marguérite Pays, and until he went to the German embassy. Here he remained for an hour in conversation with Schwartzkoppen whom he had not seen for 18 months. From the attaché's memoirs, it seems that Esterhazy attempted to force the attaché to tell Mme Dreyfus that her husband was in fact guilty. Schwartzkoppen gave him a brusque refusal and to all intents threw him out. Later that day Schwartzkoppen made a clean breast of the whole matter to Münster, who was much relieved to find he himself was not seriously involved, and reported to Berlin. Nine days later Schwartzkoppen was gazetted to the command of the 2nd Kaiser Franz Guard Grenadier regiment, and recalled to Berlin.

On leaving the embassy, Esterhazy went to the rendezvous where he was approached by two men. One was Gribelin in his dark glasses, the second was du Paty wearing a false beard. (Henry waited their return in a cab, having warned Gribelin not to let du Paty talk too much). Esterhazy recognised both clowns. To du Paty, he said: 'I do not know who you are, but I tell you that I am about to be the victim of a frightful machination', to which du Paty replied, 'If we were not convinced of it, we should not be here. But how do you know what it is about?' Esterhazy then produced the 'Espérance' letter. Throughout the conversation he pretended to know nothing beyond this. He expressed surprise at the handwriting of the *bordereau* of which he was shown a facsimile; it so much resembled his own, he said. He claimed to know something of Sandherr, but Gribelin sharply stopped him from claiming to have worked for the Statistical Section, an interesting light on the Staff-Sergeant, an enigmatic figure throughout the case. At the end of an hour they separated, du Paty rejoining Henry in his cab.

Henry saw that it was not enough to tell Esterhazy not to talk; he must be told what to say. It is clear that from now on he kept in touch with Esterhazy, unknown to du Paty. It is impossible to elucidate the contacts between them from October 1897 onwards. Esterhazy claimed later that they were intimate and continuous, but no reliance can be placed on his statements and there is no evidence for this one, save that he was undoubtedly put in possession of most of the facts of the Dreyfus case and of what was known against Dreyfus. Henry told Gonse in July 1898 that he had seen Esterhazy only twice, just before his duel with Picquart, and it is obvious that he tried to avoid meeting him: had he done so, he could scarcely have escaped the notice of the Sûreté agents.

The day after his farcical meeting with Gribelin and du Paty, Esterhazy approached the War Office and asked for an interview, which he was granted on the 25th. He was seen by General Millet, director of infantry, to whom he said that he had been denounced to the Dreyfus family by a Lt.-Col. Picquart. He agreed that his handwriting resembled that of the *bordereau*, and continued with an amount of confusing detail. General Millet, himself not at all clear on this emotional story, which reduced Esterhazy occasionally to tears, advised him not to get excited but to write to the War Minister if he believed it useful.

That evening Esterhazy sent Billot a long letter setting out his grievances, in fact copying it out from an original in the hand of du Paty. The original he kept.

On the same day, the *Service du Renseignement* received from the Sûreté a note that on the 23rd, the afternoon of the Montsouris meeting, Esterhazy had spent an hour in the German embassy, a fact he had not divulged to his would-be protectors. Du Paty was now extremely loathe to have any more dealings with Esterhazy, but Gonse told him to consult with Henry about preventing the fellow from talking.

At this point one sees that, with the possible exception of du Paty, the main actors were conspiring with each other and at the same time each distrusted his allies. Du Paty alone seems to have represented the 'blameless fool' in the conspiracy.

At the end of October, the Dreyfusist adherents were increasing, but they by no means formed a party, not even a coherence. Although the phrase 'the Syndicate' came readily to the lips of anti-Dreyfusist journalists, it was not until November that it began to be commonly used.

Scheurer-Kestner returned to Paris on 22 October and was at once invited by Billot. He put Billot off and tried to see Faure, but failed to persuade Leblois to allow him to mention Picquart. Eventually he got to the Elysée on the 29th after Faure had received a letter from Esterhazy, written on his own initiative and couched in the most extravagant language, which perplexed and irritated him. He was very short with Scheurer,

stood on his own constitutional position and at the most
promised no more than a 'benevolent neutrality'. But he held
his tongue. Nothing escaped from the Elysée Palace as it had
from the War Office.

On the next day, Scheurer-Kestner lunched with his old
friend Billot. Neither was quite frank. Scheurer-Kestner spoke
of Esterhazy, but not of Picquart: Leblois would not allow it.
Billot on the previous evening had had a note from du Paty on
Dreyfus's alleged admissions and also new evidence against
Dreyfus. Scheurer-Kestner did his best to throw doubt on the
members of the Statistical Section and on Gonse, whom Billot
insisted was wholly trustworthy. Further Billot declared that
Dreyfus had admitted to having relations with foreign military
attachés. Scheurer-Kestner laughed this to scorn. 'Really I
didn't think you as simple as all that'. 'You don't know a
quarter of the case', retorted Billot, 'Gonse is not a suspect; he
has Jewish relatives'. They parted on bad terms, and Scheurer-
Kestner promised to take no steps for a fortnight.

When he saw Méline on 2 November, Scheurer-Kestner
limited his activity to bringing specimens of Esterhazy's
writing. Méline said he was no expert, and the two men parted
engaged to say nothing. And since Méline was watched over
more carefully than Billot nothing emerged.

On 31 October, having received no acknowledgment of his
letter to the Elysée, Esterhazy wrote a second time to Faure.
Once more he demanded justice, but this time he threatened.
Unlike du Paty and Henry, Esterhazy had a sense of humour,
and now entered heart and soul into the mad conspiracy. He
invented a veiled lady who communicated with him by letters
in a disguised hand—they were in fact written to his dictation
by his young cousin Christian—and gave him information at
night in odd quarters of the city. This high-souled woman he
now produced for the edification of the President. She had, he
said, given him a photograph of a document which later came
to be known as the 'liberating document'. 'The generous
woman', he wrote to Faure, 'who has warned me against the
horrible plots mounted against me by the friends of Dreyfus
with the help of Colonel Picquart, has succeeded in procuring
for me, among other documents, the photograph of a piece

which she has removed from this officer. This document, stolen from a foreign legation by Colonel Picquart, is most compromising for certain diplomatic personages. If I am given neither support nor justice, and if my name is made public, this photograph, which is today in a safe place abroad, will at once be published'. Perhaps nothing better reveals the confused and credulous minds of the President, the Prime Minister and the War Minister than that this rodomontade was taken seriously. On 1 November Billot telegraphed through Boisdeffre to Picquart's General in Tunisia to question him about a photograph stolen by a woman. At the same time Gonse ordered the seizure of Picquart's correspondence in the post. On 5 November, Esterhazy yet once more wrote to Faure, stressing the fact that the publication of the document would mean either war or the country's humiliation.[1]

The third and last letter to the President was handed to Billot, who told General Saussier to have the writer interviewed. The next day, 7 November, Saussier received Esterhazy personally and with his habitual courtesy. Although he believed Dreyfus to be innocent, he was old—he retired two months later —and far too prudent to mix himself up in public brawls. So he heard Esterhazy's tale without comment, and after considering it for three days ordered him to stop writing letters and to send the photograph of the 'liberating document' to the War Office.

On the day of the Saussier-Esterhazy interview, Scheurer made his final appeal to Méline. He had at last wrung from Leblois his consent to the mention of Picquart. He offered to show the Prime Minister Gonse's letters to Picquart. Méline declined: 'I do not wish to read them'. 'Ah', exclaimed Scheurer, 'neither Gambetta nor Ferry would have refused to listen to

---

[1] Whether, as Picquart said at the Zola trial (cf. p. 190) and as others believed, the 'liberating document' was a photograph of the *canaille de D* letter is a question not worth pursuing, since no answer can be given. Its only interest lies in its influence on Faure and Billot. In any case Esterhazy does not appear to have relied on it, since, according to Marguérite Pays, he had a weightier document, which he called 'the Imperial-Guard', and which he kept hidden in the lining of his service cap when Bertulus arrested him in the following July. Nobody ever saw the document, Esterhazy never revealed it, and it may never have existed. (cf. p. 219).

me'. Méline shrugged his shoulders and told him to make formal application to the Minister of Justice. That evening Barthou issued a press note to the effect that Scheurer had given no documents to the Prime Minister, and therefore the Government could only adhere to the verdict of 1894.

Scheurer was left with his dilemma. To make a formal appeal to the Minister of Justice he must offer new evidence: except for Esterhazy's handwriting he had none, and the experts who had already identified that of the *bordereau* with Dreyfus's were unlikely to modify their opinions. Demange wanted Scheurer to reveal the communication of secret documents to the 1894 court and to denounce the real traitor, whose identity he did not yet know. Leblois rejected this scheme, since Billot would simply believe that Scheurer had been primed by Picquart.

Their hesitations were not to be prolonged. Lazare had already issued the second, and public, edition of his pamphlet, with a discussion of the writing of the *bordereau*, and on 9 November Mathieu Dreyfus, who, be it remembered, knew nothing of Esterhazy or Picquart, put out for sale on the streets facsimiles of the *bordereau*. Three days later a member of a financial house named Castro bought a copy and at once recognised the writing of Esterhazy, with whom he had done business. This information was passed to Mathieu, who consulted Scheurer, and was now introduced to Leblois. On the latter's advice, Mathieu prepared a denunciation of Esterhazy to the Minister of War.

On 9 November, at a formal Cabinet meeting with Félix Faure in the chair, there was a brief discussion of the Dreyfus case. Méline, after the press note of 7 November, had been asked to clarify the position to the Chamber. Neither Esterhazy nor Picquart was mentioned. It was decided to stand by the policy of *res judicata*. Darlan, the Minister of Justice, asked to see the file of the 1894 court-martial, since, in the event of an appeal being lodged, he would have to know whether Dreyfus had been condemned legally, and further, since he might be interpellated, he must have the information necessary for his reply. Darlan was in fact by no means sure that the judgement of 1894 had been regular. Billot consented, but a few days later, supported by Méline, withdrew his consent on the ground that it was better that Ministers should not know the roots of the case, a singular comment in view of Cabinet responsibility. This was enough to add to Darlan's suspicions.

On 30 November Méline dropped Darlan after he had received an adverse vote in the Senate on a minor administrative error. He was replaced by an obscure senator named Milliard. Thus the whole Cabinet, save Faure, Méline and Billot, remained in the dark.

During the next few days Scheurer decided to apply to the Minister of Justice. To prepare the way, he wrote to Ranc an open letter, which was published in the *Temps* on 15 November. Unluckily he was anticipated: for on Sunday, 14 November, the Corsican deputy Emmanuel Arène published in the *Figaro*, over the signature *Vidi*, an article in which, without naming anyone, was set out the whole Dreyfusist story: the question of the handwritings, the communication of the Secret File to the judges, the existence at large of the real traitor, who was not a member of the War Office but a titled officer in garrison not far *from* Paris, well known in the capital. It also referred to the *faux Henry* as a forgery.[1]

On the Monday (15th) *Vidi* was answered in the *Libre Parole* by an article signed *Dixi*. This article was brought to Drumont by Esterhazy, but whether he or Henry was the author cannot be verified, although only someone in the Statistical Section could have provided the material. It claimed that a plot had been devised by a high officer, xy, at the War Office, i.e. Picquart, who had worked out a scheme of correspondence with Dreyfus. Dreyfus from The Devil's Island had been able to show how he had forged the handwriting of an innocent, if somewhat wild, officer. *Dixi* accused xy of being in the pay of the Syndicate, and of suborning junior officers to procure the handwriting of the victim. The plot was ready when xy was suddenly, for unknown reasons, transferred from Paris. But he had come back in June, and, with his accomplice, a lawyer, i.e. Leblois, he had met the Syndicate again. In any case, the *bordereau* was only one of a hundred documents on which Dreyfus had been

---

[1] The imbroglio in which all the characters were involved from November onwards can be understood with difficulty and only by examination in detail. Thomas (*L'Affaire sans Dreyfus*, pp. 450–500) alone has some clarity.

condemned. In short, the article exposed the line the Statistical Section was about to follow.

That evening Esterhazy walked into the War Office and handed to the officer on duty a packet containing the famous compromising photograph. At the same time Mathieu Dreyfus was addressing a letter to Billot denouncing Esterhazy as the author of the *bordereau*. The public was at last seized of the case.

The Cabinet agreed to Billot's proposal for an enquiry into Esterhazy, whose name most of them now heard for the first time. In the Chamber on 16 November, in answer to a deputy, Billot was non-commital. He did not say that Dreyfus was guilty, merely that further research had not shaken his faith in the principle of *res judicata;* but that he had invited Scheurer-Kestner to make a formal application to the Minister of Justice, and that, since the Dreyfus family had made public accusations, they had been asked to justify them. For the rest, he uttered a few platitudes about the honour of the Army and the security of the State. The deputies thought he had been weak. A Nationalist senator tried to raise the matter at the Luxemburg. The Senate rejected his motion, while Scheurer sat silent, but with an air of confidence.

On 17th Saussier ordered an enquiry. Esterhazy was not even put under open arrest, and he now hurried from editor to editor relating a number of fables which he did not trouble to make consistent. The press embroidered his story to their own taste. The usual lunatics, by the dozen, wrote to editors offering to give evidence. Scheurer-Kestner, in his unwise spurning of the journalists, had done nothing to enlist them in the cause. The better papers, such as the *Temps*, held to a strict neutrality. Only a few editors dared to protest—Rodays of the *Figaro*, Yves Guyot of the *Siècle*, and the contributors to the new *Aurore*. Scheurer was bespattered with obscene abuse by Drumont, Rochefort, Alphonse Humbert and 'The Monk' of *La Croix*.

Méline's attempt to keep the case out of politics was already futile, but he did not recognise that it was too late. Everywhere deputies found themselves spied on by journalists: a smile or a cordial word exchanged with Scheurer brought a deluge of vituperation from Drumont. Billot found himself pilloried daily or his hesitations and accused of pilfering the secret funds. The abuse was always vulgar and never witty. Drumont was far too much in earnest, and Rochefort had lost his former verve.

Now it was the turn of the German and Italian Ambassadors to protest yet again. Their protests were received with polite grimaces. No publicity was given to their statements, nor to confirmations by the French Ambassadors in Berlin and Rome.

7

Picquart had been kept in the dark by Leblois as to his revelations to Scheurer-Kestner, and he appears to have remained wholly in ignorance of Scheurer-Kestner's activities. In October he was due for his annual leave. Orders were sent to General Leclerc in Tunisia, first to keep him at Sousse, then to send him to Bizerta to organise the surveillance of foreigners. As soon as it was known that Scheurer was about to see Félix Faure, it was guessed that he would mention Picquart, who would then be summoned from Africa. Therefore on 29 October, on the excuse that Arab bands were collecting on the Tripoli border, orders were telegraphed once more to Leclerc to send Picquart there. Did they hope he would be killed? Gonse and Billot indignantly denied it. General Leclerc, puzzled by the eccentricities of the War Office, sent for Picquart and from him learned what had happened to him. Leclerc forbade him to go farther south than Gabes.

About a week later, on 7 November, Esterhazy wrote an insulting letter to Picquart, accusing him of bribing non-commissioned officers to hand him samples of Esterhazy's writing, and of having stolen War Office papers to hand over to the friends of a traitor. A copy of this he audaciously sent to the War Office. On 10 November he went further: he sent Picquart an anonymous note written in capital letters, of which part ran: 'Take care; whole work discovered; withdraw quietly; write nothing'. On the same day he telegraphed to Picquart 'Stop the demigod; all is discovered; case very grave. *Speranza*', while on the same evening he sent a still further telegram: 'Proved that the *bleu* was manufactured by Georges. *Blanche*' (the Christian name of Picquart's cousin Mlle de Comminges). The telegrams were of course seized in transit and passed to the War

Office. Photographs were taken and prints sent to the Sûreté, whose chief Cavard jumped to the conclusion that Picquart was associated in some plot.

Picquart received the two telegrams on 11 November and 12. The first to reach him was that signed *Blanche*. Not understanding it, he tore it up: but the *Speranza* one shook him; he saw that some friend of Esterhazy was pursuing him, and asked to have the *Blanche* telegram repeated. On 15 November he applied directly to the War Office by letter for the matter to be investigated. The anonymous letter he did not receive until 17 November. Realising that it might be compromising if a search of his quarters was ordered, he destroyed it. He did, however, see that the writers could only come from the narrow circle of those who knew of the *petit bleu*. Of what was happening in Paris he still had not the faintest idea. He telegraphed to the War Office for leave to come to Paris. The telegram crossed one from the War Office ordering him to report there.

Chapter Six

The Esterhazy Court-Martial

1

The enquiry into Esterhazy had been entrusted to the General in charge of recruiting in the Paris district, Brigadier-General Gabriel de Pellieux, a man of forty-five, young for his rank, tall, well set up, pleasant in face and speech. Yet another Alsatian, he had brains, courage and energy; his fault was impetuousness.

He opened his enquiry on 17 November, on which day he saw Mathieu Dreyfus and Esterhazy. To Mathieu he was courteous, but said little. Mathieu had little to give except a facsimile of the *bordereau* and specimens of Esterhazy's handwriting. Pellieux heard Esterhazy's rodomontade without expression. On the next day he heard Scheurer-Kestner and asked whether he had any documents. Scheurer replied that he had none, but that Leblois would explain, and now for the first time he mentioned Picquart, with whom he admitted he had had no contact, but whose evidence he regarded as indispensable. Leblois, when he appeared, told the General more than he should have done, more than he told Scheurer. He showed Pellieux Gonse's letters to Picquart and talked freely. Pellieux, who had seen some of the War Office papers, believed that Picquart had disclosed the *petit bleu* to his lawyer, who had then communicated it to Scheurer. Pellieux handed in his report on 20 November, to the effect that there were no serious proofs against Esterhazy, as neither Scheurer nor Leblois had anything but his handwriting, and that since the *bordereau* had been attributed to Dreyfus in 1894, nothing should be done. At the same time he indicated grave faults against Picquart, who appeared to have disclosed confidential documents to an unauthorised person, Leblois.

Meantime, on 17 November, the German ambassador told

the Foreign Minister, Hanotaux, that before leaving Paris Schwartzkoppen had sworn that he had never had any dealings with Dreyfus. To this Henry replied—to Paléologue of the Foreign Office—that the Statistical Section had always said that the link between Dreyfus and the German embassy was Panizzardi. On November 23, Count Tornielli, the Italian ambassador, wrote to Hanotaux that Panizzardi would be forced to write to the press if letters alleged to be written by him, pointing to Dreyfus either by name or initial, were published. Boisdeffre at once told the Cabinet that Tornielli's letter could not be accepted because Panizzardi was a suspect, and that the War Office possessed three letters of his, one of which had the name Dreyfus in full. He insisted that Tornielli's request should be declined. Thus the *faux Henry*, one of the alleged letters, remained hidden.

Already Billot had telegraphed to Leclerc to interrogate Picquart as to whether he had made such communications. The reply had been: only to Leblois. Pellieux now asked that Picquart be heard. Summoned by telegram, he left Tunis on 23 November.

Billot ordered Pellieux to re-open his enquiry, and on this occasion to make it an official one. Pellieux naturally had no hesitation in consulting the head of the Statistical Section— Henry. And Henry had no trouble in putting forward the story he had concocted, that Picquart often had Leblois with him in his room at the War Office. He had, Henry said, seen the Secret File with the *canaille de D* letter on the table between them, as well as other files. But he seems not to have revealed the existence of the *faux Henry*. It was Gribelin who, unknown it appears to Henry, mentioned it to Pellieux. Pellieux went to Gonse, who was now keeping the file and showed him the forgery. Pellieux was of course at once convinced of Dreyfus's guilt, and in consequence of Esterhazy's innocence.

At the same time Pellieux gave Henry permission to carry out a search of Picquart's lodgings in the Rue Yvon-Villarceau. Nothing of any interest was found among his papers, but it made a news story and cast early suspicions on Picquart. There was no search of Esterhazy's rooms.

The second enquiry opened on 23 November, and differed

from the first. Mathieu was harshly treated; Esterhazy was ordered to hand over the letters of the veiled lady. Henry, Lauth and Gribelin were heard on the subject of Picquart's dealings with Leblois.

On his arrival in Paris, Picquart was met by his friend Lt.-Col. Mercier-Milon, who brought him an order from Boisdeffre that he was to see nobody before appearing at the enquiry. He therefore did not see Leblois, and when he came before Pellieux on 26 November knew nothing of what Leblois had revealed. Pellieux allowed him to depose everything he knew about Esterhazy. Shown the *petit bleu*, Picquart said that he thought the writing on the outside had been clearer: he did not perceive that it had been tampered with. Pellieux was severe with him and told him he had committed a grave misdemeanour. When dismissing him, he forbade him to make contact with Leblois, an instruction which Picquart so scrupulously obeyed that he burned unopened a letter from the lawyer. On the following day, when Picquart wished to discuss the *bordereau*, Pellieux refused on the usual grounds that the Dreyfus case was closed. He then showed him the *Speranza* letter (the letter forged by Henry in the spring to place in Picquart's file), which Picquart had never seen, and questioned him on a number of minor matters in his private life. Throughout he treated him as an accused man. Picquart was given no hint of the accusations made by his late colleagues, except that he had one day been seen showing the Secret File to Leblois. He was able to prove that on that day Leblois was not in Paris. There was no confrontation. At the end he was granted permission to talk to Leblois.

Almost at the same time as Picquart was being examined, a packet of letters written by Esterhazy between 1881 and 1884 to a Mme de Boulancy, a distant relative who had been his mistress and whom he had zealously plundered, was passed by her lawyer to Scheurer. In these Esterhazy told his correspondent exactly what he thought of the French and the French Army: 'Our great leaders, ignorant poltroons, who will once more go to populate the German prisons'; 'the people are not worth a cartridge to kill them, and all these little beastlinesses of drunken women to whom men surrender confirm my opinion wholly'; 'if this evening I were told that I should be killed to-morrow as a captain of Uhlans, sabring the French, I should certainly be perfectly happy'. He looked forward to 'a red sun of battle in Paris taken by assault and handed over to pillage by a hundred thousand drunken soldiers; that is the feast I dream of. May it come to pass'. Scheurer took the letters to Pellieux, who tried to laugh them off, but under Scheurer's anger arranged that Bertulus, an examining magistrate who had been left to him by the Minister of Justice, should make a legal seizure of the letters for the Esterhazy file. Mme de Boulancy was summoned by Pellieux, who bullied her but failed to shake her testimony.

On 29 November the *Figaro* published the letters, with one in facsimile facing the *bordereau*. Esterhazy was shaken to the roots. He thought all was over and talked wildly of running for it. One of the police agents shadowing him warned the Préfet of Police, who passed on the warning to the War Office. Billot was thoroughly alarmed. If Esterhazy fled, it was as good as a confession, and he, Billot, would have to explain why the 'Uhlan', as he had now come to be called, had been left at large. Somehow Esterhazy was warned what flight would imply, and stayed. He insisted that the letters were forgeries, and the anti-Dreyfusist press took up the cry: there was nothing of which the Jews were not capable.

Meanwhile Pellieux was completing his report. He had one sultry interview with Scheurer, to whom he said that Ester-hazy's writing could not be compared with a mere facsimile of the *bordereau*. When Scheurer pointed out that the original was in the War Office, he answered calmly that to ask for it would throw doubt on the authority of the *res judicata*. At the same time he admitted that he had been shown a conclusive proof of Dreyfus's guilt, though he did not identify this conclusive proof as the *faux Henry*.

As was guessed from what he had let fall, his report, presented to Saussier, who merely forwarded it to Billot, while severe against Picquart, exonerated Esterhazy. For the War Office, what the world thought of Esterhazy was no matter for con-sideration; he was a crook, a liar, a low-living ruffian, whom they would willingly dispose of. Their sole aim was to prevent a

revision of the 1894 court-martial, and a report clearing Esterhazy of the authorship of the *bordereau* was enough. On the
other hand, if Esterhazy, as he had threatened far and wide,
were to sue Mathieu Dreyfus and Scheurer for libel, the case
would go before a civil jury, and no one could tell what might
then come to light. Esterhazy's lawyer, Maître Tézenas,
observing the harm the Boulancy letters were doing to his
client's cause, recommended him to ask for a court-martial. If
he were acquitted of the charge of treason, as in view of
Pellieux's report he certainly would be, he would be not only
rehabilitated but safe. This plan appealed to the War Office,
since it would avoid the unreliable civil jury and at the same
time confirm the verdict on Dreyfus. They agreed, and Esterhazy in an eloquent letter to Billot, which Pellieux rashly lent
an editorial hand to, applied to appear before a military court.
It was the ratification of a bargain. Should the War Office desert
him, he could always expose their support of him at this point.

On 4 December Saussier, on Billot's recommendation, rejected Pellieux's findings of 'No Case', and signed the order to
proceed against Esterhazy.

It is clear that from December 1897 all the leading actors
in this obscure drama were so involved with each other that not
one could break away. For Billot and Boisdeffre, as well as for
Mercier, still commanding his corps at Le Mans, any re-
opening of the Dreyfus trial, any bringing of documents before
the eyes of civilian judges, experienced in the handling of
evidence, would entail disaster, perhaps even criminal proceedings. Du Paty de Clam had to fear not only his conduct of
the case in 1894, but now his commerce with Esterhazy. Gonse,
who had allowed so many unjustifiable activities, was in no less
danger, and moreover he had given hostages to Henry. Henry,
although he had kept himself in the background, could be
betrayed by some unpredictable speech or action of Esterhazy.
As for Esterhazy, his peril was perpetual, but he had a grip on
both Henry and du Paty, not to speak of his new supporter,
Pellieux, and could use them against their superiors.

If one asks how this could happen, the answer is that it goes
back to the whole conception of the duties of the Statistical
Section, a secret department working on obscure and often

sordid tasks, whose officers and agents knew they would be disavowed by their superiors if they made a false step. Their superiors on the other hand shrank from knowing too much of the Section's activities, though they were ready enough to take the kudos for any successful coup. Henry's advice to Picquart not to worry his chiefs, and his counsel to du Paty that there were things which an officer does on no more than a hint, expose the whole structure of distrust. It is probable that Billot, Boisdeffre and Gonse were, either through shame or diffidence with each other, failing to talk the case over frankly. Indeed it becomes clearer, as the series of enquiries and trials proceeds, that, far from there being a concerted plan or even any serious knowledge of the evidence, they had in fact avoided discussion. Gonse almost certainly never revealed much of his own or Henry's proceedings to Boisdeffre. Billot, on the other hand, partly deceived—he certainly seems not to have suspected the *faux Henry*—partly flinching from coming to grips with the Chief of Staff, technically so much more versed in the business of the Army than he was, failed to work out a policy of his own to lay before the Cabinet. And an inherent loyalty to the uniform forbade him to enquire too deeply into Mercier's delinquency of 1894. Thus each man said as little as possible to the others and allowed matters to drift on a course laid for them by their subordinates and by the maleficent fanatics of the press and parliament.

2

Du Paty had seen Esterhazy several times since their original interview. From mid-November he ceased to have direct contact, either, as he alleged, on orders from Gonse—Gonse denied that he knew anything about the du Paty–Esterhazy connection until the following July—or from fear that he was taking too great a risk. But he continued to communicate through the agency of Marguérite Pays and the cousin Christian. He had removed his false beard after the interview at the Montsouris Park, but he met Christian in dark corners of the city, on bridges or in public lavatories, where messages were read and answers written by match-light.

Christian had swallowed his cousin's stories whole. He believed that the rogue was what he said he was, the victim of a plot, and that everything must be done to save him. In spite of the fact that Esterhazy was now living in open concubinage with a common prostitute, he was shocked when Esterhazy's wife threatened to divorce him. He put himself completely at Esterhazy's disposal and, apart from writing the letters his cousin dictated, in August he had handed over to him another 17,000 francs, bringing the total up to 50,000: he had not yet seen a penny of the profits Rothschilds were to make for him.

As for du Paty, it was not until the end of November that Gonse revealed to him the whole matter by showing him both the file Picquart had compiled on Esterhazy and the file Henry had concocted against Picquart, as well as the Dreyfus file as it now was. Du Paty later admitted having misgivings. He did not believe that Picquart was in any way dishonourable, and said so. He was only half-deceived by the *faux Henry*: he said that Panizzardi had never written a capital D like the initial to 'Dreyfus', and he told Gonse he believed it to be a trap. Lastly, du Paty was surprised to perceive, from a comparatively rapid glance through the commentary shown to the judges of 1894, that it in no way resembled the one he had made. He had no opportunity to examine it more thoroughly, for a week or so later, when Mercier happened to be in Paris, Gonse, on Boisdeffre's orders, handed it to Mercier, who promptly burned it.

On 4 December, when the deputies entered the Palais Bourbon, they read on the notice-boards the order to charge Esterhazy. At the opening of the session Castelin requested Méline to make a statement which would reassure the Army, public opinion and the Chamber. Méline replied: 'I shall say at once the decisive words in this debate: there is no Dreyfus case'. After a burst of applause he went on: 'At this moment, there is not and cannot be a Dreyfus case'. (A Socialist: 'At this moment!') 'An accusation of treason has been made against an army officer; this particular question bears no relation to the other. The examining judge can propose either an appearance before a court, or an ordinance stating that no case lies'. He

then launched out into a disquisition on constitutional principles and legal procedure.

Castelin asked Méline to stress the absence of connection
between the cases of Dreyfus and Esterhazy. Méline said he
would accept a motion. At this point Count Albert de Mun rose.

Albert de Mun was a retired cavalry officer, handsome,
devout, humourless, eloquent and philoprogenitive. He formed,
with the two priests in the Chamber, Gayraud and Lemire, the
tiny group of Christian Democrats, but he was the Jaurès of the
Right. As a soldier he had been horrified at the excesses of both
sides during the Commune of 1871; he had resigned from the
Army and flung himself into social work, becoming one of the
founders of the Catholic working-men's clubs, long before the
Republicans had recognised there was such a thing as a social
problem. 'He resigned from the cuirassiers to enlist in the
gendarmerie', said Drumont caustically. Throughout his
parliamentary career he had represented the Church far more
than the Monarchy. The anti-clerics had so feared his influence
in Brittany that again and again they had unseated him on the
ground of clerical pressure, and each time he had been re-
elected. He had more than once made his position clear as the
champion of the Church against the Revolution and the
principles of 1789. He had welcomed the Ralliement and placed
his hopes in the advent of a Catholic Republic, of which the
Méline Government seemed to be the harbinger. Like many
honourable men, like Scheurer-Kestner, he had implicit faith
in the honour of an army officer. Attacks on the Army, whether
from Drumont or from Ranc, disgusted him; he looked on them
as treasonable. And, like many others on both sides, he made
the crude error of confusing the honour of the Army with the
honour of half a dozen officers. The fact that he himself was the
pattern of honour, the fact that he was liked as a man by all
sides in the Chamber, and the fact that he was eloquent, caused
him to be heard with respect.

From this time, December 1897, de Mun, the representative
of Catholicism—had not a bishop proclaimed he had received
'*le mandat imperatif de Dieu*'?—became the champion of the
General Staff.

De Mun summoned Billot, who was not present in the

Chamber, to avenge the Army and to defend Boisdeffre against the charge he had told Esterhazy that he would cover him. Simple-minded, he raised the question of the occult power which was undermining the confidence of the soldier in his leaders; he looked across at Reinach. He received an ovation, not only from his friends but also from the Left and Extreme Left.

Billot was fetched, and after a short adjournment mounted the tribune. He had already spoken twice on this infernal question. Now he staked his all on giving the answer which would end the clamour for ever. 'Dreyfus', he said, 'has been rightly judged and unanimously condemned by seven of his peers on the evidence of twenty-seven officers. The case has been regularly tried. On my soul and conscience, as a soldier and the head of the Army, I hold that verdict truly delivered and Dreyfus guilty'.

Seven motions were put forward by the various groups. One from de Mun, asking the Government to put a stop to the attacks on the 'Army', was defeated by the narrow margin of 18; another, that the Chamber should not interfere in purely judicial questions, found only 90 supporters. The comparative peace of the past 18 months was breaking up like icicles in a thaw. The Chamber was not dividing on party lines, and, as so often happened, chaos followed. At length a composite motion was put together, with Méline insisting on a vote of confidence. 'The Chamber, acknowledging the *res judicata*, associating itself with the tributes paid to the Army by the Minister of War, approving the declarations of the Government, and blaming the leaders of the odious campaign undertaken to disturb the public conscience, passes to the order of the day'. The whole was carried by a majority of nearly 250. Méline was confirmed in his confidence that he now could and would keep the case out of politics. Billot and Boisdeffre could congratulate him and themselves. They had not realised that de Mun, the supporter of the Army as well as of the Government, had in fact taken the case out of the Army's hands and thrown it into the political dogfight.

Scheurer had as yet made no move. He was disgusted with Billot's evasions. He put down a notice to interpellate Méline and Billot in the Senate. The case was now exciting other countries than France, and on 7 December the Luxemburg Palace was thronged with foreign journalists, while half the deputies had come over from the Palais Bourbon. Scheurer went into action at a complete disadvantage. Picquart had refused to allow Leblois to give Scheurer Gonse's letters, and had forbidden the mention of his name to the Senate: he wished to remain the good soldier, and he had not yet perceived that his seniors, as well as his late colleagues of the Statistical Section, intended to destroy him. Nevertheless Scheurer spoke well, declaring that he had begged Méline to undertake the revision himself: moreover, it was not true that Dreyfus had been well and truly condemned: documents had been shown to the judges but not to the defence. Billot retorted that Scheurer had no evidence that the *bordereau* was the only basis of accusation against Dreyfus. Of the Secret File he did not breathe a word. The Senators lapped up his statement. Méline added that the 'Government had acted with perfect correctness; its sole guide was the Law'. Scheurer, and Trarieux who supported him, were heard in dead silence; the Senators thought that their hearts were better than their heads, and they gave the Government a unanimous vote of approval. In neither Chamber was the matter re-opened before Parliament rose on 23 December.

3

In the criss-cross of charges and counter-charges of espionage, bribery, falsification, mendacity and illegality, with the anti-Dreyfusists at one moment crying for action, at another for silent respect for the *res judicata*, with Rochefort boldly stating that the German Emperor was himself involved, with Ministers sometimes professing the regularity of the 1894 trial, at others admitting further unspecified charges against the traitor, at others again holding tenaciously to the sanctity of the judgement and never very sure whether they were lying or merely telling half-truths, it is little wonder that in Paris—for the case hardly as yet interested the provinces—Parliament and society, inflamed by a reckless press, began to take sides. None except the handful of Dreyfusists in part, and the War Office staff again in part, had any evidence on which to base an opinion. Hence rumour pursued rumour, fantasy fantasy. Yet as Christmas passed and Twelfth Night approached, it became clearer that the case or cases could not remain sealed up in the judicial circle, and that they must in the end involve the Government, the Chambers, the Judiciary, the Army and even the Church. The old conflicts of doctrine were reappearing; Jacobinism was once more stripping for battle against the Ancien Regime. And only five months ahead lay the general election. Could Méline hold out until the crucial month of May was passed? The politicians of the Centre and the Radicals were resolved to prevent the Dreyfus case from becoming a question for the electorate. None the less, the Radicals had no intention of permitting Méline an easy passage. Now that de Mun, representing Church and Army, had thrown down the challenge from the Right, they would not shrink from attacking them both, not on the particular issue, but on general principles of doctrine.

At this hour the Church in France had not yet spoken. The French ecclesiastical hierarchy was far too experienced, and far too cautious, to intervene. Cardinal Richard, Archbishop of Paris, invited by some University professors to lend his prestige to the cause, said that it was not the duty of the Church to interfere or to call in question the uprightness of Republican justice. Cardinal Lecot of Bordeaux, when pressed by Canon Chaîne, recommended silence and neutrality. Some priests protested against the demagogic pretensions of the Assumptionists and their anti-semitism. 'For the observer', wrote the Abbé Pichot, 'there are scarcely any Jews favourable to Dreyfus. And of those who should be blamed, it is the rich and powerful Jews, the great Jewish newspapers, for not siding with their co-religionists'. 'I have thought', he added, 'of possible reprisals, and I have asked myself with anguish if the attitude of *La Croix* would not bring reprisals'. Several—Archbishop Sueur, Bishops Fuzet and Mignot—regretted that they could not control the Assumptionists. They were helpless. The Dreyfusists, rebuffed, began to look elsewhere, to the University.

It must be emphasised that in January 1898 there was as yet no movement in favour of Dreyfus, because, except for the few who had been the recipients through Leblois of Picquart's opinions, there was no evidence that Dreyfus had not been justly, even if not legally, found guilty. It was the irregularity of the proceedings, and not the presumed innocence of Dreyfus, that alarmed and angered men like Trarieux and Waldeck-Rousseau in the Senate, and a few journalists such as Cassagnac, Yves Guyot and Clemenceau.

It must also again be stressed that in itself the Affair was of minor importance from a governmental point of view: it merely gave an opportunity for the Opposition to sow the wind. Each Minister had his own important tasks to fulfil. The Budget for 1898 was not yet near completion, and the Government must obtain provisional credits to carry on. Hanotaux, moreover, had been embarrassed by the rumours of the *faux Henry* and the name of Panizzardi. The Italian Ambassador, Tornielli, had warned him that any letters believed to emanate from his military attaché, in which Dreyfus was mentioned, were forgeries. He had wrung from Hanotaux a promise that no paper claimed by a friendly Power to be false should be made public. To the Cabinet Hanotaux said that he believed Panizzardi to be lying, but prudence was imperative. In any case, the Cabinet could hardly disbelieve Billot, and they had all seen previous newspaper tumults pass away. Moreover they bore no particular love to either Reinach or Ranc. The policy of silence was accepted.

4

Méline has never been called a great statesman, but he possessed some of the statesman's qualities. He knew why he was head of the Government: his business was to guard and preserve the existing structure of society against those who would break it down in favour of one of their own systems. In particular he was there to resist the Radical proposal, considered dangerously revolutionary, to substitute income-tax for a large part of the indirect taxes. For 18 months he had successfully resisted all attacks. His passage had not been altogether easy, but the Ralliés and some of the Conservatives had supported him without fail. These, added to the 250 Progressists and

Liberals of his own following, had assured him the necessary majorities. He had made no bargain with the Right, but he had refrained from hostility to the Church and the Religious Orders. The Radicals of course accused him of betraying the Republic, and in May, Delcassé, a Progressist, had moved that the Government should rely only on a majority of Republicans, but he had failed to carry the Chamber. Méline's single danger lay in the appearance of some unexpected, eccentric, controversy, some question of principle, which might split his own group.

Now, for the first time, he was faced by a problem turning on that awkward word, justice, a word calculated to excite demagogues and preachers to violence. Worse, it involved one of the great institutions of state, the Army, which, whatever its faults, was popular. Even more disturbing was the fact that its defenders were drawn from both wings of the Opposition; on the one side de Mun, the acknowledged representative of the Church, on the other Cavaignac, the Radical proponent of income-tax, while the Dreyfusists, although few in numbers, were drawn from his own party. And the elections would take place in less than five months. If his Government were defeated by a combination of Conservatives and Radicals, it would almost certainly be succeeded by a Radical Government, which in May would have in its hands, through the Ministry of the Interior, all the levers to exercise political pressure on the voters. For these reasons he chose what appeared to him the course of wisdom: to entrench himself behind the judgement of 1894, the *res judicata*, and to refuse to hear anything which might weaken that resolve. He undoubtedly knew of the *faux Henry*, but the question of Dreyfus's guilt or innocence was irrelevant; it was a question of the conduct of his trial. Hence he must on principle refuse to hear anything about the materials of the case, either from Scheurer-Kestner or from Billot. And in pursuit of his policy of neutrality he must ignore the accusations of the Dreyfusists and yet refuse to oblige the anti-Dreyfusists by attacking them.

5

The summary of evidence for Esterhazy's court-martial was

entrusted to a retired army major called Ravary, who opened his examination at the Cherche-Midi on 8 December and continued it up to 30 December. Gonse and the officers of the Statistical Section gave evidence, largely against Picquart and Leblois. Esterhazy, having been stiffened by the information that Ravary had been primed—he said later by du Paty—told his customary story and proliferated accusations. Marguérite Pays, Scheurer, Reinach, Mathieu Dreyfus, were all heard. The weak spot was the *bordereau*. None of the available professional experts wished to be mixed up in the Dreyfus case. But they were assured that the examination of the *bordereau* was only to decide whether it was in the handwriting of Esterhazy. On this they got to work, dealing simultaneously with the Boulancy letters. Then an incautious note from du Paty raised the suspicion in Esterhazy's mind that the verdict on the Boulancy letters would not be given until after his court-martial, and he guessed that the perfidious War Office, while securing his acquittal on the *bordereau*, would get rid of him through the other correspondence.

The experts, under pressure, concluded that the *bordereau* was a poor copy of Esterhazy's writing, and went on to say that the Boulancy letters might equally be the work of a forger. Ravary's summary cleared Esterhazy, but, on Henry's testimony, accused Picquart of showing the *canaille de D* letter to Leblois, and stated that the *petit bleu* was a fraudulent document. Nevertheless, in order to allay public opinion, Saussier was persuaded to order a court-martial on Esterhazy. But was the hearing to be held *in camera* or in public? The War Office insisted that defence secrets required a closed hearing. After much argument a compromise was reached, that only Esterhazy and the civilian witnesses, though not the handwriting experts, should give their evidence in public. Scheurer-Kestner and Trarieux were both outraged at the news and published letters of protest in the *Temps*, but without avail.

Mathieu Dreyfus was naturally represented by his brother's counsel, Demange, who now knew much more than he had in 1894. For Mme Dreyfus, Demange recommended a rising young advocate, Fernand Labori, ambitious, vigorous, handsome and noisy. 'Labori', said Barrès, 'is not an intellect—he is a temperament'. The court of seven officers, presided over by General Luxer, assembled on 10 January in the same room in which Dreyfus had been tried. Since the Minister of War had publicly declared on three occasions that Dreyfus was a traitor, their minds were already made up: moreover, in view of the Pellieux and Ravary conclusions, they had no alternative to acquitting Esterhazy. Demange and Labori were refused leave to plead, on the ground that the case did not concern Alfred Dreyfus.

By five votes to two the court decided to hear the military witnesses and the experts *in camera*. Esterhazy made charges right and left, and became confused in his own evidence, but nobody pressed him. He refused to identify 'the liberating document'. During Picquart's examination, Pellieux intervened to prevent the mention of Billot or Boisdeffre. The court was rough with Picquart until one of the junior judges remarked: 'I see that Colonel Picquart is the real accused. I request that he be allowed to offer all the explanations necessary for his defence'. Picquart then completed his evidence. He did not know, and would not know until the following day, the accusations made against him by his late subordinates, Henry and Lauth. Faced by Henry, he rebutted the charge of communicating the Secret File to Leblois, and Leblois supported him. The court believed both to be lying. There was a curious exchange between Tézenas, Esterhazy's lawyer, and Mathieu Dreyfus. The former said that Paris had been inundated for some days with foul pamphlets, a manoeuvre against justice, and that 300,000 francs had been spent. 'Not a word of truth in it', replied Mathieu. 'Then sir, how much?' asked Tézenas. 'That's my business', retorted Mathieu. 'I defend my brother as I intend. It is my right'.[1]

After hearing Tézenas's speech for Esterhazy, the court found

[1] The part played by money in the Affair remains and will remain obscure. It is certain that a great deal changed hands on both sides. Reinach is very discreet, but Mr Wickham Steed told me that when, as correspondent of *The Times*, he was transferred from Rome to Vienna, the Viennese Jews openly said that Reinach had bled them for the cause. On the side of the anti-revisionists, it is certain that Mme de Loynes financed in part the Ligue de la Patrie Française, just as by will she left money for the benefit of Maurras's *Action Française*.

him not guilty. The audience broke into applause, and outside the prison the court gave 'the martyr of the Jews' an ovation with shouts of 'Long live France! Down with the Syndicate!' Trarieux at the Rennes trial said: 'Esterhazy has been acquitted: he has not been judged'.

On the following day Pellieux permitted Esterhazy to publish the findings of the experts on the Boulancy letters. On this day too—13 January—Billot ordered Picquart under fortress arrest to Mont-Valérien.

The partisans of revision had not coalesced. Some knew one part of the case, some another. Picquart had the greater number of threads, though by no means all, in his hand. He had shown them only to Leblois and had talked with none of the revisionists. Only now did the basic material factors begin to be known. On 7 January Reinach dared to publish the Ormeschville report of 1894, which gave the lie to Billot's declaration of 7 December that the *bordereau* was not the only evidence against Dreyfus. On 12 January, with the Ravary summary of evidence for the Esterhazy trial, the *petit bleu* came to public knowledge. Enough was now known for the revisionists to become a coherent body and work out a plan of campaign. The precipitating element of this cohesion was at hand.

Chapter Seven

The Intervention of Zola

1

The most widely read and most heartily detested novelist of the day was Émile Zola. The list of his novels, of which sin was the obsessive theme, had been extending since 1868. He was regarded with horror by the Catholic conservatives, with contempt by other writers. 'Zola', wrote Anatole France, 'has no taste, and I end by thinking that lack of taste is that mysterious sin of which the Scriptures speak, the greatest of sins, the only one which will not be forgiven'. He had recently completed his trilogy *Lourdes, Rome, Paris* and was casting about for a theme when the Dreyfus case re-emerged in November 1897. He had written two articles on Dreyfus for *Figaro;* then de Rodays, the editor, thought by the owners to be too Dreyfusist, was replaced. After this Zola published a couple of pamphlets which fell flat. The acquittal of Esterhazy roused him, and he set feverishly to work. It is possible that his self-esteem, which had never been low, led him to believe that he had but to speak. Probably he did not foresee the furies that '*J'Accuse*' would raise. As was said, he was always throwing bombs and was surprised when people were hurt. It is also possible he had not realised that, if he were taken at his word and prosecuted, he would not be the centre of the trial, that the real drama would be played by other actors, and that his words would seem fustian against the exchanges of the confronted witnesses. A recent critic has said: 'Whatever he may have done for the Dreyfus family, it was nothing to what the Dreyfus family did for him'. In so far as his support of Dreyfus made him acceptable to many writers who had hitherto shrunk from him, it is true. Yet his action must not be underestimated. His trial forced into the light much that had been hidden, and removed many of the barriers to revision.

During two nights and a day after Esterhazy's acquittal he composed a long open letter to Félix Faure. In it he arraigned the War Office, Mercier, Billot, Boisdeffre, Gonse and chiefly poor romantic du Paty de Clam; he attacked Pellieux and Ravary and the handwriting experts at the Esterhazy trial. He accused the War Office of running a campaign in the *Eclair* and *Echo de Paris* to cover their tracks. He accused the first court-martial of violating the rights of the defence, and Esterhazy's court-martial of acquitting him on orders from the War Office. 'As for the people I accuse, I do not know them; I have never seen them. I bear them neither ill-will nor hatred. For me they are no more than entities, spirits of social evil. . . . My fiery protest is only the cry of my soul. Let them dare bring me to the Assize Court and may the examination be made in the light of day. I wait!' He took it to the office of the *Aurore* on the evening of 12 January. Vaughan, on Clemenceau's suggestion, ran the headline 'J'ACCUSE' and placed it on the front page. It was on sale at eight next morning, and by evening 200,000 had been sold.

Méline was taken completely by surprise. Since he had refused to look into the case, he was angered at the accusations against the various officers. But he was careful. At first he thought the sensible line was to do nothing, as in the past. But on reflection, and after talking to his ministerial colleagues, he realised that it was impossible to ignore the article, with the patriot press in eruption and the Chamber warming up to overthrow the Government. De Mun had at once given notice to interpellate Billot, and Billot and Boisdeffre knew they must act.

Two days later, the 14th, the Chamber resumed its sittings. Brisson, once again re-elected President, in his address made a few comments on the perils of dictatorship, and announced that he had received notice of an interpellation from the Comte de Mun. The Government bench was empty except for Cochery, the Minister of Finance, who was expecting to deal with the urgent matter of the overdue Budget. The Right noisily backed de Mun in his demand for Méline and Billot. 'The Army', roared de Mun, 'will not be kept waiting'. Méline, when he appeared, said that he well understood the indignation of the

Chamber: Zola would be prosecuted, in spite of the fact that what Zola actually wanted was to prolong the agitation. De Mun insisted on summoning Billot, who added nothing save a few platitudes to Méline's declaration. Jaurès, amid hostile murmurs, remarked that the Government was handing the Republic over to the generals.

It was the turn of Cavaignac, who hoped to overthrow Billot. He asked why the Government had not published Lebrun-Renaud's account of Dreyfus's confession: it escaped him that this confession, if it existed, should have appeared in January 1895. In reply Méline, while not denying the existence of Lebrun-Renaud's report, said that to follow Cavaignac on to this ground would lead to the re-opening of the case, and in Parliament. All he need do was to hand Zola over to public justice. The man who had been Prime Minister in 1895, Dupuy, held his tongue. Although Cavaignac's reference to a confession had reassured a number of members, his motion of censure on Billot was defeated. Méline got a vote of confidence, but well over 100 members abstained from voting.

On the same day, in the Senate, Scheurer, vice-president for as long as anyone could remember, was defeated at the annual re-election.

On 18 January Billot, after a full meeting of the Cabinet, requested the Minister of Justice to lay an information against Zola and the manager of the *Aurore*, Perrenx. The charge was skilfully drawn. It was confined to the passages which accused the judges at Esterhazy's court-martial of acquitting by order a criminal whom they knew to be guilty: 'the first court-martial may have been unintelligent, the second is criminal'. Thus the trial would be restricted to matters on which the defence could produce no evidence, and by eliminating the accusations against du Paty and Mercier would keep the Dreyfus case remote from the proceedings.

2

The excitement caused by Zola's letter was not confined to the Chamber. It was a signal to the anti-semites. From 17 January onwards Jules Guérin, the leader of the anti-semites in Paris, set on foot a series of anti-Jewish demonstrations in the provinces beginning with Nantes, Rennes, Bordeaux, Tournon, Moulins, Marseilles, Montpellier, Angoulême, Privas, Toulouse, Angers, Châlons-sur-Marne, Saint-Malo, Luneville, Epinal, Bar-le-Duc, Grenoble, Niort, Le Havre and Orléans, which were in turn the scene of riots by students, ne'er-do-wells, and hirelings, and in which the shops of the few Jews were smashed and pillaged.

In Paris there was little but demonstrations. The only serious outbreak occurred, as might be expected, in Algeria, where the trouble began on 18 January in Algiers. After four days' looting of shops, the mob, inflamed by agitators, swept down on the Jewish quarter and sacked it. Lépine, the Governor, who had been sent from the Préfecture of the Police in the previous October with the mission of discouraging trouble of this kind, was powerless to keep order, as were the Préfet and the Maire; the police were overwhelmed. These scenes were repeated on a lesser scale at Constantine and Oran as well as in smaller towns. The inspirers of the violence, Morinaud and an Italian named Max Régis, were neither restrained nor arrested.

On the revisionist side, the article in the *Aurore* had been followed by a petition against the violation of procedure in the trial of 1894 and the manifest incapacity of the court-martial on Esterhazy. It called for a revision of the Dreyfus case. It was signed by many men, savants, writers, philosophers, painters, teachers and students—by Grimaux, Anatole France, Monet, Reclus, Émile Bourgeois, Lucien Herr, Renan's son-in-law Psichari, the two young Halévys, Élie and Daniel, Marcel Proust, whose *Jean Sauteuil* contains his impressions of the trial: in all some three thousand names. There would have been many others but for fear of reprisals. 'Yesterday', wrote Clemenceau in the *Aurore* of 18 January, 'one of our most distinguished secondary schoolmasters said to me: "You'll get no one from the schools. If I gave you my name, that ass Rambaud [Minister of Public Instruction] would send me to rot in the depths of Brittany".' Nevertheless the so-called intellectuals were far from unanimous. A great number were hostile, among them Brunetière, Lemaître, Barrès, Degas (almost blind, revelling in hearing the *Libre Parole* read to him each morning),

Coppée, Forain. 'The Dreyfus case' said Albert Thibaudet, 'was a tumult of the intellectuals'.

Except for Guérin's bands of ruffians, the case had roused no interest among the workers of Paris. The Socialist leaders were both cautious and far from unanimous. Guesde and Chauvin suggested to Jaurès that he should take up the case as the spokesman of the party. Either because he knew Guesde to be jealous of him and feared desertion after he had committed himself, or possibly from reluctance to break with his right-hand man, Millerand, Jaurès refused, on the ground that he was not yet convinced. Certainly the Socialist Union was not of one mind. Vaillant and his Blanquists, whose constituents were the small Paris shopkeepers, would not come out in a Jewish cause. Others were themselves anti-semites. The Allemane group was for revision. Jaurès's group was split; Millerand, its most powerful member, was for the Army and against revision. Those Socialists who were closest to the Radicals followed their patriotic line. In the end the policy which Guesde, dropping his first advice to Jaurès, recommended, was adopted: since Dreyfus belonged to the capitalist class, the enemy class, let the rival factions of the bourgeoisie, the opportunists and the clericals, fight it out. 'Between Reinach and De Mun, maintain your full liberty' (Manifesto of 19 January). After the event the Socialists were to claim that they were the first in the field for revision, but their votes during the six months betray them.

22 January, according to a political correspondent, 'will remain without precedent in our parliamentary annals since the Convention'. Cavaignac had once again pressed for the publication of Lebrun-Renaud's report, and also one by Gonse which he alleged bore the date of 6 January 1895—a letter from Gonse did exist, but Gonse had only just written it. Méline once more perceived the shadow of a Right-and-Left coalition against him. He admitted that on the evening of Dreyfus's degradation Lebrun-Renaud had made a report such as Cavaignac indicated, but he refused to read it; the judgement had been legal and could not be questioned: and he swept into an attack on those who slandered the generals.

He had admitted the existence of a confession, which probably he had never seen. That was enough for the Chamber. Amid immense applause, Cavaignac withdrew his motion. At that moment Jaurès dashed to the tribune and broke into a violent harangue against Méline, against the 'Jesuit generals protected by the Republic'. 'We are dying of equivocation and cowardice, in the lies and cowardice of the incomplete charges against Zola'. Rebuked by Brisson, he returned to the attack, scarlet in the face, thundering against the Ministers and the generals. A noisy, truculent member of the Right, the Comte de Bernis, called him a member of the Syndicate. Jaurès retorted that Bernis was a miserable coward. Bernis moved to the centre of the Chamber, on which twenty Socialists flung themselves at him and the Right rushed to the rescue. Gérault-Richard slapped the Comte's face. The ushers vainly tried to part the shouting combatants. Bernis freed himself and, running up the tribune steps, hit Jaurès on the back of the head. Brisson, after frenziedly and impotently ringing the presidential bell, clapped on his hat and closed the sitting. The Palais Bourbon military guard marched in and swept out the struggling and vituperating members.

At the next session, the deputies, shame-faced, sat in silence. Jaurès put a series of questions to Méline: had the first court-martial been given documents not shown to the defence? Why was there systematic use of *in camera* procedure? What was he afraid of? Méline refused to answer questions, and justified his attitude by saying: 'The Government will not substitute itself for the justice of the country'. Once again he fell back on his impregnable entrenchments, the separation of the powers and the *res judicata*. Later, a few members said to Jaurès: 'What a pity this business broke out just before the election'.

On this same day, 24 January, von Bülow, the German Foreign Minister, told the Budget Committee of the Reichstag that he did not desire to enter into French domestic affairs: he would limit himself to a formal and categorical denial that there had ever been relations of any kind between Captain Dreyfus and any German agent. In Rome an analogous statement was made by the Foreign Under-Secretary to the deputies, and a few days later William II called on the Marquis de Noailles, the French Ambassador in Berlin, and repeated Bülow's declaration. Hanotaux passed these on to Méline and Billot. Even if they believed the statements, they were now far too deeply involved to be able to act.

Billot and Boisdeffre decided to deal with Picquart before the Zola case came on. Although properly he should have gone before a court called by his own commander in Tunis, he was described for these purposes as an officer on the staff, temporarily detached. The Court of Enquiry was presided over by General de Saint-Germain, a squat, ill-bred dwarf, intimate friend of Mercier. Picquart was accused of all the old crimes, of showing the Dreyfus and the two other files to Leblois, of having handed him Gonse's letters. Leblois, called, successfully destroyed one of the accusations, but the President refused to allow him to confront Henry, Lauth and Gribelin. Gonse, very hostile, said that Picquart should have been relieved of his duties instead of being sent to Tunis. Alone General Galliffet spoke boldly and warmly for Picquart. Picquart addressed the court in his own defence, rebutting the charges one by one, and ended: 'If it is desired to thrust me out of the Army, I bow to the wish, fortified by my own conscience. The court will weigh whether Lt.-Col. Picquart should be hunted from the Army while Major Esterhazy still walks the streets with his rank and his decorations'.

The court, by four to one, found that there were grounds for dismissing Picquart from the service for grave infractions of discipline. He should at once have been released. Instead he was sent back to Mont-Valérien. Billot, who should immediately have accepted or rejected the findings, delayed in the hope that Picquart would show discretion at the Zola trial.

The trial of Zola and Perrenx was called for 7 February.[1] Zola's counsel was Maître Labori, profuse as usual. Perrenx,

[1] French legal procedure differs from English in a number of ways. As regards evidence, a witness makes his statement in full, and without examination by counsel. Article 319 lays down: 'The witness cannot be interrupted. The accused or his counsel may through the presiding judge question him after his deposition, and say, as much against him as against his evidence, everything which may be of use to the defence of the accused'. In cross-examination, questions to witnesses are thus put through the judge, who can refuse to put them, or worse, put them in a form different from that put by counsel, though in practice it seems that

the manager of the *Aurore*, was represented by Albert Clemenceau, younger brother of Georges, but Georges Clemenceau himself, although not a member of the Bar, was authorised to appear on behalf of the newspaper. As has been seen, the policy of the defence was to justify *all* the charges made in *J'Accuse*, whereas that of the Minister of War was to confine the case to the Esterhazy court-martial. Thus the defence wished to call almost 200 witnesses, not only Mercier, Billot, Boisdeffre, Gonse, du Paty and the officers of the Statistical Section, but the Cabinet Ministers of 1894, the judges of 1894, Casimir-Perier, Pellieux and Ravary, Picquart, Leblois, Esterhazy, Lebrun-Renaud, many journalists, philosophers and savants, Panizzardi and Schwartzkoppen: in short, anyone who could throw light on the 1894 trial.

Billot did not want to appear, and as a Minister he need not. Boisdeffre wished to prevent the officers from attending. Billot showed him that they must, but that Boisdeffre, by refusing to release them from 'professional secrecy', could close their mouths.

The Dreyfusard writers charge that the Judge, Delegorgue, a round and rosy man, took his orders from the Minister. It may be so, but he was wholly correct in preventing the evidence, as far as he could, from straying away from the specific accusation of Zola.

7 February saw the Assize Court invaded by an excited crowd of journalists, lawyers, army officers, society women— the fashionable first-night audience. Guérin had patrols of his anti-semite roughs outside the Palace of Justice, ready to cheer

---

frequently he does not intervene. But the remotest contacts with the case are admitted. To blacken du Paty, Labori produced a witness to say that du Paty many years earlier had got him ten days' C.B. for writing an essay to show that brains, not force, ruled the world. But the witness was found to have identified the wrong officer.

Possibly the least satisfactory practice is that hearsay evidence, what some third person has told the witness of the acts or conduct of the accused touching his guilt, is admitted and given probative effect. This was particularly bad at the Rennes trial of Dreyfus in August–September 1899, where the statements of at least 20 out of the 100 witnesses were of this character; sometimes they had no factual basis whatever, sometimes they were contradicted by the person they were quoting.

See Lord Russell's comments on the Rennes trial; cf. pp. 237–8.

or hiss any recognised face. The witnesses waiting in the corridors divided into two opposing groups: between them the lean and sinister Esterhazy, in civilian clothes, stalked to and fro, cut by both sides. The jury consisted almost entirely of tradesmen. As soon as they were empanelled, the Advocate-General, Van Cassel, asked that the trial be limited to the single charge on the indictment, the insult to Esterhazy's judges. 'There is no right to question even indirectly the *res judicata*. Behind that lies the wish to provoke a revolutionary revision'. Counsel for the defence protested, but not strongly, their chief object being to get the military witnesses into the box. In this they were aided by the Judge, who rejected Billot's attempt through the Minister of Justice to prevent the appearance of witnesses other than those concerned in the Esterhazy trial—Lauth, Gonse, Pellieux and Gribelin. Delegorgue ruled that the military witnesses should appear. Esterhazy tried to avoid going into the box, but the Judge enforced his appearance.

Esterhazy had been enraged by the cool attitude of the officers towards him. He spoke about it to someone, possibly Pellieux, and on the third morning Boisdeffre came up and shook him by the hand. Others followed his example. None the less they did not like it, and as soon as they could, left him alone. He felt the slight, became irritated, and suddenly burst out to a group of civilians, who were talking to him: 'They bore me with their *bordereau*. All right, yes! I wrote it! But it was not I who invented it; I did it by order!'

On 8 February, when Labori called Lucie Dreyfus, Delegorgue, since she had nothing to say concerning the Esterhazy case, refused to question her. On this, Zola, his moment come, demanded the freedom 'granted to murderers and robbers; they can defend themselves, they can call witnesses'. Delegorgue interrupted him: 'You are aware of Article 52 of the law of 1881', to which Zola returned angrily, 'I don't know the law and I don't want to know it'. There was at once an uproar, in the midst of which he explained that he rebelled against the sophistries of a hypocritical procedure. It took some time to restore silence and then Lucie Dreyfus was asked to leave the box. She was followed in it by Leblois, who told what he knew about the *Blanche* and *Speranza* telegrams, about du Paty and the 'veiled lady'. Scheurer, the next witness, wanted to read the correspondence between Gonse and Picquart, but was forbidden.

Boisdeffre was heard the following morning: he claimed, for reasons of State, the right to answer only those questions he could answer without endangering security. He whitewashed everyone except Picquart, who had been blameworthy in accusing Esterhazy without being able to discover any serious proofs. As for Dreyfus, he said that while the 1894 case was outside the discussion, 'later facts had confirmed his own certainty'. In allowing this statement, Delegorgue had accepted evidence on a matter on which Lucie Dreyfus had been silenced. Gonse, who followed, sheltered behind the plea of professional secrecy: the exchange of letters with Picquart had nothing to do with Dreyfus, to whose case he would not think of referring. (Reinach that morning had published several of these letters in the revisionist papers). Lauth and Gribelin took up against Picquart the accusation that he had shown secret War Office papers to Leblois. Confronted with Leblois, Gribelin stuck to his story that he had seen them together in October 1896: Leblois proved that he was in Germany at that time. Then came Mercier.

Shortly before the trial, Mercier at Le Mans had had several conversations of considerable frankness with his corps artillery commandant, General André, a firm Republican and anticlerical. Mercier had no doubt about the existence of the 'Jewish syndicate', since some years earlier he had been prevented from prosecuting a well-known army contractor who had cheated the Government. Now, called on to give evidence in the Zola case, he told André that in 1894 he had had in his hands crushing proofs of Dreyfus's guilt, but these proofs, if produced in open court, would inevitably lead to war with Germany at the moment when the new guns were not ready and the Germans were in possession of the French plans. In view of the risk, his only solution was to give the judges the evidence in secret. 'It was serious for me; it was an abuse of authority, I knew. Between the safety of my country and judicial crime, I chose the crime.' But now that the war plans had been redrafted, and France was once again on equal terms, the case could be reviewed and judged in open court. The court can 'say if I am blameworthy for having, even at the price of my peace of mind, wanted to assure the security of France.[1]

Possibly he intended, if driven to the wall, to admit what had been done in 1894. But Labori botched his cross-examination. By misquoting the *canaille de D* letter and suggesting that it was a postscript, he gave Mercier a loophole. He disclaimed all knowledge of what Labori was talking about, and then withdrew behind the verdict of 1894.

On 10 February four of the judges of 1894, and Ormeschville, were called, but Delegorgue refused to allow them to give evidence. The main witness of the day was Henry. He had not wanted to appear, but the defence succeeded in their request. On reaching the box, he said he was ill: 'I have eighteen campaigns behind me and I have every right to have a touch of fever!' He took his time over answering questions. Asked about the Secret File, he replied that he had had it from Sandherr, but refused to state its contents. 'It was the file of the Dreyfus case?' 'No, the Dreyfus file had been sealed up since 1895.' Confronted with Leblois as to the alleged conferences with Picquart, he got muddled and contradicted himself, until Gonse, saying that he was a very sick man, secured his withdrawal.

Pellieux, convinced as he was by the *faux Henry*, could not do otherwise than insist on Esterhazy's innocence: Picquart himself, he said, had been deceived by a combination of forgeries. Since he was speaking of the marrow of the case, he was listened to attentively, and his decisive bearing was convincing. He pointed out that the court-martial which tried Esterhazy could, after they had seen his own and Ravary's reports, do nothing except acquit him. He stated emphatically that Esterhazy's judges had been honourable, and that he was proud to

[1] The phrase 'the war plans' can only refer to the credit to the War Office of 300 million francs for an unspecified object, in fact for the new 75 mm Q.F. gun. Although most authorities deny that Mercier was alarmed at the possible betrayal of the gun, he was in this instance undoubtedly sincere. In May 1894 he had ordered the mock-up of a battery: after January 1895, as a mere Corps Commander, he had no connection with either Bourges or Puteaux arsenals, but it is impossible for him to have forgotten the earlier versions of the 75 and the secrecy attached to it.

have been 'their leader'. Zola, who had been silent since his outburst on the second day, broke out: 'France can be served by both the sword and the pen. General de Pellieux has doubtless won great victories. I have won mine. By my works the French language has been spread through the whole world. I have my victories. I bequeath to posterity the name of General de Pellieux and the name of Emile Zola. Posterity will make its choice'. The demonstration was alas! irrelevant, and Pellieux remained master of the field.

One other witness appeared that day, but was not heard. This was an elderly lawyer named Salles, who had heard from one of the judges in 1894 that Dreyfus had been convicted on documents not shown to the defence. Delegorgue, having elicited that his evidence did not touch the Esterhazy trial, refused to hear him. Every attempt by Labori and Albert Clemenceau was cut short with: 'The question will not be put'. Salles left the box.

On 11 February it was the turn of Picquart, still held, pending Billot's decision, at Mont-Valérien. Here he had been sent two officers to advise him that his future depended on what he said to the court. The first, Colonel Maurice Bailloud (who—by then 'a rosy old Punch of a man'—was to command the French Expeditionary Force at the Dardanelles in 1915), was shamed by Picquart's friendly manner and did not deliver the message. To the other Picquart simply answered that he would tell the truth. Furthermore, Bertulus, the lawyer seconded to advise Pellieux, was asked by Gonse to let Picquart know that if he, so to speak, remained in the military family, as everyone desired, and held his tongue, his career would not be ruined. Picquart coldly replied that he would do his best to reconcile his duty as a soldier with his duty as a witness.

He was wearing uniform. Tall, thin, with an impassive face, he told an enthralled audience of his discovery of the *petit bleu* and his first amazed examination of the Dreyfus Secret File, which contained no proofs. Of his conversations with Gonse, Boisdeffre and Billot, of Henry's betrayal, of the *faux Henry* and the Weyler letter, he said not a word. In examination by Labori, he pointed out that no one had ever told him that Esterhazy could not be the author of the *bordereau;* no one had ever told him to stop his investigations. He hinted, no more, that Esterhazy had been protected. Pellieux had shown him the so-called 'liberating document': it was the same as that alleged to have been shown by him to Leblois, the *canaille de D*.

Picquart had burned his boats and could expect no mercy. From this moment the centre of the case swung away from Zola, away from Dreyfus, to Picquart. As Pellieux said: 'Without Picquart the case would not exist'. From this moment the members of the Statistical Section set about him. Gribelin asserted that he had seen Picquart and Leblois with the Secret File open between them. Lauth swore that Picquart had tried to force him to say that the *petit bleu* was in the hand of a military attaché, and further had tried to persuade him to fake the photographs to show that the *bleu* had passed through the post: he said he believed, but would not swear, that Picquart had himself planted the letter in Bastian's bags. Clemenceau tore most of this to pieces, but Lauth resolutely maintained his statements.

On the following day Henry was confronted with Picquart. Once more he repeated that he had seen the file with his initial on the cover lying on the table between Picquart and Leblois. Cross-examined, he was led on to say that the *canaille de D* letter was sticking out and that he recognised it. Picquart replied that it was impossible to know it at a distance. 'I could recognise it at ten paces', said Henry. Picquart said that he formally challenged the statement, whereupon Henry ex-claimed: 'There's no arguing about it, particularly if one is accustomed to seeing a document, and I've seen this more than once. I maintain formally what I said, and I say again, Colonel Picquart has lied'. For one moment Picquart nearly lost control of himself; he raised his fist to strike but let it fall again, merely remarking: 'You have no right to say that'. The Judge blandly interrupted: 'So you two disagree'.

Clemenceau angrily protested at Delegorgue's remark, before turning to Henry. Going back to the witness's evidence of two days earlier, he showed that Henry then denied that the file with the '*canaille*' letter had anything to do with the Dreyfus case, and had said that the Dreyfus file had been under seal since 1895 and had never to his knowledge been opened. How did he reconcile that with his current statement that the letter he saw between Leblois and Picquart was the '*canaille*' letter, and part of the Dreyfus file? Henry replied that it had nothing to do with the Dreyfus case. 'However, I will explain this file. It is a long time since I took responsibility for it. *Allons-y*. Here goes'. He went on to say that Sandherr in 1894 had told him to collect in one file all documents relating to espionage. 'I found eight or nine pieces, of which one was highly important, very confidential, ultra-secret. Sandherr kept it from November until the 15th or 16th December, when he gave it back to me: in the interval he had had a few photographs taken of it. I then put all the documents of the file into an envelope, marked it "*Dossier secret*" with the letter D and my initials on the back. This lay in my cupboard until Gribelin got it out for Picquart. When Sandherr gave me back the file I asked him why he no longer needed it. He showed me a letter, making me swear never to talk about it and added: "I have several pieces besides this one; I keep them beside me, and if need be I shall use them". I have never heard anything more about this [ultra-secret] file; the Colonel never handed it over to me. He spoke of it only the once, on 16 December 1894'.

Henry had successfully blurred the traces. Neither Labori nor Clemenceau appears to have done any serious work on the case. They do not seem to have understood what Henry was saying; they did not pursue the line of the *canaille* letter. They let Henry go.

On the same day Demange in the witness-box uncovered a little more. Delegorgue was momentarily caught napping. To Labori, Demange admitted that had he believed the Dreyfus judgement to be legal, he would not have applied for an annulment. 'What makes you think it illegal?' asked Labori.

'Because M. Salles learned from a member of the court that the judgement was null and void'.

Albert Clemenceau quickly put in: 'Is that because a secret document was shown to the judges?' And before Delegorgue could stop him, Demange whipped out: '*Mais oui, parbleu!*' Later Stock, the publisher, stated on oath that a member of the court had told him that four documents had been communicated. Delegorgue cut him short.

By the end of the fourth day the revisionists, seeing that some light was gradually filtering through to the original case, were inclined to congratulate themselves: they even began to believe that Zola would be acquitted, though, considering the body of the indictment, it is difficult to see the grounds for their optimism. In any case they had reckoned without the power of the anti-revisionist press. In all the popular newspapers the reports were, as usual, abridged, and concentrated on the more dramatic aspects. According to the views of the editors, awkward statements were omitted, favourable ones enlarged: there was no hesitation about falsification when required. Beyond this, the unhappy jury received veiled threats: an unlucky juryman, having been discovered to be one of the Rothschilds' tradesmen, was denounced by Drumont as being in the pay of the Jews, and judiciously went sick.

During the trial the anti-revisionists invited the professional Republican patriot and poet, Paul Déroulède, founder in 1882 of the now defunct Ligue des Patriotes, to return to the field of action. From his adherence to the Boulanger cause in the eighties had sprung his permanent feud with Clemenceau. Hence he willingly accepted, and during the rest of the case appeared in court as the leader of the anti-Zola claque. In the corridors the Nationalist advocate Auffray worked up tumults of his fellow-barristers and army officers. Each day outside the precincts the crowd increased to watch Guérin's ruffians jeer, pelt or even assault the witnesses on Zola's side.

Meanwhile the case dragged on. From 12 to 17 February were heard those who wished to testify to Zola's virtues— Jaurès and his friends. The evidence of the handwriting experts was taken: on one side were ranged Bertillon, 'the stubborn defender of the unintelligible', and his overawed or venal fellows: on the other, brought in by the defence, the expert palaeographers of the Ecole des Chartes and the Institut, who demolished the prosecution's witnesses and, as one man, swore that Esterhazy was the writer of the *bordereau*. The dreary case seemed scarcely to move. By 15 February *The Times* correspondent, Fullerton, was writing: 'This affair is even beginning to affect business. The shops are suffering, timorous foreigners hasten their departure and postpone their arrival...foreign orders are falling off from a supposed uncertainty of punctual execution'.

On the afternoon of 17 February Picquart was recalled. He gave it as his permanent opinion that Esterhazy could, from many sources, including the firing-practices he had attended, have procured all the information described in the *bordereau*. Pellieux and Gonse in confrontation asserted that the information about Madagascar could not have been obtained by Esterhazy, since at the time when the Madagascar expedition was being planned—August 1894—he was at the artillery ranges. Picquart remarked that surely the *bordereau* was of April, whereon Pellieux sharply replied that it was not, and appealed to Gonse to confirm him. Picquart was shaken; he could merely tell Delegorgue what he had always heard, that the document had been written in April, and had always accepted it as of that date. On this Labori asked Gonse why Ormeschville in his indictment had accused Dreyfus of procuring a document on Madagascar in February (before any confidential work on Madagascar had been done): Gonse stammered that he could not explain, but he stuck to his statement. Labori—it shows how little he understood—failed to take up the point, which could then and there have destroyed the prosecution's case of 1894.

Throughout the trial Pellieux had been becoming more and more irritated. In complete honesty he had accepted the *faux Henry* as genuine. He could not understand why his chiefs— Billot, Boisdeffre, Gonse—with such a weapon at hand, were reluctant to produce it and preferred to shelter behind the *res judicata*. It does not appear that he at any time took up the point with Gonse. Now, however, having seen the handwriting experts covered with ridicule by the palaeographers, having seen Gonse contradicting himself in the box, he determined to play the *coup de maître*. On the plea that the defence had read a passage from the Ormeschville indictment of Dreyfus, he claimed to speak not of the case itself, but to adduce further evidence. He then related that at the moment of the Castelin interpellation of 1896 the War Office had received a positive proof of Dreyfus's guilt. So far as he recalled it, it ran: 'There is going to be an interpellation on the Dreyfus case. Never say anything about the relations we were in with this Jew'. He went on: 'The revision of the trial has been sought by a roundabout way; I give you this fact; I affirm it on my honour, and I call for the support of General de Boisdeffre'. There was a howl of joy from the anti-revisionists. Zola and Clemenceau at once demanded the production of this document. Pellieux was furious that his mere word was not accepted. Gonse asked to speak, and confirmed Pellieux's statement, but insisted that this proof, which was real and absolute, could not be brought into the public court.

Pellieux, abashed, and angry at Gonse's veiled reproof, tried to regain control of the situation. When Delegorgue said that Boisdeffre's evidence could be taken next morning, he shouted to his orderly officer to fetch Boisdeffre at once. Then, turning back to Zola's counsel and the audience, he roared that he would not be interrupted, that he would be believed. 'No proof has been brought of secret communication to the judges. . . . The newspapers [i.e. *Figaro*] have abridged Ormeschville's indict-ment'. Clemenceau expressed surprise that, in all his speeches, Billot had never mentioned this decisive letter. Pellieux shouted: 'General Billot does what he likes; it's none of my business. But there are other pieces, as General de Boisdeffre will tell you'.

Delegorgue hastily closed the hearing. That evening the noise outside the court was worse than ever. An attempt was made to get hold of Leblois, who escaped with difficulty. Zola and his counsel left by a side door.

On the following morning Boisdeffre, having approved Gonse's refusal to produce the document, made a brief and dignified appearance in the box. 'I confirm the deposition of General de Pellieux in all its points as exact and authentic. I have nothing more to say. I have not the right. You, gentlemen, are the jury; you are the nation. If the nation has no confidence in its Army's leaders, in those responsible for the national defence, they are ready to leave the heavy task to others. You have only to speak. I will say nothing more. I ask leave to withdraw'. It was, of course, a threat, and the wretched jury-men knew they could not resist. How could they ask for the resignation of the Chief of Staff? Delegorgue refused Labori permission to cross-examine.

Picquart, recalled later in the day, said it would be well to verify the authenticity of some of the documents, notably the one which had reached the War Office at the moment when it became necessary to show serious proof that another than Esterhazy had written the *bordereau:* for 'the moment at which it appeared, the absolutely improbable terms in which it was conceived, gave every reason to think it a forgery. This is the piece of which General de Pellieux spoke yesterday'. It will be remembered that Picquart had had from Billot's lips a version of Henry's fabrication.

This concluded the material body of the evidence, though not the trial. After Boisdeffre, Esterhazy was called. He had been thoroughly coached by Pellieux. His orders were to refuse to speak. Gaunt and yellow, he stood in the box and faced Albert Clemenceau. Clemenceau had prepared a list of questions covering his career, his letters about the French, their Army and their generals, about the *bordereau.* To none did Esterhazy reply. Implacably and remorselessly his adversary questioned him. The spectators grew restive as through forty minutes the ordeal went on. After the last question they gave Esterhazy an ovation, which was loudly renewed as he left the court. Prince Henri d'Orléans congratulated him on his courage, and Guérin's boys carried him shoulder-high to his cab.

On this afternoon, Maurice Paléologue overtook Henry on the latter's way home, looking very unwell. Henry said he had a return of fever, and then broke out against Pellieux. 'One doesn't throw secret papers into a public hearing . . . Gribelin had no idea what General de Pellieux was going to use it for . . . Gonse whispered to me: "What an ass!" I felt suffocated'. Paléologue repeated this to Armand Nisard, at the moment the permanent head of the Foreign Office, and Nisard replied: 'The document is a forgery'.

On 21 February the final speeches began. That of the Advocate-General was cold, dull and flat. Zola replied. Egotistical and romantic, although claiming to speak for Dreyfus, he spoke of himself. 'He began', wrote Fullerton of *The Times*, 'with an insult to the Prime Minister and at the same time to the jury; and such glorification of himself must have displeased the unpretentious men who form the jury'. Even

Reinach, his admirer, admits that the 'I' was superabundant. Labori followed, and continued on the next day. He spoke quietly, tracing the whole history of the case from the arrest of Dreyfus: he implied that the generals had been mistaken, and that someone, not in the War Office, but a friend of Esterhazy, had forged the evidence. Finally, on the evening of the 22nd, Clemenceau rose on behalf of Perrenx. Throughout their speeches the counsel had been interrupted by Déroulède and his claque. Clemenceau pursued his way unmoved; he had faced Dèroulède before when they exchanged shots in 1892 and both missed. He stuck to his theme that he did not know whether Dreyfus was guilty or innocent, but that it was invincibly evident that he had been condemned by violation of the law: and 'illegality is a form of iniquity, since the law is a guarantee of justice'. This did not answer the charge against Zola and Perrenx but it brought out the higher issues. The jury retired. That morning each had received an anonymous offer of ten thousand francs if Zola were acquitted.

They returned to the court forty minutes later and gave their verdict. By a majority they found both the accused guilty, while on the question of extenuating circumstances they were equally divided. In face of the indictment, they could not have found otherwise; no evidence had been offered against Esterhazy's judges.

The verdict was greeted with a howl of joy, echoed in the corridors and taken up by the street: 'Up the Army! Down with the Jews!' Zola was condemned to the maximum sentence under Article 31 of the Press Law of 1881: imprisonment for twelve months.[1] Perrenx got four; both were fined the maximum, 3,000 francs.

'Yesterday', wrote the *Berliner Tageblatt* on the following morning, 'the French Army won its first victory since its defeat in 1870–71'.

---

[1] Zola appealed, and on technical grounds the appeal was allowed. He stood his trial again at Versailles on 18 July, and was again condemned to the maximum penalties. On the night of 19 July he set out for London, where he remained for 18 months. He went much against his will and only under the heavy pressure of his friends. It is said that his expenses during his period in England were paid by the Viennese Jews.

Chapter Eight

The Death of Henry

1

At this point it is well to consider how far the facts about the trial of Dreyfus were known to the general public. Readers of the press had seen poor facsimiles of the *bordereau* and of Esterhazy's writing. They could have read Ormeschville's summary of evidence, an unconvincing document. From the reports of the Zola trial they could conjecture that at the court-martial of 1894, documents not available to the defence had been shown to the judges, but evidence of this divulgation was far from clear, and in any case the contents of the documents were unknown. They may have read some of Esterhazy's letters to Mme Boulancy, but these were irrelevant except as to Esterhazy's character. As for the *petit bleu*, its existence was unknown to all save some of the War Office staff and to Picquart: even the leading revisionists never heard of it until Picquart was dismissed from the service.

On the other side, there was Picquart's not very illuminating evidence at the Zola trial, which had been stoutly challenged by a number of officers. As to the Secret File, the story given by Henry had completely obscured the matter. There was Pellieux's deposition as to subsequent irrefutable evidence against Dreyfus, confirmed by Gonse and Boisdeffre. Furthermore, Schwartzkoppen had been transferred to Germany, a significant removal.

On top of all this confused evidence there were the rumours that letters from Dreyfus to the Kaiser and one from the Kaiser to Münster were, either as originals or photographs, in the possession of the War Office, that vast sums of money were being sent to France by foreign Jews, and so forth. And there was always the fear of war with Germany.

'Fanaicism begins at the point where evidence stops short'. In Society everyone had his opinion and everyone clung to it tenaciously, coloured as it was by his own political and social prejudices. In these circles the case from being a subject of conversation swelled into furious discussion, and from discussion to open quarrels. Families were torn apart; engagements broken off by partisan parents; old friendships were ruptured; partnerships dissolved. 'Whatever you may say or do', wrote Paul Cambon, then on leave from Constantinople, 'you are classed as a friend or enemy of the Jews and the Army'. Agitated hostesses wrote on their cards of invitation requests that the Affair should be treated as taboo.

Outside these circles the effects of the trial were small. 'I am bound to admit', wrote Clemenceau on the morrow, 'that the working classes appear to take no interest whatever in the question.' *The Times* correspondent had already noted that, amid all the appeals to violence by the anti-semites, 'there prevails a sort of indifference. . . . Anti-semitism has not penetrated the masses. . . . The shopkeeper fights a very easy battle with them (the Jews), and does not really fear them'.

Apart from Paris the country was little interested. As yet the provincial bourgeoisie were immune; they did not catch the infection until the appearance of the Waldeck-Rousseau Ministry in June 1899, and the Rennes court-martial. The provincial artisans and the peasants were never roused. Many of them did not read newspapers. Duclos, later the Communist leader, says in his memoirs that although he, a Jew, was brought up near Lourdes, he knew nothing about anti-semitism or what was a Jew. In the provinces, it is true, there were the whipped-up anti-semitic riots in Nantes, Rennes, Lyon, Rouen, Marseilles, Clermont-Ferrand and other towns, chiefly of students and ne'er-do-wells intent on plunder: the only serious trouble was in Algeria, where the outbreak of mid-January had hardly died down, and where, in spite of the urgings of Barthou and Méline, the authorities found themselves impotent to quell the anti-semites.

In Parliament indifference reigned. On 18 February, after hearing Boisdeffre's evidence with its threat of resignation, Jaurès tried to raise the scare of a military *coup d'état:* 'the Republic has never run so great a danger'. His fellow-Socialists were cool.

Did the Left at any time believe that the danger existed? It is difficult to be definite. Undoubtedly cooler men of great political experience entertained the idea. Paul Cambon, looking at the attitude of the soldiers to revision, thought that a revival of Boulangism might occur: 'It may be that a general will be found to take up a spectacular defence of the honour of the Army. But', he added, 'it is true, I don't see the general'. In fact there was none. All the soldiers desired was to be master in their own house, without interference from the politicians, to whip their own dogs, and for that they were ready to go to lengths, but not to extremes, not to revolt. As isolated as monks from the main currents of civilian society, the generals did not know enough to decline the help of political charlatans who hoped to use them for their own purposes.

Thus there was mutual misunderstanding. The civilians, the Senators and deputies, were no less ignorant of the Army. They did not attack it on the score of incompetence: they accused them of the one thing from which every general on the active list would have drawn back in horror; rebellion. The members of the Army committees in the Chamber and Senate did not know their business, and they permitted freedom to their fellows to attack, on political grounds and for electoral purposes, the institution they should have protected.

There were even weaker foundations for the attacks on the Church. Anti-clerical writers presented the Church as a reactionary body allied to the Army in conspiracy against the Republic. The evidence is thin. The single body which justifies the charges of anti-clerical writers was the Assumption Order, plebian and violent, which did so much harm to Vatican policy; which was deplored by many bishops; and over which they had no control. For the Vatican, Dreyfus was a minor matter, of the smallest importance in comparison with the doctrinal warfare which raged during these years throughout the whole Catholic Church.

2

In the French Parliament the disposition to damp down the

Zola and Dreyfus cases remained. On the day after the verdict two deputies put forward a somewhat academic motion on the predominance of civil power over the military. Méline, while admitting that the generals had been drawn on to say too much, maintained they had been provoked to exasperation by Zola's counsel. He claimed that the incessant accusations made by the Dreyfusards were responsible, and that the Jews who had so rashly undertaken the campaign were themselves the provokers of anti-semitism—they and 'this intellectual élite which seems to take pleasure in adding venom to raw hatred'. While he rejected the idea of reprisals, he said that, where circumstances demanded, disciplinary measures would be taken. The speech was greeted with immense applause from all sides. The deputies, with the elections so near, were not likely to respond to the jeers of Clemenceau, who in his daily column was lashing the hypocrisy of those who professed liberal ideas while failing to put them into practice.

Naturally the anti-revisionists made no bones about their victory; they triumphed noisily. They believed that revision was dead. They were wrong. In spite of the verdict, the Zola trial had demonstrated to those who read the full report of the proceedings that much was being concealed. If the politicians ignored the omens, the despised 'intellectuals' read them aright. Immediately after the trial there came into being the League for the Defence of the Rights of Man and the Citizen. Its earliest members were found among professors from the Ecole des Chartes, who had heard from the palaeographers at the Zola trial of the fatuity of Bertillon and company; from the Collège de France; from the Ecole Normale Supérieure, brought in by its Socialist librarian, Lucien Herr; there were serious publicists, such as Yves Guyot, former Minister, economist and editor of *Le Siècle*, and Françis de Pressensé, and a few Senators, Ranc, Trarieux. Particularly notable is the large proportion of Protestants among the leading members. The Protestants knew well that they were as odious as the Jews to militant Catholicism. The League's growth was not rapid, but it had excellent speakers, who began to carry their mission beyond the boundaries of the Seine. Slowly its influence began to be felt.

The League's statutes had been drafted by Trarieux and the

eminent Catholic savant, Paul Viollet, who became its first secretary. Viollet suggested that a master-stroke against the Right would be for the League to put forward the re-admission of members of the teaching Orders to the State Schools. The League committee rejected the proposal unanimously, and Viollet sadly resigned. This early manifestation of anti-clericalism by the committee set the future course. Within five years the League was to become as fanatic and as treacherous as its enemies.

Meanwhile Méline's disciplinary measures were being taken. On 26 February Picquart was dismissed from the service for grave professional faults; his pension was commuted to rather less than £100 and, being no longer liable to recall to the Army, he would wear uniform no more. He was released from Mont-Valérien. Leblois was relieved of his duties as assistant Maire of the VIIth arrondissement: he was also suspended for six months by the Paris Bar Council on the grounds of professional misconduct in communicating to Scheurer-Kestner the confidences of his client, Picquart. Even Demange escaped censure only by the vote of a majority. Grimaux, senior professor of chemistry at the Polytechnic and the Agricultural Institute, was removed from his chairs, at the Polytechnic by Billot, at the Institute by Méline: he had rashly testified on Zola's behalf.

In the world of journalism, where no holds were barred, inter-professional abuse led to frequent duels, of which the most prominent was that between Clemenceau and Drumont. Both were ageing; they fired three times, and three times they missed. It is fair to say that in all these encounters there were no deaths and very few wounds. One duel had some importance. For his insult at the Zola trial, Picquart challenged Henry. Henry refused to meet him, on the ground that Picquart was a dishonourable person. Pellieux told Esterhazy to challenge Picquart. Picquart, in turn, refused to cross swords with Esterhazy. During the negotiations between seconds, Henry called openly at Marguérite Pay's apartment to discuss matters with Esterhazy, with whom he had hitherto had no acknowledged contact. In the end Henry accepted Picquart's challenge. They met on 4 March, when Henry received a slight wound in the arm.

3

As has been seen, Picquart, since his arrival in Paris, had had little contact with the revisionists. He had seen Leblois only once before the Esterhazy trial, and only met Scheurer, Mathieu and Mme Dreyfus on the first day of the Esterhazy trial. To Mathieu he said: 'You need not thank me; I obeyed my conscience'. Forty-eight hours later he was in Mont-Valérien. Now he was free from the bonds of discipline, and as a free man he could openly join those who were working on behalf of Alfred Dreyfus.

During the Zola trial he had three times seen Bertulus, the examining magistrate who had been lent to Pellieux. Bertulus had been requested by the War Office to look into the telegrams sent to Picquart in Tunisia, *Blanche* and *Speranza*. Further, Picquart himself had laid an information against a person unknown for forging these telegrams. On several occasions in the past Bertulus had helped Sandherr and Henry on legal points. When Picquart took over the Statistical Section, Bertulus had thought of making his acquaintance, but was warned off by Henry, who told him Picquart was difficult to get on with, a hair-splitter who made trouble, a type the magistrate had no love for. Now, beneath a free-and-easy manner Bertulus was extremely acute. After talking to Picquart, he found that the man against whom he had been warned was clear-headed, intelligent, and so far as he could judge reliable.

Picquart, admittedly, had never seriously examined the Dreyfus file. With his eyes firmly fixed on Esterhazy, he had failed to discover the false dating of the *bordereau*. Knowing the part du Paty had played in the original examination of Dreyfus, he now jumped to the conclusion that he was the person whose interest it was to save Esterhazy, that he was the author of the telegrams and the mainspring of the accusation against himself. He conceived a violent hatred for the man who was in fact about to become his fellow-victim. He imparted his suspicions to Bertulus. Bertulus saw du Paty, who assured him he knew nothing about the telegrams or the veiled lady. His statement on the telegrams was confirmed by the experts who compared his handwriting with that on the originals in the Post Office.

F

Nevertheless, du Paty's lack of common sense and his inability to hold his tongue were again to betray him. Since Esterhazy's acquittal, he had begun to suspect him of being, if not a traitor, at least a rogue and a blackmailer, and he regretted having involved himself in his defence. Furthermore, he had an inkling that Henry was also secretly trafficking with the ruffian. Unable to be silent, a few days after the condemnation of Zola he had told Henry of his suspicions of the *faux Henry*, about which he had already spoken to Gonse.

Henry had intended that this famous document should never be seen except by those to whom he had shown it. He had cursed Gribelin for telling Pellieux of its existence. Now that the light-headed du Paty was on the right track, the whole of his great construction might crumble. From the moment that du Paty came to him with his suspicions, Henry decided to deal with him as he had dealt with Picquart. Du Paty's unwise confidence was made a couple of days before Henry's first open contact with Esterhazy. At that meeting Marguérite Pays let slip that the only mistake they had made had been the *Blanche* and *Speranza* telegrams. Henry, who had not known their origin, and had believed them to be part of the Esterhazy–du Paty collaboration of November, took the story to Gonse. Gonse demanded an explanation from du Paty, who denied all knowledge of the matter, and said that Esterhazy's mistress was a *drôlesse*. Not content with sowing suspicion of du Paty in Gonse's mind, Henry went on to complain to his subordinates, Lauth and Junck, that by his clumsiness and arrogance du Paty was responsible for all the recent trouble, and thus he created round him an atmosphere of distrust. At the same time, knowing the unreliability of the fantastic Esterhazy, and afraid that in a wild moment he would divulge to du Paty the truth about the telegrams, he warned Esterhazy that du Paty was speaking ill of him. Thus, of those who were playing some part in the affair of Alfred Dreyfus, Henry remained the only one not to be suspected either by his seniors or by his juniors. Du Paty slowly discovered that he was being cold-shouldered and avoided. Proud as he was, he suffered, and his sufferings were visible. 'He looks as if he was crucified', said one. This was in April.

Bertulus not only failed to discover anything about the telegrams, but he began to grow suspicious of the people to whom
he was attached. Gonse had filled him with false information.
He had told him that Mathieu Dreyfus had tried to bribe
Sandherr, and at the same time he gave him a bunch of papers
which included Sandherr's accurate account of the interview,
with its testimony to Mathieu's innocence. Pellieux had involved him with a married woman, Picquart's mistress, by
pretending that she was the famous veiled lady. He suspected
that he was being given deliberately false scents, and guessed
that he was thought a nuisance. Being an intelligent and
persistent man, he decided to lie low for the time being, while
showing all his accustomed affability to those who were trying
to mislead him. At this point an incident wholly foreign to his
business opened up a new line of enquiry.

Christian Esterhazy had gone back home to the Bordelais.
He had received none of the profits promised him by his cousin,
and, from all he could hear, Esterhazy was in very low water.
Esterhazy had told him that as soon as he was clear of the great
conspiracy against him all would be well, but his letters offered
little more than vague promises. Christian's mother was well
aware that Mme Esterhazy had refused to live with her husband and had begun divorce proceedings. She and Christian
asked for the repayment of the 50,000 francs they had handed
over.

Esterhazy returned a threatening letter, and to Christian's
mother he sent one accusing her son of frequenting prostitutes.
Christian at once came to Paris, and on 23 April called on
Esterhazy at his mistress's flat. Esterhazy bluntly told him the
money had flown, and threatened to denounce the young man
as an unregistered moneylender: in addition he spoke of committing suicide. Christian had witnessed this scene before and
was not alarmed. Receiving confirmation from Rothschilds that
they had never had a penny of his money, he went, on the advice
of an acquaintance, to see Labori, to whom he related the whole
story of his collaboration with Esterhazy, as well as that of
Pellieux and du Paty; at the same time he agreed that Labori
should pass the information on to Mathieu Dreyfus. Christian
also sought out Trarieux, who was one of the Senators for his

own department. Trarieux, not, as was Labori, bound to professional secrecy, repeated the story to Picquart, Leblois and
Reinach. But the revisionists could not be sure that Christian
would not retract what he had retailed to Labori and Trarieux
in an hour of agitation. They decided that Picquart should pass
the story to Bertulus, who as an examining magistrate could
subpoena Christian to testify. There for the moment the matter
rested.

4

Parliament rose on 7 April. In the Chamber, Brisson, in his fare-
well presidential address, ignored the question which had been
agitating society: instead, he made a fierce attack on clerical-
ism, stressing his distrust of the perfidious Ralliés.

The month preceding the opening of the elections was quiet.
Only in those constituencies where active Dreyfusards or anti-
Dreyfusards were standing was the case mentioned. One unhappy Radical who was rash enough to announce himself in
favour of revision was at once disavowed by Léon Bourgeois and
Cavaignac, who both won the praises of the anti-semite press
for their patriotism. The Radicals remained unyieldingly anti-
revisionist; their chief newspaper in the South, the *Dépêche de
Toulouse*, owned by the Sarraut family, jeered at Zola and
supported the Army, while remaining doctrinally sound on
anti-clericalism.

Brisson's attack on the clericals had certain justifications.
Two years earlier, Leo xiii had confided to Etienne Lamy, a
Catholic Republican, the task of federating and leading the
various Catholic groups with a view to the elections of 1898.
Unhappily, of the dozen or so organisations, the strongest in
numbers, wealth and influence was the 'Justice-Egalité',
founded and controlled by the Assumptionists. This organisation rejected the recommendation to pool the Catholic resources. They came to the election in the spirit of no compromise
with the Republic and refused Lamy's policy of negotiation
with Republican candidates. They not merely preferred Royalists, but even Radicals, to Ralliés. Their action is reckoned to
have given as many as sixty seats to the Radicals.

The electors polled on 8 and 22 May. The results showed no great change in the groups in the Chamber. The Republicans lost a few seats, the Radicals a few more. Lebon, Minister of Colonies, was beaten by a combination of Dreyfusards and Conservatives, while Reinach was defeated at Digne. Guesde lost his seat at Lille, and Jaurès his at Carmaux. Of the 581 Deputies in the Chamber, 205 were new. Among them were Drumont, Morinaud, instigator of the Algerian riots, and two other proclaimed anti-semites, who had been elected for four of the six Algerian seats. They advertised their arrival at the Palais Bourbon by shouting 'Down with the Jews' and moving ostentatiously to the Extreme Right of the semi-circle, where they were joined by the group of Nationalists who had hitherto sat with the Socialists at the Extreme Left.

In spite of this superficial appearance of identity with the previous Chamber, the position of the Government was uncertain. The changes had indicated a slight movement towards the extremes: there were fewer Radicals and more Socialist Radicals. Much depended on intangibles, and although no one wanted to revive the Affair, it lay like a small cloud on the horizon of the Chamber. The Government Republicans, who had now adopted the title of Progressists, felt that it was the moment when they should assert their predominance. Their demonstration at the opening on 1 June took the form of proposing against Brisson, for the presidency of the Chamber, Paul Deschanel, a youngish Progressist deputy from Eure-et-Loir, a Republican of unimpeachable republicanism, whose ambitions had led him to steer a dexterous course between conservatism and radicalism, and between the Dreyfusists and their enemies. Deschanel defeated Brisson by a single vote, and his victory was confirmed by two subsequent ballots, each with an increased majority. Brisson, President for the last four years, the scourge of the clericals, was now up in arms, ready to seize the first chance to overthrow Méline. On 14 June the usual motion requiring an outline of Government policy was put down. The Opposition attacked the Prime Minister for relying on the Right for his majorities. Méline replied that he had never sought or bargained for Right support, and on a motion of confidence carried the House by a majority of 23. Here was Brisson's opportunity. He put up two Radicals to add a rider that the Government should rely on a purely Republican majority, a motion which Delcassé had proposed in May 1897 and lost. Méline resisted the amendment, but a number of his followers, who no doubt had posed to their constituents as unyielding Republicans, dared not vote against the motion. Twenty-six having voted their confidence in Méline, now voted against him, while a further 20 took refuge in abstention. The Government was beaten by 49, and Méline went with his resignation to Félix Faure.

Méline had been a far from unsuccessful Prime Minister. He had been in office for more than two years; in the last 23 years only two other Cabinets had lasted as long. Some useful work had been done: some reforming Acts added to the Statute Book. But for the Case his reputation would be higher than it is. Yet it is difficult to see how, by any other policy than that of entrenching himself in the *res judicata*, he could have survived the last six months. Had he let the Radicals in on the eve of the elections, he would have lost the confidence of his party and earned the anathema of all conservative Frenchmen.

His successor was not easy to find. In the end, much against his will, Faure had to send for the author of the crisis, Brisson, whom he should have summoned in the first place. Brisson quickly got together a Cabinet in which, except for Delcassé at the Foreign Office, the main portfolios were in the hands of Radicals such as Sarrien, Minister of Justice, Brisson himself taking the Ministry of the Interior. He came before the Chamber on 30 June, and after a studiously careful declaration, from which all Radical policies except the supremacy of the lay State were omitted, he received a vote of confidence by a majority of 110.

The transfer of current business from the old to the incoming Cabinet appears to have been as superficial as was usual in these circumstances. Méline said nothing to Brisson about the Affair. Hanotaux, infuriated at having to make way for Delcassé, whom he considered in every way his inferior, passed on none of the representations and warnings of the German and Italian Ambassadors.

Superficially it appeared odd that the Chamber which had

rejected Brisson for its President a month earlier should now give him a handsome vote of confidence. The reason was that Cavaignac had accepted the Ministry of War. Godefroy Cavaignac, son of the general who had put down with much bloodshed the revolt of the unemployed workers in June 1848, had been brought up from childhood to regard himself as the future Cromwell of the Republic, the reincarnation of the purest pures of 1793. He prided himself on his honesty and inflexibility, along with other appropriate virtues, including impenetrable solemnity. He had the long, lean head of a greyhound, a touch of whisker, and sad, staring eyes: a cruel journalist had nicknamed him 'Corporal Werther'. He had been one of the four junior deputies who in 1892 had forced the Panama enquiry and had won much praise for his virtuous speech, as well as the detestation of Clemenceau. In January 1898 he had spoken in the debate on Zola, when he had told the Chamber that there existed 'contemporary evidence' of Dreyfus's admissions. Since Dupuy, who should have known of these admissions, sat silent, Cavaignac believed that what he had said was true. Known as the adversary of revision, he was now acceptable to both the Right and the Radicals, the former believing that he would run the Brisson Cabinet. 'Brisson', wrote Drumont, 'is a dummy on which Cavaignac will sit'.

Indeed Brisson seemed bulliable. In addition to the normal transfer of Préfets on demands from his Radical followers, he was weak enough to yield to Drumont and his anti-semites, and withdrew Lépine from the governorship of Algeria.

From his assumption of office Cavaignac decided that he himself would have done with the shilly-shally methods of Billot and Méline. He would clear up the Affair by a personal examination of the Dreyfus dossier. Credulous and obstinate, and having already convinced himself of Dreyfus's guilt, he took the papers at their face value. He ignored the fact that Lebrun-Renaud had not reported the alleged confession after the degradation of 1895, and accepted as a genuine report the note that the Republican Guardsman had written at Gonse's dictation less than a year ago. He was not, however, convinced that the *bordereau* was in the handwriting of Dreyfus; it resembled Esterhazy's; but, since Esterhazy was not a gunner, the information must have come from Dreyfus. Therefore he assumed that the two had collaborated.

This theory absolved him from having to support Esterhazy as the alternative to Dreyfus; he had no love for Esterhazy, whom he looked on, quite rightly, as a bad soldier. As for the other documents, he accepted the application of the *canaille de D* letter to Dreyfus, and swallowed the *faux Henry* without a second thought. Last of all he seized on another of Henry's manipulations, the letter of 1896 in which Henry had changed the letter 'P' to 'D', 'who has brought me a number of interesting things', re-dated by Henry 'March 1894'. He had informed the Cabinet of his intentions. Brisson was dubious: like Méline, he believed that the *res judicata* would suffice; to fall back on a later document would question 'the majesty of judgement'. Cavaignac was obstinate. He invited Brisson and Sarrien to the War Office, and laid before them some sixty or so pieces from the Dreyfus file. They let him have his way.

Armed with his three documents, he came before the Chamber on 7 July, to answer yet another interpellation by Castelin. 'I am completely certain of Dreyfus's guilt', he announced, to the applause of the Radicals and Socialists. Without uttering Esterhazy's name, he went on to say that this officer had been acquitted in error; he was, in fact, the writer of the *bordereau;* he would be dealt with. But this in no way exonerated Dreyfus, who had been justly condemned. He then read to the silent deputies the three documents he had selected from the file, suppressing only the phrases which would identify the foreign military attaché. It is said that Méline turned paler than his wont; from the wording of the *faux Henry* he recognised the piece which Tornielli had assured Hanotaux was a forgery of Panizzardi's handwriting. Then Cavaignac went on to give a version of Dreyfus's confession to Lebrun-Renaud. Once again Dupuy made no comment. At the end the Chamber rose spontaneously and cheered the War Minister to the echo, Radicals vying with Nationalists in patriotism. Brisson declared that Cavaignac had spoken in the name of the Government, and invited the Chamber to vote the *affichage* of his speech.[1]

[1] *Affichage* means the printing of a member's speech and its distribution to each of the 35,000-odd communes in France, to be posted up outside each Mairie.

On the demand for a vote on the proposal, the motion was carried by 545 to 0; three Radicals abstained. So did Méline: to vote for the motion would have been the denial of his past judicious policy. So too did 15 of the 50-odd Socialists. No one had remarked that the most striking document, the *faux Henry*, had been known ever since Pellieux gave it at Zola's trial, and that even then many had qualified it as suspect. But the deputies wanted to be convinced, to be quit of this menacing case, and they accepted Cavaignac's insistent statement with the enthusiasm born of relief. That evening Cavaignac signed the order for an official enquiry into the conduct of Esterhazy.

Two days later Picquart, after consultation with Reinach, Labori, Demange and Trarieux, sent to Brisson an open letter, communicated to the press, in which he wrote that he felt it his duty to say that two of the letters quoted by Cavaignac did not refer to Dreyfus, and that the third displayed all the marks of a forgery. This thesis he was prepared to defend before any competent tribunal. The undoubted good faith of the War Minister had, he said, been taken advantage of.

Before Billot left the War Office he had set Gonse to put together in one file all the documents relevant to the Affair. Gonse had naturally called in Henry, who supplied him with everything, including all the papers he had forged or tampered with. One document was missing: the deciphering of Panizzardi's telegram to Rome of 2 November 1894. Gonse told Henry to obtain a copy from the Foreign Office. In April Henry casually dropped in on Paléologue and asked him for a copy. Paléologue said shortly that he could supply it only after application through the usual channels, but he dictated to Henry a version from memory. Henry, putting the dictation in his pocket, returned to Gonse and told him that the Foreign Office would not supply the copy. After Billot had also failed to get it from Hanotaux, Gonse, instead of making a formal approach, sent for du Paty and asked him to recollect it. Du Paty, foolishly, allowed himself once more to become the tool of Gonse and Henry, and produced some vague recollection of the first erroneous deciphering which the Foreigh Office had later discarded. He refused, however, to admit the phrase about the messenger being warned. On this, Gonse concocted a version which ran: 'Captain Dreyfus arrested. War Office has proof of his relations with Germany. All precautions taken'. He showed it to Billot and Boisdeffre, and then added it to the file, with a note that it had been reconstituted by du Paty from memory: no mention was made of the final Foreign Office text.

All these documents, amounting now to nearly 400, had been handed over to Cavaignac, together with a numbered list of the contents, when he took office. He had taken as the chief of his military secretariat the temporarily unemployed Brigadier-General, attached to the War Office, Gaudérique Roget, a meridional with all the temperamental garrulousness of the Provençal, who had reported unfavourably on Dreyfus in 1893. He also included among his aides Captain Louis Cuignet, a member of the Fourth Bureau, who had been employed by Gonse to copy the *catalogue raisonné* of the documents. These two officers had both come to the War Office within a few weeks of Henry's arrival; they knew him well and liked him. To Roget, who, like others, could not resist the fascination of the case, and had already received many confidences from Henry, Cavaignac gave the duty of reconstructing the whole case from its beginning. Roget, looking at the *petit bleu* in the course of his examination, discovered a hitherto unnoticed fact: in the superscription Esterhazy's name had been tampered with. (It will be recalled that Picquart, when shown the *petit bleu* by Pellieux, had observed a peculiarity in the writing of the name.) Roget thought that something else had been there before, and that Esterhazy's name had been written over it. He had no reason to know that Henry had been at work. He showed his discovery to Gonse, who saw no significance in the fact. Roget, however, jumped to the conclusion that Picquart had deliberately written in Esterhazy's name over another.

5

Two days after the appearance of Picquart's letter, on 11 July, Bertulus at last secured the appearance of Christian Esterhazy before him. The young man was reluctant to give evidence: all he would say was that he had heard that Marguérite Pays was responsible for the two false telegrams. Bertulus at length persuaded him to produce the file of letters which had been handed to Labori. From these Bertulus found that he had sufficient to warrant the arrest of Esterhazy.

For the moment he was held back. Cavaignac, furious at Picquart's open letter of 9 July, determined to have done with this tiresome gadfly. He ordered the prosecution of both Picquart and Leblois on the almost forgotten charge of showing and examining confidential military documents, and with the agreement of the Cabinet ordered Picquart's arrest. He permitted Bertulus to proceed to a search of Esterhazy's dwelling, hoping that the documents with which the rogue had threatened the Ministers and the Staff would be found; but he would allow no matters to be dealt with other than the false telegrams. Finally he ordered Captain Cuignet to make a thorough examination, in the light of Picquart's public statement, of the documents handed over by Billot.

Bertulus guessed that, if he were not to be stopped, he must act at once. That evening, 12 July, he went to 45 Rue de Douai and under the eyes of Marguérite Pays proceeded to a seizure of Esterhazy's papers. There were many, and before he and his men had finished, Esterhazy arrived. Bertulus at once told him he was arrested and ordered him to be searched. Esterhazy tried to bluff it out, but did not intimidate the magistrate. The search went on until towards midnight, when Esterhazy was committed to the Santé and Marguérite Pays to Saint-Lazare.

Picquart only heard by chance of the order to prosecute him during the afternoon, and nothing of that to arrest him until he was told by Trarieux, on whom he happened to call. Trarieux kept him for the night. In the meanwhile the law officers called at his lodgings and searched them—in his absence an illegal action. On the afternoon of 13 July he went to the Palais de Justice and surrendered to the police. He too was conducted to the Santé.

The mass of papers which Bertulus seized and put under seal threw little light on the telegrams or the heart of the Dreyfus case, but they demonstrated that some members of the Staff had collaborated in Esterhazy's defence; there were notes from Pellieux, du Paty, and Boisdeffre's orderly officer, Pauffin de Saint-Morel, while one obscure note in which occurred the words 'Bâle' and 'Cuers' postulated that Esterhazy had received information from a source in the Statistical Section. But many notes were unsigned, and there was nothing to connect Esterhazy or Pays firmly with the *Blanche* and *Speranza* telegrams.

The arrest of Esterhazy, as well as that of Picquart, gave many members of 4 Rue Saint-Dominique food for thought. Boisdeffre conveniently went sick. Gonse was to follow his example at the end of the month. Neither had as much cause as Henry. He had seen the folly of Pellieux's evidence in February, but he had hoped that the blunder had been forgotten. Now it had been disinterred by this infernal ass Cavaignac. 'The Minister would have done better not to read those letters', he murmured in Gonse's hearing. He had Gonse and Roget well in hand, but Cuignet was working through the Dreyfus file. And now, worst of all, Esterhazy was in jail, subject to the keen intelligence of Bertulus; and Esterhazy was capable of betraying anyone, either to save his skin or from sheer malicious humour. Henry made one attempt to cover himself when, at the beginning of May, as part of his scheme to discredit du Paty, he had disclosed to Roget the meeting with Esterhazy at the Montsouris Park, underlining the fact that he himself had not then spoken to Esterhazy, and that he had met him in the flesh only at the time of his duel with Picquart.

Cavaignac also was in an ill humour. Bertulus, by his rapid action, had snatched away his prey. He sent a sharp note to the Minister of Justice, Sarrien, who passed it on to the examining magistrate. Bertulus calmly replied: 'I have arrested a criminal without other domicile than the bed of a prostitute'. The military Court of Enquiry on Esterhazy was adjourned *sine die*.

Cavaignac sent for du Paty, who was a distant relative, and asked him about his connection with Esterhazy. Du Paty confessed to the Montsouris Park and other meetings, claiming that his superiors knew about them; but he denied all knowledge of the false telegrams and of the 'liberating document', save that he knew that another officer had also had dealings with Esterhazy. This officer he refused to name, but it seems that he had Boisdeffre's orderly officer, Pauffin, in mind. Gribelin, also questioned by Cavaignac, simply referred him to du Paty. Gonse said that he had only just heard of the Esterhazy interview from Henry, whom he had told off; as for du Paty, he must have been out of his mind: neither Boisdeffre nor himself would have sent du Paty, too, before a Court of Enquiry, but he knew that if he did so, Bertulus would at once join du Paty with Esterhazy and Marguérite Pays in the charges of forgery. The one action he might have taken he did not. He did not ask Sarrien to remove Bertulus and substitute a more pliable examining magistrate. It may be that it went against his principles; it may be that he recalled similar substitutions which had led to the resignation of Ministers.

On 15 July Bertulus had Pays brought to the Santé to be present at the opening of the sealed packets of papers in Esterhazy's presence. She impudently asked him why at their previous meeting he had not questioned her; she would have told him that she was the writer of the *Speranza* telegram. Later she retracted the statement. Next day, in the presence of Esterhazy, Pays and their lawyer Tézenas, the papers were examined.[1] Esterhazy admitted that one draft was that of a letter he had written to Boisdeffre, but he refused to sign the summary of evidence unless the General's name was omitted. It was a threat to the War Office, should they not protect him, and he knew that Tézenas would report it. Further, he gave no names, but merely indicated the writers or addresses by their rank.

Cavaignac had bethought himself that the Esterhazy papers might contain matters of interest to the War Office. He allowed Henry, designated by Gonse and Roget, to call on Bertulus as the War Office representative. On 18 July Henry went to Bertulus's chambers. The magistrate, who had begun to see that some, as yet mysterious, link existed between Esterhazy and his visitor, could only show him the papers already examined; among others, the rough note with the words 'Bâle' and 'Cuers'. Henry was taken aback. Bertulus saw his change of face, and in a flash of intuition said: 'You'll never make me

[1] Esterhazy was lucky. Had the examination taken place eight months earlier, he would have had no legal adviser. The law of 8 December 1897 made the presence of the prisoner's counsel obligatory at the preliminary examination. The law had taken nearly four years to reach the Statute Book. Further, he would have had no lawyer if his case had been before a military court.

believe that Esterhazy could know the story of Cuers and Bâle interview from his own sources. Who but you, or someone close to you, can have told him?' He went on to deal with the charges against Esterhazy and du Paty, and spoke of the forged telegrams, on which Henry stammered out that they had been despatched by those two officers. Pressed, he begged Bertulus before going any further to help him save the honour of the Army, to do nothing before talking to General Roget. Bertulus replied that he would gladly talk with Roget, but insisted that the officers who were compromised must be sacrificed.

On Henry rising to leave, Bertulus pushed his advantage: 'Let du Paty blow his brains out, and let justice follow its course against Esterhazy. He has once been acquitted irrevocably as a traitor, but he is a forger! And that's not all. There is still you. I have read one letter in which Esterhazy draws a terrible portrait of you. If that letter falls into the hands of your enemies, it will be seen that everything you have said is a lie, that for long you have had contacts with Esterhazy. Some minds could easily go so far as to hold that the man who documented Esterhazy was none other, Henry, than you!'

Henry was overwhelmed: bursting into tears, he flung his arms round the magistrate, crying, 'Save us! save us!' The astonished Bertulus pushed him back into his chair. After a silence, Henry groaned: 'Esterhazy is a bandit'. Quickly Bertulus retorted: 'Is he the author of the *bordereau*?' Henry only [replied: 'Don't press me (*N'insistez pas*). Before all, the honour of the Army'.

Bertulus had only half-penetrated Henry's secret. Believing that he had him in his power, he let the soldier go: it was a bad error. Henry quickly recovered from the shock, and made a mendacious report to Gonse and Roget. When, now quite jaunty, he reappeared at the examination of Esterhazy and Pays on 26 July he brought Junck with him from the Section. As the seals were broken, they coolly examined the documents and took away no more than two as of security interest. Again reporting to Gonse, who by now had taken refuge in a nursing-home, they said that Esterhazy had made a good impression, and that Bertulus had said that though he was a rogue, he was not a traitor—words that Bertulus later denied. Esterhazy went through his examination with skilful bravado. To Bertulus, who remarked that he could not think what Henry was looking for, he said impudently that it was the 'Imperial Guard', but he did not explain what he meant. Both he and Pays denied all knowledge of the telegrams. Christian, who was present, he insulted.

As a result, Bertulus felt that he needed further weight to the indictment. He advised Picquart to prefer a charge against du Paty of complicity with Esterhazy and Pays in forgery, while at the same time he at length persuaded Christian to bring an action for malversation of funds against Esterhazy. Esterhazy breathed again: the linking of du Paty with himself made him believe that he could rely on War Office support.

Meanwhile the anti-Dreyfusard journals, fully alive to Bertulus's hunt, were fulminating against him and demanding his withdrawal from the case. Cavaignac tried to have the case against du Paty brought before a military and not a civil court. The Public Prosecutor, following him, applied to the courts to dismiss Bertulus from the case, on the ground that he had no *locus standi*. The judges could find no good reason for this, but since they themselves could examine the evidence against Esterhazy and Pays, they did so. They reached the conclusion that the evidence was too flimsy, and on 12 August found for the accused. Whether pressure had been applied by Cavaignac is unknown, though it seems probable: Tézenas, on the day before the judgement, had told Esterhazy that he would be free, and advised him to get out of the country at once, since he still had to face the War Office enquiry as well as Christian's suit. But Esterhazy, strong in the feeling that he had Henry in his grip, refused. The Dreyfusists had once more met defeat: they had not yet found their way to the centre of the maze.

While Esterhazy was being examined, Picquart and Leblois had been undergoing (13 July—20 August) a similar experience in the matter of communicating and receiving security matter. Their examining magistrate, Fabre, was honest but a stickler. He picked on the fact that, at the time Picquart had put his interests and his defence in the hands of Leblois, he was accused of nothing, and was an officer on duty. Moreover, Fabre heard all the War Office witnesses and was shown all Picquart's correspondence which had been stopped and copied. At one meeting, Henry, confronted with Picquart, made an effort to come to terms. 'What a pity', he said, 'that we haven't been able to reach an arrangement'. Fabre cut him short. Later, Picquart, who still believed that du Paty was the sole villain of the piece, said to Henry: 'You have been a tool; perhaps you don't think so?'

Fabre, no more than any other outsider in the case, understood the significance of the prosecution; he was shown none of the documents or files which, according to the witnesses, were so dangerous that war with Germany would follow their publication. After consultation with his chief, Fabre found against both men on the connected charge. In consequence Picquart would automatically accompany Leblois before a civil tribunal: if, as Cavaignac had hoped, the charges had been separated, Picquart could have been sent before a court-martial, which would have faithfully dealt with him. Refusing temporary release, Picquart returned to the Santé.

Cavaignac had long reached the pitch of exasperation. He had been publicly given the lie: the Dreyfusards were more and more active, and it was not in his nature to think that he could be mistaken. He believed that the Army, for which he was responsible, was being gradually undermined by the remorseless sapping of the Syndicate. On 11 August he appeared at a dinner given by Brisson to the Cabinet, with a note he had prepared. It was his intention to bring the whole revisionist group before the High Court of the Senate under the Constitutional Law of 2 August 1875, on the charge of attempts against the security of the State. The accused would be not only Picquart and Leblois, but also Scheurer-Kestner, Trarieux, Mathieu Dreyfus, Bernard Lazare, Christian Esterhazy, Zola, and all the Dreyfusard journalists—Clemenceau, Ranc, Reinach, Guyot and the rest. On a joking enquiry from Vallé as to why he had not included the lawyers, he added: 'Of course, and Labori and Demange'. The Cabinet was staggered. Brisson exclaimed: 'It's mad, preposterous', and said he would refuse to look at such a proposal even if it were brought to him officially.

Two days later, the 13th, Captain Cuignet, who for a month had been going through the Dreyfus file piece by piece, reached

Henry's masterpiece. It was evening and he had a lamp. When he came to look closely at the document, he was surprised to perceive that while at the head and tail of the letter the feint lines were blue-grey, those in the body were grey-claret. He took up the letter prepared by Henry for comparison, the letter assuring Schwartzkoppen there would be only one Jew at a dinner-party, dated in Henry's hand 14 June 1894. He saw that here the feint lines at the head and tail were wine-tinted, while those in the body were blue-grey. Cuignet was a friend of Henry; but at the same time he was a disciplined soldier. Next morning he reported his discovery to Roget. Roget, who himself had had some doubts about the letter, led Cuignet to Cavaignac, and Cavaignac suffered the exquisite horror of seeing that the document which was placarded outside every one of the thirty-five thousand mairies, and which he had guaranteed, was false.

6

Henry was on leave. Cavaignac wanted the truth: as he said later, an official examination carried out by a judicial officer would have led to a superficial enquiry, where the accused would have been so protected by procedure that the truth would not have emerged. He decided to wait until he could carry out the examination himself. He confided in nobody, not even in Brisson, not even in Boisdeffre. He had a number of political engagements in the provinces, but before he left Paris he ordered Esterhazy to appear before a military court on 24 August.

Before the court Esterhazy took a strong line. He admitted all the faults of his private life. He stood on the ground that he had obeyed the orders of the Cabinet and the General Staff. The Jews had offered him 600,000 francs to betray his Army chiefs, but he would not. He called du Paty. Du Paty owned to helping him in the confection of the letters to the President and to correcting the article by 'Dixi'. On many points he was hesitant, and moreover he refused to uncover Gonse, Henry and even Gribelin. Esterhazy had no such scruples; in his defence he named Henry as one of the party at Montsouris Park. He went on to a farrago of truth and lies: everything he had done, every line he had written, had been at the direction of the War Office. After confusing the judges, he succeeded in holding up the case until he could produce a letter from du Paty with the damning line: 'General Boisdeffre is not uninformed that I have had indirect relations with Major Esterhazy'. The bewildered and browbeaten court at last delivered its verdict. By three to two they found that Esterhazy should be dismissed for habitual private misconduct. On the charges of failure in respect of honour and discipline, they acquitted him by four to one.

Cavaignac, who received the findings through Zurlinden, Military Governor of Paris, Saussier's successor, had no intention of sparing the culprit, in spite of the fact that he was condemned on no more than one charge and that by a majority of one—the so-called 'majority of favour'—which normally led to the defendant's receiving the benefit of the doubt. He ordered Esterhazy's dismissal from the service.

During the court of enquiry Esterhazy must have come to the conclusion that his life-lines were becoming frayed and precarious. He began to prepare his retreat. One evening he went to the Paris correspondent of the London *Observer*, Rowland Strong, and in the course of the conversation told him that he had written the *bordereau* at the request of Sandherr for the purpose of providing evidence against the traitor Dreyfus, against whom Sandherr could find nothing but 'moral proofs'.

Meanwhile Cuignet had made a further test of the two forged letters and had verified his previous opinion. Finding that Henry was to pass through Paris on 30 August, Cavaignac ordered him to report to the War Office on that day, and telegraphed for Boisdeffre, who was still on sick leave. When the latter was shown the documents, he felt that they were susceptible of a reasonable explanation; but neither he nor Gonse thought of warning Henry.

On 30 August, at 2.30 p.m., Gonse brought Henry to Cavaignac's room. Boisdeffre was present, and Roget, who took a note of the examination. Cavaignac alone interrogated. Told that the two exhibits showed signs of being mixed and altered, Henry said that he had received them on the dates he had inscribed, June 1894 and September 1896. Cavaignac offered him a chance by suggesting that he had in fact reconstituted both letters at the same moment in 1896. Henry missed the hint, and affirmed that he never kept any paper longer than ten days without reconstructing it: he had, he said, mislaid the 1894 exhibit and found it again some days after he had given that of 1896 to Gonse. Having thus lost the chance of clearing himself of no worse than an error he might easily have made if he had in fact been dealing with the torn fragments of both letters at the same moment, he could only stammer when Cavaignac, implacably, pressed him on the question of facts: 'What do you want me to say?'

'What you have done'.

'I did not manufacture the papers'.

'You put the fragments of one onto the other?'

Henry then went so far as to say that he had cut bits out of one to insert in the other: nothing more.

'What you say is belied by the material facts'.

Failing to understand the tenour of Cavaignac's questions, Henry embroiled himself more and more deeply. At last Cavaignac gave him the clue: 'The squares on the fragments of paper are of different shades'.

Lost, Henry could only offer denials, first of tampering, then of fabricating. 'I acted for the good of the country'.

'That is not the question I asked you . . . you had better tell everything'.

'I received the heading and a few words'.

'What words?'

'Words which had nothing to do with the case'.

'So this is what happened. You received in 1896 an envelope with a letter of no significance in it; you destroyed the letter and you fabricated the other'.

'Yes'.

The interrogation had taken nearly an hour. Cavaignac ordered Roget to keep Henry under his eye in the next room. Boisdeffre sat down and wrote out his resignation as Chief of Staff. 'I have just received proof that my trust in Colonel Henry, head of the Intelligence Service, has not been justified. This trust, which was absolute, has led to my deception, and to my declaring to be genuine a piece which was not so, and to my handing it to you as such. In the circumstances, I have the honour to ask to be relieved of my duties'. Cavaignac in vain tried to dissuade him. Boisdeffre rejoined that no one but he had had the misfortune to swear to a jury that a forgery was genuine and to claim that he was ready to resign if he were not believed. He insisted. His brilliant career, of which the peak was the Franco-Prussian alliance, was ended. He retired to his family house in Maine. Except for his appearances, tired and disillusioned, at the subsequent trials, he was seen no more. He survived until 1919.[1]

The imperious Cavaignac had already broken every rule of procedure. He should now have rung up the Military Governor and ordered Henry's removal to the Cherche-Midi prison. He could himself have ordered his arrest. Instead, he agreed with Zurlinden to put the man merely under fortress arrest at Mont-Valérien, with no charge proffered. An officer was summoned and Henry despatched under escort by cab, first to his home. To Mme Henry, while he hastily packed his bag, he is reported to have said: '*Je suis perdu, ils me lâchent.*' At this date it is impossible to identify the *ils*.

To Colonel Féry, who escorted him to Mont-Valerien, he said: '*Quel malheur d'avoir rencontré sur mon chemin de pareils misérables.*' While they waited for Cavaignac's orders, Roget asked him a few questions. Henry repeated firmly that he had had no accomplice. Later, Roget said that Henry had dropped no names, nor did he show any consciousness of wrongdoing. Asked whether Esterhazy had ever had relations with Sandherr, he replied that only once had he seen him at the Section when he had come to Sandherr with some documents he had picked up by chance, a fact which he had never revealed to Picquart.[2]

Cavaignac at length informed Brisson, who was overwhelmed. That evening those of the Cabinet who were in Paris

---

[1] Boisdeffre's place was temporarily filled by Sub-chief General Renouard. No permanent appointment was made until Freycinet became Minister of War, in October, when General Brault, a soldier of high reputation, was appointed. Gonse was replaced by General Delanne. Henry's place at the Statistical Section was taken by Major, later Lt.-Col. Rollin, who had been in the Section some years earlier. Lauth, his tour of staff duty terminated, went back to the Dragoons in November.

[2] This seems to have been true.

dined with Delcassé. Cavaignac told his story. Then, after a silence, Vallé broke out: 'Come, this means revision'. 'Less than ever', came back swiftly from Cavaignac.

Cavaignac, it will be revealed, was the Deputy who had brought up the alleged confession by Dreyfus in the Chamber in January. His statement had never been denied by Dupuy or Boisdeffre, or, of course, by Mercier. Thus he remained convinced of the existence of the complicity of Dreyfus with Esterhazy. Even now he was unable to explain Henry's work to his own satisfaction. With no insight into the motives of common men, he began to think that Henry had forged the Panizzardi letter to conceal something that could not be shown, perhaps the famous letter from the Kaiser. No doubt, had he had the opportunity, he would have renewed his examination of Henry. He was not to have it.

On the following day, 31 August, Henry in his cell asked for some notepaper. He then wrote and had despatched to Gonse a letter: 'I have the honour to request you to be good enough to come to see me here. It is essential that I talk to you'. Then during the afternoon he wrote a letter to his wife. 'I see that, except you, everyone is going to desert me, and yet you know in whose interest I acted. My letter is a copy and there is absolutely no touch of forgery. It only confirms information given me a few days before. I am absolutely innocent; it is known, and everyone will know it later, but at the moment I cannot speak'. Later he scrawled: 'My beloved Berthe, I feel quite mad, a terrible pain is pressing my skull, I am going to take a bathe in the Seine . . .'. It was three o'clock on a burning afternoon. He took off his jacket, lay down on his bed, and with his razor cut his throat. The orderly bringing his supper at six o'clock found his dead body, drained of its blood.[1]

That day the Cabinet had met four times. A note had been

---

[1] Later a rumour was picked up and printed that a senior officer had visited Henry and taken away a number of papers. Another story involved his friend Junck, whom the Dreyfusard papers (e.g. *Le Siécle*) did not flinch from saying had murdered him. Junck had in fact been with Mme Henry at the time. As a result of the rumour, Jules Cambon, Ambassador in Washington, advised that Junck's appointment as military attaché there should be cancelled. Neither story has any foundation.

issued through Havas on the previous evening, stating that Henry had admitted forging the letter of 1896 and that he was confined to Mont-Valérien. Now the Ministers argued over Boisdeffre's resignation. Brisson, scandalised at what had occurred, demanded a complete change of the senior War Office staff. Cavaignac refused. They agreed to wait for the return of Léon Bourgeois, who was in Switzerland. Revision was not discussed. At one meeting Félix Faure signed the order dismissing Esterhazy from the service. On leaving the last of these meetings Brisson went to glance over the latest telegrams. He found one from the commandant of Mont-Valérien reporting Henry's suicide. He telephoned to Zurlinden, who confirmed the report. On returning to his room, he found Cavaignac, who had come back to agree to the resignation of Boisdeffre. Cavaignac had not yet heard of the suicide, but the news made no impact on his mind. Ignoring the information, he spent an hour with Brisson arguing the terms in which Boisdeffre should resign.

On 2 September Henry's body was taken to his native village of Pogny. The burial took place two days later. Monsignor Latty, Bishop of Châlons, forbade a religious service, and instead the Maire made a patriotic and moving speech.

On 1 September the world had the news. All those papers which had hitherto maintained neutrality came out for revision, and even the Nationalist and other hostile journals accepted it as inevitable, except those of Drumont and Rochefort. One of the judges of 1894, Gallet, announced publicly that his eyes were opened.

Pellieux, when he read the Havas message, was seized with fury, and poured out his wrath in a letter of resignation from the Army. 'Sir, The dupe of men without honour, with no hope of keeping the confidence of my subordinates, without which command is impossible, while on my own side I have lost faith in those of my superiors who set me to work on forgeries, I have the honour to request you to allow me to retire on the ground of length of service'. Zurlinden, upset by the tone and terms of the letter, sent for him, tried to calm the agitated man, and told him he would keep the letter for two or three days to allow him to think it over. Eventually Pellieux withdrew the letter, but not before giving a version of it to a Monarchist newspaper. It is said that when Mercier heard the news, he uttered one word: '*Foutu!*' and tore up the telegram.

For one person Henry's suicide was the end: Esterhazy. Hearing the news on the evening of 31 August, he walked out to Saint-Denis early next morning, took a train to Maubeuge, where he shaved off his huge moustache and slipped over the Belgian frontier on foot. He went on to Brussels and thence to London.

Yet in spite of the quasi-unanimity of the press, nothing happened. Brisson seems to have been paralysed with indecision and inertia. Did he shrink, as he had already done, from challenging his formidable War Minister? It is said that, being a practising Freemason, perhaps the only one of the old Gambettists who had not resigned from that peculiar institution, he hated to move before consulting the brethern at 16 Rue Cadet, who in turn needed to consult the provincial lodges. In any case no move was made. Sarrien, Minister of Justice, was favourable to revision, but wanted the request to come from Cavaignac. Cavaignac, obstinately clinging to his opinion that the discovery of the forgery made no difference to Dreyfus's guilt, resolutely refused to make any application. Since both Sarrien and Cavaignac were immovable, Brisson sent a message to Mathieu Dreyfus, telling him to present through Lucie Dreyfus a petition for the re-opening of her husband's case. Further, he sent Léon Bourgeois, who had now come home, to soften Cavaignac's resistance. Bourgeois, most persuasive of men and an old friend of Cavaignac, failed. Cavaignac argued dourly, and ended by saying he would resign. He then called on Brisson, who himself offered to resign in favour of Cavaignac if he would consent to revision. Cavaignac rejected the offer, and a few hours later sent in his letter of resignation, which he also communicated to the press. It ended, 'I remain convinced of Dreyfus's guilt'. The anti-revisionists, reading it, raised their heads.

An as yet little known journalist, Charles Maurras, set forth in the Royalist *Gazette de France* the thesis that Henry's forgery was in fact an act of intellectual and moral nobility. He was the heroic servitor of the great interests of the State. Maurras promised that Henry should be avenged. 'Your unlucky forgery will be acclaimed as one of your finest deeds of war'. This initiative, though it did little for Henry, sent Maurras along the path he was to follow with success for more than forty years.

Chapter Nine

Lucie Dreyfus's Appeal

1

With the death of Henry, the period of what might be called the 'detective novel' side of the Affair ends, although the discussion and interpretation of the documents continue in an atmosphere of misunderstanding and mendacity. From September 1898 the leading figures are the politicians and the judges. Sometimes it is the judges in contention with the politicians, sometimes part of the judiciary in alliance with the Dreyfusards against their fellow judges supporting the anti-revisionists. The ten months following the death of Henry are months of confusion.

During the nineties the eminent critic Emile Faguet published two small books, entitled respectively *La Culte de l'Incompétence* and . . . *Et l'Horreur des Responsabilités*. Faguet pointed out that under a centralised administration, with each Ministry the jealous guardian of its own prerogatives, the tendency was for officials to avoid acting, on the ground that the action did not lie within the sphere of their competence; behind this they were able to shelter from responsibility. It was from this shirking of responsibility rather than from ill-will that the successive delays in dealing with the cases of Dreyfus and Picquart proceeded. Through month after month, lest they compromise themselves, Ministers shrank from using their powers and threw the onus of decision on to the members of the Courts of Appeal. It was, of course, cowardice, in which the majority in both Chambers followed them. Yet it is arguable that the consequences of political action, in what was essentially judicial business, might have done serious injury to the Army. That a great number of the senior Army officers were deceived is a fact; that of these perhaps the greater number wished to be deceived is probable. The men who misled them were in two groups: in one, those who expected to make their reputations out of the case; in the other, those who put loyalty to their superiors above every other consideration. As du Paty was to say before the Court of Appeal at the final revision on 22 March 1904, the opposition of the second group to revision arose from the fact that the disclosure of the communication of secret documents to the judges of 1894 would lead to the accusation of Mercier, and his former subordinates were obliged to cover him until such time as he accused himself.

Henry's mortal remains were buried, but his works lived on, and he had heirs. He had owned to nothing beyond the forgery of the *faux Henry*. No one had asked what else he had done, and there still lay, with others in the file, two key papers, the *petit bleu* with the name Esterhazy erased and written in again, and the letter quoted by Cavaignac in which the initial 'P' had been changed to 'D'. His heirs, who perhaps hoped to profit from the case, were Captain Cuignet and General Roget; they assumed the role of leading advocate of the Staff thesis and determined enemy of Picquart. Gonse, who by his frivolity and stupidity had contrived the fall of his friend and patron Boisdeffre, and who had not resigned, was put on half-pay in October, and remained unemployed until his retirement in 1903.

2

Brisson, in spite of his recent conviction that the Dreyfus case must be re-opened, remained in an agony of indecision. The Cabinet wanted him to take the War Office himself and promote Vallé, the under-secretary, to the Ministry of the Interior. But Brisson considered, probably rightly, that if revision was to take place, it must be supported by the head of the War Office, and that only a soldier could undertake the task without stirring up trouble in the Army. He invited old Saussier, who declined; that wasted four days. In the meantime he had invited Félix Faure to return from his holiday at Le Havre. The President recommended the Military Governor of Paris, Zurlinden, who had shown signs of treating the case on its merits, and who, though he had once for a few months been Minister of War, was not a politician. On Brisson's invitation, Zurlinden accepted, but with the proviso that he should be given time to study the Dreyfus file himself before recommending revision.

Zurlinden, naturally enough, consulted those members of the Staff who were versed in the peculiarities of the file—Roget and Cuignet, whom he took over from Cavaignac's secretariat. Roget, proud of his earlier perspicacity, showed Zurlinden the *petit bleu* with the erased and rewritten name. Like Roget, Zurlinden jumped to the conclusion that it was the work of Picquart in his desire to hunt down Esterhazy. Neither man seems to have thought that Henry might have been responsible. Hence within a fortnight Zurlinden was convinced that the charge of treason against Esterhazy was, in spite of his flight, baseless. Further, he believed, wrongly but with some justice, that if a revising court recondemned Dreyfus, he himself would be made the scapegoat by the civilian ministers. On 17 September he resigned.

Soon after he reached the War Office, Zurlinden had ordered an enquiry into du Paty's relations with Esterhazy. It was taken on 9 and 10 September by General Renouard, acting Chief of Staff. Du Paty admitted that he had acted on his own initiative, under Henry's influence. 'Henry has a broad back,' returned Renouard. He implied that the influence had been reciprocal, a suggestion resented by du Paty, since 'it leads to the idea that I suggested Henry's forgeries'. He insisted that his superiors knew what he was up to, because on 18 November 1897 they had forbidden him to make personal contact with Esterhazy.

Gonse in evidence said that he knew nothing about du Paty's connection with Esterhazy until informed in July 1898. As in all his evidence at the many enquiries and trials at which he appeared, he had no other motive than to protect himself: again and again he lied, without perceiving that each lie contradicted an earlier one.

Renouard reported that du Paty deserved to be reprimanded severely, but that account should be taken of his past and his devotion to his superiors. Zurlinden thought that du Paty was a liar. He put him on half-pay and informed Brisson that he intended to order the Governor of Paris to open an enquiry into the 'origin and sophistication of the *petit bleu*', against Picquart. Brisson forbade him to do so until the Cabinet had discussed the matter.

On the same day Brisson pitched on a General Chanoine, recommended to him as a revisionist, as Zurlinden's successor. According to an English journalist who saw him at Rennes, Chanoine 'looked like a Nonconformist Member of Parliament who had accidentally strayed into a Covent Garden ball'. He was told that revision was already decided on by the Cabinet, and he accepted the decision.

Nevertheless, within a few hours of his arrival at the Rue Saint-Dominique, without informing the Prime Minister, he signed the order to lay an information against Picquart which Zurlinden had drafted before he returned to the Military Governorship of Paris. Zurlinden, now back at the Invalides, promptly acted on the order which Brisson had forbidden him to give, and put in motion the prosecution of Picquart. He also refrained from telling Brisson when he called on him. When Brisson heard of it, he was outraged, but once more flinched from accusing the generals of disobedience and bad faith. Nor did he revoke the order.

Chanoine had given the order with such speed because Leblois and Picquart were to appear on 21 September on the charges following the Fabre examination. When the criminal court sat on that day, the prosecution asked for an adjournment, partly on the ground that the 'door was now open to revision', partly on the ground that Picquart was now charged with forgery. Labori opposed, pleading that the new charges were part of a plot by the War Office staff. Picquart, having been permitted to speak, looked straight across the court at Gonse and Pellieux, and said: 'It is possible that this evening I shall go to the Cherche-Midi. It is probable that this is the last time, before being accused in secret, that I shall be able to speak in public. I wish it to be known that should there be found in my cell either Lemercier-Picard's rope[1] or Henry's razor, it will be murder; for a man such as I am could never for one instant think of suicide'.

---

[1] Lemercier-Picard, otherwise Moïse Lehmann, a spy and a blackmailer, who tried to sell an obvious forgery to Reinach in 1897 and eventually disposed of it to Rochefort. He committed suicide a few days after Henry, whom he was wrongly believed to have helped over the concoction of the *faux Henry* (Thomas, *op. cit.* note 20, pp. 569–70).

The court adjourned the case. Picquart returned to the Santé, whence in due course he was transferred to the Cherche-Midi and put in solitary confinement to await court-martial.

The Dreyfusard papers broke out in fury at Brisson's latest capitulation to the War Office. Clemenceau whipped the Cabinet with his tongue, denouncing the whole gang of *Radicaille* as more jesuitic than the Jesuits. Even Zurlinden, disturbed at the outburst of rage, and anxious to cover his treachery, said publicly that the Cabinet could have adjourned the prosecution of one who would be an important witness in the imminent revision. Brisson, sunk in his habitual inertia, took no steps. Sarrien, however, called together the committee on revision, three Appeal Court judges and three civil servants from the Ministry of Justice, to consider Mme Dreyfus's application. They split evenly, the judges opposing revision, the civil servants favouring it. Sarrien, not the man to take a decision when his chief hung back, told the Cabinet that this amounted to a rejection. For once Brisson refused to listen. He insisted that the committee was purely consultative, and that the initiative in revision was the business of the Cabinet. The argument went on all day and the next. On 26 September the Cabinet members present voted: Brisson, Bourgeois, Delcassé and three others for; Sarrien, Lockroy, Peytral, Viger against; Chanoine abstained.

Brisson had won. Sarrien forwarded Lucie Dreyfus's application for a revision of her husband's case to the Court of Criminal Appeal.

During this week, Rowland Strong published in the London *Observer* an article giving the gist of his conversations with Esterhazy, in which the officer had asserted his responsibility for the *bordereau* (under Sandherr's orders) and for the *Blanche* and *Speranza* telegrams. These revelations were printed in the *Temps* of 23 and 27 September, and in the *Figaro* of 4 October. Esterhazy at once played his old game of denying everything, and through Arthur Newton—it was inevitable that he would fall into the hands of this shady English solicitor—threatened the *Observer* with an action for libel and succeeded in getting five hundred pounds. The revelations do not appear to have had the slightest influence on public opinion. In November he published, through Fayard, his version of what had happened, *Les Dessous de l'Affaire Dreyfus*, in which he attempted to portray himself as the counter-espionage agent of Sandherr, passing false documents to Schwartzkoppen. He was lavish in abuse of all the senior officers, but now warm in praise of Henry.

2

While Brisson pondered and procrastinated, tempers were rising. Not only was the Paris press abounding in abuse and counter-abuse: the press of foreign nations was now taking a hand. Having seen the conduct of the Zola case, having heard the accounts of Henry's confession and suicide, and now hearing from Esterhazy in London that he had indeed written the *bordereau*, inevitably the foreign journalists and their editors took the Dreyfusard side. But instead of confining their criticism to discussion of the known facts and to reports of day-to-day information, they attacked the French nation as a whole. Naturally Frenchmen, whether Dreyfusard or anti, Left or Right, resented these impertinences and hardened in their own attitude to the case. The anti-revisionists accused their opponents of being sold to the foreign enemy, of being *sans-patrie*; the revisionists accused the Army of putting itself above the country's laws.

At the same time the political sky was darkened by disturbances wholly foreign to the Affair. From early September, for more than two months, Delcassé was involved in serious controversy with the British over the appearance of the Marchand expedition at Fashoda on the Upper Nile. Since he had no cards in his hands, he could only hope to save his face in the negotiations, but his task was not eased by the noisy support of the French press.

To this diplomatic trouble were added labour conflicts, a strike of the building hands working on the site for the Paris Exhibition planned for 1900, which was joined by other workers in the building trades to the number of 20,000. The leader of the Anti-Semitic League, Guérin, had recently got onto the pay-roll of the Duc d'Orléans. Hoping to create anarchy from which the Royalists might profit, he infiltrated his own men into the strikers with orders to incite attacks on blacklegs. Simultaneously the secretary of a railway union, Guérard, who had been one of the adherents of the general strike, called out his whole union. Brisson drafted 60,000 troops into the capital and occupied the railway stations.

There was thus enough explosive opinion in Paris, in the last two weeks of September, to make nervous people foresee some outbreak, some new '*Grande Peur*', a prelude, if not to another 1789, at least to riots. The Duc d'Orléans's followers, watched by the Sûreté, were known to be rather more active than usual in their amateur plottings, as if they expected an opportunity for trouble. Then, on 25 September, Déroulède, now Nationalist Deputy for Angoulême, who had recently begun the reconstitution of his Ligue des Patriotes, began calling public meetings in which he poured out threats against Clemenceau, Jaurès and Reinach, and claimed that if Dreyfus were brought back he would be lynched. On 2 October there was a street-fight between his followers and some Dreyfusards and the police had to interfere. Wild rumours of a military plot passed from mouth to mouth. The Socialist leaders took alarm. Momentarily sinking their differences and jealousies, Guesde, Jaurès, Millerand, Fournière, Allemane, Viviani, Briand, met together on 16 October. There was no representative of the Blanquists. With the conventional romantic belief in the Revolution, they decided that, should the Nationalists demonstrate outside the Palais Bourbon on the day the Chamber re-opened, they would call out 'the people' and form a committee of vigilance. Within a few days manifestos appeared from the Socialists, the Ligue des Patriotes and the Anti-Semitic League, all promising a bloody riot outside the Chamber on 25 October. The Ligue des Droits de l'Homme, perturbed at the prospect, hastily collected the more reasonable Socialists, who, aided by the cold sense of Guesde and Millerand, threw cold water on the bellicose enthusiasm of Jaurès.

3

The Court of Criminal Appeal[1] got to work on Lucie Dreyfus's appeal immediately after receiving the order from Sarrien. Its president was an Alsatian named Loew, a man of integrity who had long foreseen that the case might come to his court, and had refused to hear private confidences from friends. The Procureur-Général, Manau, having read the documents submitted to the court of 1894, and seeing the emptiness of the case, asked to see the secret dossier. Chanoine refused, and on a more formal application from Sarrien refused again, on the grounds of security; the refusal was an insult, but Brisson weakly submitted to it. Loew, having read Manau's preliminary agreement to the appeal, appointed the junior member of the court, Bard, to be the *rapporteur*. The anti-revisionist press broke into a volume of threats against the judges, obviously sold to the Germans. Unmoved, the judges went on with their work, and the full meeting of the court to consider the case for revision was set down for 27 October.

Brisson had summoned the Chambers for 25 October, before the Criminal Appeal Court had reached its conclusion as to whether there were grounds for revision. The Cabinet was in a bad situation. Its acceptance in June by the Republicans had been solely due to their trust in Cavaignac. Cavaignac had first deceived them, along with the whole Chamber, and during the vacation had resigned. The *raison d'être* for Brisson's Cabinet had gone.

On the morning of the re-opening of the Chamber the groups held their private meetings. The Radicals were torn between their dislike of revision and their need to support a Radical Cabinet. At the Republican meeting Barthou proposed that the group should vote against the Government, which had sought through Cavaignac the support of the Nationalists and anti-semites and now, since Henry's suicide, had made a *volte-face* and was asking for the Republicans' support against its earlier allies: he had no confidence in its ability to meet the crisis.

[1] The Appeal Court (*Cour de Cassation*) consisted of three Chambers, the Court of Criminal Appeal, the Court of Civil Appeal, and the Court of Petitions (*Requêtes*), today defunct. They all sat in the Palais de Justice.

The Chamber opened in the afternoon. A noisy mob had already gathered round the Palais Bourbon and in the Place de la Concorde, while the Tuileries Gardens were occupied by cavalry, and the approaches to the Chamber guarded by a strong police force. Drumont, according to the Socialist Clovis Hugues, was listening for 'the drums of Augereau'.[1]

Brisson was faced by five interpellations. He said he was already to discuss them, and claimed the honour of lifting the Affair out of the political field into the judicial. He was at once attacked by Déroulède, who accused him of having outlived a mandate which had been accorded him only because of the presence of Cavaignac. It was time to turn him out, even if in doing so, and in spite of its respect for the Army, the Chamber included General Chanoine in their condemnation of the Ministry.

Chanoine at once asked to speak, and from the tribune announced that he held exactly the same opinions as his predecessors in the Government, and would here and now resign his office. Then, hurriedly leaving the stand, he fled from the building.

His action, which had obviously been concerted with Déroulède, was unpardonable. Chanoine had given no warning to Brisson of his intention, and had outraged parliamentary convention. In spite of the frantic applause of the Right, the Republicans for the moment rallied to the Prime Minister. Brisson spoke angrily of Chanoine's treachery and demanded that the Chamber uphold him in his determination to sustain the civil power. After an interval for consultation, the united Republican groups, Republicans, Radicals and Socialists, brought forward a resolution in which, having stressed the supremacy of the civil power and their confidence in the loyal obedience of the Army to the laws of the Republic, they agreed to adjourn for two days. Had this been voted without discussion, it would have been passed: but one deputy after another rose to argue and add riders. Barthou listened for some time, and then intervened to say that neither he nor his group could

[1] On 18 Fructidor (4 September, 1797), General Augereau, in obedience to Buonaparte then in Egypt, occupied Paris in support of the tottering Directory.

give their confidence to the Government. After a confusion of motions, one of confidence was defeated. The Chamber adjourned for a week and the Cabinet resigned.

Outside the building Guérin had tried to bring his gangs into action. The police would have no nonsense. Guérin and some 500 demonstrators were arrested.

Chanoine, the cause of the crisis, was forgotten: he was left 'at the disposition' of the next Minister of War. No job was found for him. He had already taken care of his friends—it shows how little spontaneous was his resignation. General Roget was given command of the 17th Infantry Brigade of the Paris garrison.

Four days later the Court of Criminal Appeal gave its judgement on Lucie Dreyfus's appeal. By ten votes to four it declared that the appeal was well founded, and that the Court would now proceed to a further investigation of the Dreyfus case. But it refused to follow the request of the Procureur-Général that the sentence on Dreyfus should be suspended.

4

Félix Faure consulted the Presidents and Vice-Presidents of the two chambers as to Brisson's successor. The primary need was a Prime Minister strong enough to prevent attacks on the Army. Ribot would not do: he was already known as a quasi-revisionist, and his wife was reported to look on Picquart as a hero. On the other hand, the Republican groups of both Chamber and Senate put out a manifesto that they would only give their support to a Cabinet which maintained the authority of civil government, the separation of the powers and the free exercise of the judicial authority. Therefore the revision could not be postponed. Félix Faure invited Dupuy, who, whatever his behaviour in 1895 against Casimir-Perier, could, with the right Cabinet, manipulate parliamentary opinion. To lend him strength he must have a Minister at the War Office capable of soothing both civil and military susceptibilities. Thus Freycinet, who had been largely effaced since the Panama scandal, was pressed to return to the office he loved.

Dupuy, on 4 November, promised to rely on Republican

support alone, and to introduce no *ad hoc* laws of circumstance. More than four-fifths of the Chamber voted approval; but at once his troubles began. A motion was put forward to transfer the Dreyfus appeal from the Court of Criminal Appeal to a united Court of the three Chambers, Civil, Criminal and Petitions. Dupuy said that, having declared that justice should be respected, he would not give an example of disrespect. The declaration sounded well, but in fact Dupuy had resolved to place all future responsibility on the Criminal Appeal Court. He refused to allow Dreyfus to be informed that his appeal had been before a court and had been admitted. The Criminal Appeal Court, hearing of this, ordered that Dreyfus should be informed by telegraph, and further that he should be invited to prepare his defence. The order caused something of a sensation. Who were these bold men? The anti-Dreyfusard press informed their readers that Reinach had but to command for the judges to obey and began a new campaign of vilification.

The Court proceeded to take the statements of the witnesses, first the five War Ministers, Mercier, Billot, Cavaignac, Zurlinden and Chanoine. Billot was evasive, Cavaignac full of argument, Zurlinden and Chanoine negligible. Mercier alone fought. He admitted that he had secured no confession from Dreyfus through du Paty, but he accepted Lebrun-Renaud's statement. Asked why, in that case, he had not made a report, he coolly answered that, since the case was finished, it was unnecessary: 'It could not be foreseen that a whole race would later line up behind Dreyfus'. Asked about the communication of the secret dossier at the trial, he claimed that since Mme Dreyfus's application had not mentioned this, the matter was irrelevant, and refused to say yes or no. Yet he was driven to deny that any of the papers read by Cavaignac in July had figured in the trial of 1894. Since the *canaille de D* was one of these papers, he lied. He, and several of the others, held to the opinion that Esterhazy could not have obtained the information given by the documents listed in the *bordereau*. One new item of evidence against Esterhazy was suddenly produced—a letter written by him from Châlons gunnery range on 11 August 1894, on paper which, when examined by three paper experts, proved to be of exactly the same make as that of the *bordereau*.

While the Appeal Court was beginning its examination of witnesses, the War Office had already got far in the proceedings against Picquart for forgery of the *petit bleu*. Before an officer named Tavernier, the same witnesses from the Statistical Section made the same imputations. But on this occasion the handwriting experts refused to follow the line dictated to them: unanimously they reported that the name 'Esterhazy' had been scratched out and written in again, and they refused to connect the rest of the *petit bleu* with either Schwartzkoppen or Picquart. Picquart had been heard by Tavernier nine times between 23 September and 22 October, but he had been confronted with no witnesses and had not been allowed to consult his lawyer, Labori. For seven weeks he was in solitary confinement, permitted to receive no visits save from a few close relatives. From 22 October to 5 November he heard nothing more of the case against him. Labori at length applied to Freycinet for permission to consult.

Freycinet is perhaps the most ambiguous character in the history of the Third Republic. Of a distinguished southern Protestant family, he had done good work as an officer in the Ponts-et-Chaussées under the Second Empire. In 1870–71 he had been Gambetta's organiser at Tours, when he had produced some order in the wild chaos of the last months of war. Unlike Gambetta or Ferry, he had never been a doctrinaire politician, never a preacher of crusades. As a private member of the Senate, he abstained more often than he voted. He had been Prime Minister on four occasions and, more relevant to the situation in 1898, he had been the first civilian Minister of War, a portfolio he had held from 1888 to 1892. He was properly speaking a technician, an executive who had strayed into politics. His misfortune was that he was weak and that he disliked violent controversy. He looked timid, and on every occasion when he found himself in a seriously difficult position, he resigned and disappeared. Yet in many ways he was valued. He had a gift of persuasion, and his passion for Army matters was genuine. During his four years at the War Office, he had striven to modernise the service, largely a question of horse-trading with the military hierarchy: in return for the reduction of national service from five to three years, he created a number of cadre units and formations and staffed them with ten new divisional generals, twenty brigadiers and a host of lower officers—the officers became founder members. But the Army remained a barrack army. If he improved the weapons he did not improve the training. In order to secure his ends he had to all intents bribed his military collaborators: certainly he had surrendered ministerial control over the senior appointments. In the opinion of Galliffet and Casimir-Perier, his activities had resulted in serious damage to the Army. Now he had come back at perhaps the most difficult moment since 1871, the indispensable man, who, it was hoped, would restore harmony between the service and the politicians.

At once he found himself in trouble. Urged by the soldiers to press on with the court-martial of Picquart, urged no less strongly by the Dreyfusists to release him, knowing that there was almost certainly no case, calumniated by the Drumonts and Rocheforts on one side, upbraided on the other by Clemenceau, who loathed and despised him, he temporised. He sheltered behind the fact that the Law of December 1879, which made it obligatory for a prisoner to be advised by his lawyer, had not been extended to the code of military law. At once Antide Boyer, a Socialist, in the Chamber, and Constans in the Senate, tabled bills and asked for their urgent consideration. They were too late. Tavernier immediately closed his examination of Picquart's case, and on 19 November Zurlinden sent the summary of evidence, which pronounced for a court-martial, to the government commissioner. He then permitted Labori to see Picquart. Freycinet once more submitted. Zurlinden set down the court-martial for 12 December.

The fact that Picquart was now a civilian made it arguable that he could no longer be tried by a military court, but his friends, mistrusting the power of argument on the military mind, appealed to public opinion: a public protest was organised. A vast roll of signatories was inscribed, including members of the Institute, professors and savants, painters, sculptors, musicians, distinguished writers, ambassadors, famous actresses. The Ligue des Droits de l'Homme sent its best speakers out to whip up adherents. Students from the Sorbonne and the Ecole Normale stood outside the Cherche-Midi shouting '*Vive Picquart!*'

The intention of the War Office to discredit Picquart, even to destroy him as Dreyfus had been destroyed, was too obvious. If, as was alleged, he was a forger attempting to fasten a crime on an innocent man, his guilt would undoubtedly be made plain in the Criminal Appeal Court. By attempting to forestall the Court's action, by attempting to produce yet another *res judicata*, they outraged a whole new body of opinion which hitherto had displayed no particular bias in the Affair.

Far worse, however, were the wider consequences. Up to now the early revisionists—Reinach, Ranc, Scheurer-Kestner, Trarieux—had done their best to limit the case to that of justice for Dreyfus. Failing to secure redress, they had been forced to find other allies. With the increase in their forces, the original case became generalised. The point at issue was no longer the rehabilitation of one man, but the cause of all men subject to military justice; from that it became swollen by propaganda to the case of the nation against the Army. A dozen officers in the War Office and the Military Government of Paris, aided by a group of demagogic politicians and journalists, had brought the Army to the situation where it had assumed the appearance of an autonomous body within the State, and had thereby marshalled against it all the elements of anti-militarism, anti-clericalism and anti-capitalism. Zurlinden, in no way a politician, but 'pig-headed as all Alsatians', trying, as he believed, to save the Army, had in fact put it in a position where it could not, short of revolution, defend itself.

Zurlinden's action shocked in particular the one body which looked on itself as the guardian of the constitution, the Senate. The four Republican groups delegated their presidents to protest to Dupuy. The Prime Minister, recognising the need for immediate decision, brought the matter up in the Chamber on 28 November. The thesis put forward by the Left was that a court-martial on Picquart, whose prosecution in company with Leblois in the civil criminal court had been adjourned until the judgement on Lucie Dreyfus's appeal had been delivered by the Appeal Court, would be acting *ultra vires*. Millerand put the case with his usual clarity: the Government had an absolute authority to vary the order convoking the court-martial; the members of the court-martial themselves could adjourn it, and if they did not use this power, then it was the responsibility of the Government to do so. The Opposition tried to shift the debate on to the villainy of the Syndicate and Jewish finance. Suddenly Poincaré, Minister of Finance in Dupuy's Cabinet at the time of the Dreyfus court-martial, was heard to exclaim: 'Really, enough of this!' and rose to speak. Poincaré, it has been said, had 'the mind of a chartered accountant'. It is true that in many ways he was narrow, but he was an upright and completely honest man, though possibly too balanced: like Freycinet, he had the reputation of abstaining from voting. Since 1895 he had returned to legal practice and had taken little part in politics. He had, however, watched, and had gradually reached the conclusion that there had been something very wrong with the court-martial of 1894, and that it behoved him to say what he knew.

'At the present moment,' he said, 'silence on the part of some of us would be undisguised cowardice'. Everyone could see that a supreme attempt was being made to prevent light from being thrown on the abusive conduct of some War Office departments, while each attack on Picquart had been made at a moment when it had all the appearance of being a reprisal. If a judicial error had been made in 1894, it was the imperious duty of the members of the Cabinet of that time to do nothing to prevent the error from being brought into the open. He called on his former colleagues by name—Dupuy, Barthou, Leygues, Delcassé. He said that none of them had ever heard of any charge against Dreyfus other than the *bordereau*, had never been told of a Secret File, had never been informed of Dreyfus's confession to Lebrun-Renaud. Cavaignac shouted that the avowals had been given to Mercier. Poincaré replied that Mercier had never spoken of them to any of his colleagues, and he appealed to Dupuy. Dupuy sat silent. Poincaré ended by saying that he knew that in breaking his silence he was exposing himself to attack. 'I do not care. I am glad to have taken this opportunity, for which I have waited too long, to unburden my conscience'. The speech was so completely honest that a great part of the Chamber, many members almost against their will, broke into applause.

Cavaignac, harassed by the jeers of the Extreme Left, now attacked Brisson for deciding on revision without consulting Parliament, and for removing the case from the political to the judicial field. Dupuy interrupted sharply: 'It should be left there now'. Later, from the tribune, he developed the theme crystallised in his exclamation. He admitted that the Government had the right to adjourn Picquart's case; but would the Chamber order him to use that right? In any case he would not accept such an order, because he would be trespassing into the forbidden field. Constitutionally the Court ruled; it could adjourn the case. It had already asked for the documents relative to Picquart, which would be given to it. Thus he thrust the responsibility on to the Court of Criminal Appeal, and though he was upbraided by Ribot for refusing to take responsibility, he secured a huge majority.

On the following day in the Senate, Waldeck-Rousseau, who had played little part in politics for the last five years, proposed that a simple law granting the Appeal Court permission to adjourn all prosecutions connected with the revision would absolve Dupuy. The proposal was narrowly defeated.

For another week the legal and constitutional arguments continued, until the solution of the problem was found. Since Leblois and Picquart still had to appear before the civil criminal court for communication of the secret dossier, it was impossible that one of them should appear before a civil and the other before a military tribunal: there might be a conflict of judgement on the same set of facts. Picquart lodged an appeal to have all charges against him transferred back to the civil criminal court. On 8 December the Criminal Appeal Court granted what was tantamount to a stay of proceedings. Temporarily saved, he remained in prison.

5

During the controversy over his court-martial, Picquart, under the guard of an officer of the gendarmerie, had appeared as a witness before the Criminal Appeal Court on four days between 22 and 29 November. He was spied on by his guard, by the clerk of the court and by other parasites, and all civilities shown to the prisoner by members of the court were reported in exaggerated form to Zurlinden and the anti-revisionist journalists. On one occasion, while Roget finished his deposition, he was kept waiting in the room of the President of the Court of Petitions. Bard, the *rapporteur*, having been asked by the President of the Criminal Appeal Court to tell the prisoner that his deposition must be postponed until the following day, went by mistake into the room of the President of the Civil Appeal Court, Quesnay de Beaurepaire, who said that the man Bard was looking for was perhaps in the room of the President of the Court of Petitions.

Quesnay de Beaurepaire must surely be the most eminent oddity among the high officials of the Third Republic. He had been an imperial legal officer before 1870, when he resigned his post, and had great difficulty in getting back on to the *parquet* under the Republic. However, he had worked his passage, and after various minor posts was appointed Avocat-Général in Paris. As a side-line he wrote novels, which are said to have been 'of the most revolting sentimentality'. His prosecutions appear to have been conducted with the maximum of dramatic fire. He had been in charge of the case against Boulanger, in which his abuse of that unsuccessful dictator revolted even the anti-Boulangists. At the trial of the Anarchist Ravachol, having asked for a sentence of death, he said to the jury: 'If you find extenuating circumstances—it would insult you to suppose that you will—you can only be impelled by the lowest and vilest of emotions: fear. Who is afraid? This evening you will be escorted to your homes by bodies of the police. But I shall proceed alone; I have no need of man's aid. You must send Ravachol to the scaffold!' Needless to say, the jury added a rider of extenuating circumstances. During the Panama scandals he again sought advertisement by resigning noisily at the moment when Carnot and Loubet, then Prime Minister, were doing their utmost to bring measure into the proceedings. He was, however, promoted by Léon Bourgeois to the presidency of the Civil Appeal Court. In the winter of 1897–98 he had been attacked by a combination of Socialists, Radicals and Nationalists, and, weakly defended by Méline, had suffered a vote of censure by the Chamber. Although he was purged by a legal committee set up by the Minister of Justice, he was raw with resentment. Further, he could not bear a case as exciting as that of Alfred Dreyfus to proceed without his intervention. He began to talk to anti-revisionists and to soldiers, such as General Roget; he entered on a course of calumniation of his colleagues of the Criminal Appeal Court. And he invented the story that when Bard came to his room to find Picquart he had said as he came in, before noticing that it was not Picquart but he, Quesnay, who was in the room: 'My dear Picquart, give me your opinion on this deposition of . . .' He invented further imaginary crimes of the Criminal Appeal Court judges. When now the Nationalists, his former enemies, sought his aid, he expected to be called on to lead the crusade to save the Army. On 8 January he resigned uproariously from the presidency of the Civil Court of Appeal.

6

In the tangled wood of truth, half-truth, insinuation, mis-interpretation and falsehood, all investigators had at one time or another become hopelessly misled. By October Reinach had convinced himself that Henry had been Esterhazy's accomplice since the beginning. From scraps of evidence and gossip, from the fact that the War Office had been losing documents during 1893, from the fact that Henry had known Esterhazy in the late seventies, from the fact that by manipulation of the Section's accounts, Henry had been able to build up a *caisse noire* of 29,000 francs, from the now partly established fact that much of Esterhazy's information about the case must have come from the Statistical Section, Reinach reached the conclusion that Henry was the major traitor, the man who sup-plied the information to Schwartzkoppen. His reasons he pub-lished at intervals in the *Siècle* between 25 October and 6 December. (They were republished in volume form, *Tout le Crime.*) He had failed entirely to guess the truth about Henry: that, before all, he was a serving officer, with the narrow loyal-ties of a not very intelligent soldier.

On the day after the last article appeared, Mme Henry wrote protesting against these calumnies on her husband.

She was taken to see Drumont, who urged her to prosecute Reinach and at once opened a public subscription, placing a streamer on the balcony of the office of the *Libre Parole*: 'For the widow and orphan of Colonel Henry against the Jew, Reinach'. In a month some 15,000 persons subscribed 130,000 francs, say £60,000, among them both active and reserve officers, including Mercier; a number of members of the aristocracy; various politicians, including the ex-Communard and present Socialist, Cluseret; journalists and writers, Barrès, Paul Valéry and Léautaud among them, and three hundred priests. Much was made later by the anti-clericals of the priests who subscribed; but 300 out of 50,000 is not overwhelming evidence of clerical anti-semitism.[1]

The incident is unimportant but for the fact that it demonstrates the strength of the anti-Dreyfusard and pro-Army sentiment which still flourished in spite of the unmasking of Henry. The revisionists complained that the anti-revisionists exploited Mme Henry's sorrows: but they had exploited Dreyfus's.

7

During these interludes the Criminal Appeal Court had been quietly taking depositions from all and sundry. They had turned Lebrun-Renaud upside-down, faced him with his empty report after Dreyfus's degradation, his silence to Dupuy and Casimir-Perier, the contradiction between the first sentence of Dreyfus's alleged confession: 'I am innocent' and the rest, and his destruction of the leaf in his notebook after rewriting his statement under the eyes of Gonse and Henry. They called various Ministers of 1894, who could say little more than that the only evidence they had seen against Dreyfus was the *bordereau*. Hanotaux preserved a discreet silence on his share in the diplomatic difficulties started by Mercier's impetuousness. Gonse and Boisdeffre added nothing to their earlier testimonies. Roget, who had taken on himself the part of mouth-

---

[1] For various reasons Mme Henry's case against Reinach was not disposed of until 1902, when the plaintiff was awarded five hundred francs.

piece for the War Office, was voluble at great length, chiefly
to the effect that Dreyfus *could* have had access to information of
value to foreign staffs and Esterhazy could not, while Picquart
was of course the villain: a judge shrugged his shoulders and
Roget took offence. By mid-November the court decided it
could go no further without seeing the Secret File. For some six
weeks the question was at intervals debated in the Chamber.
Freycinet, having seen the file, knew its emptiness. The
Nationalists fought hard to have it withheld. Eventually, at the
end of December, under stringent safeguards, it was agreed
that Captain Cuignet should show it to the court and at the
same time explain it to them.

Like practically every other man who had once got involved
in the web of documents—Picquart, Roget, and much later
Major Targe—Cuignet was by now obsessed. The Secret File
had acted on him like a witch's philtre, and with more violence
than on any of the others who became involved. At the same
time the discoverer of Henry's forgery and a friend of the
forger, he was both immensely proud of his perspicacity and
resolute to cover the dead man. Before the court he produced
the invention that Henry, both because he was honourable and
because he was a rough uneducated man, could not have
imagined the *faux Henry*: the villain was du Paty, who had been
the author of the forgery and had made Henry his cat's-paw. Du
Paty was responsible for all the errors in tactics and for all the
forgeries: it was he who had revealed the name of Dreyfus in
1894; it was he who had written the *Eclair* article in 1896; it was
he who had sent the *faux Weyler*, had written the letters of the
'veiled lady', had sent the *Blanche* and *Speranza* telegrams—all
from a desire to defend his work of 1894 and from hatred of
Picquart.

His demonstration of the documents in the file was equally
personal and eccentric. He disregarded entirely the three
documents that Cavaignac had read to the Chamber on 7 July,
including the *canaille de D* letter. But because Dreyfus had been
through the railway sub-section at the War Office, he brought
forward as genuine Panizzardi's letter of March 1895 saying
that he would shortly have the railway organisation, the letter
from which Henry had torn the date and substituted April

1894. He insisted that the version of the Panizzardi telegram of 2 November 1894, which Gonse had concocted from du Paty's memory, was authentic and that the version given by the Foreign Office was false, going so far as to contest the good faith of the gentlemen at the Quai d'Orsay. There were many other original interpretations, which it would be otiose to detail.

The judges listened to this fantastic travesty with stupefaction. Cuignet, who, if the press photographs do him justice, looked like a comic mongrel terrier, was taken aback by their attitude to his triumphant exposition. He did not perceive that he had in fact broken the case against Dreyfus.

Quesnay de Beaurepaire's posturing and lies gave the anti-revisionists a new idea. Perhaps they believed that Quesnay's attitude represented the feeling in the Civil Appeal Court; perhaps they relied on the information that the Minister of Justice, Lebret, had sounded the members of the Civil and Petitions Appeal Courts and discovered that, if the three courts sat together, the Criminal Appeal judges would be out-voted. Certainly they became convinced that if they could force the Government to remove the case from these hostile judges to a combined assembly of all three courts, they would secure by a majority a judgement against revision. To work for this, there came into existence yet another league, the Ligue de la Patrie Française (which should not be confused with Déroulède's Ligue des Patriotes), dedicated to the dismissal from the case of the Court of Criminal Appeal and the creation of a special body of the three courts. Its public sponsors were three professors, Dausset, Vaugeois and Syveton, but the true founder was Charles Maurras. It soon collected some 15,000 members, a figure which demonstrates the extent of anti-Dreyfusard sentiment. Among these were almost as many 'intellectuals' as had joined the Ligue des Droits de l'Homme, though perhaps of lesser calibre: the historians Houssaye, Vandal and Rambaud; the artists Detaille, Gérôme, Forain, besides Barrès, Mistral, Heredia, Theuriet, Lavedan, Coppée, Melchior de Voguë, Emile Faguet, and the Comtesse de Martel, otherwise Gyp. On the committee sat Cavaignac. The League's spokesman was the well-known critic Jules Lemaître, the lion of the Comtesse de Loynes's salon. Strong in the confidences which had been imparted to him, Lemaître boldly asserted that the League would loyally submit to any judgement delivered by the combined courts.

Beset by their propaganda, Dupuy saw that the responsibility for the conduct of the Affair was once more being passed back to him. And once more he and Lebret evaded the issue. They forced Mazeau, First President of the united Courts of Appeal, and a Senator, to form a committee to enquire into the charges made against the Criminal Appeal judges, and to advise. The committee spent ten days listening to the fables of Quesnay, the slanders of the underlings of the courts, and to Roget's and Cuignet's fury against the obvious disbelief in their evidence shown by the judges. At the end, while clearing the Criminal Appeal Court, the committee recommended that the judges should be protected from assuming full responsibility for the judgement they had not yet delivered, and that the other two courts should be joined to that of Criminal Appeal from now onward.

Dupuy decided to carry the destitution of the Criminal Appeal Court with a high hand. He met with an unexpected opposition within the Cabinet. Georges Leygues, the Minister of Public Instruction, stuck in his heels against this insult to some of the highest judges in the country. He was followed by the Minister of Commerce, Delombre, and by Delcassé. Their protest was in vain. The rest of the Cabinet backed Dupuy.

The bill to remove the appeal for revision to the united Courts was brought to the Chamber by Lebret on 30 January, and thence sent to a committee. The committee, having found Mazeau's report full of gaps, insisted on having further evidence.

But before the committee had reported, the Court of Criminal Appeal had nearly finished the hearing of the evidence. Among the new witnesses were four artillery experts, two retired, two active, who all declared that the terms employed in the *bordereau* could have been written only by someone who knew nothing about artillery, and that so far as they could judge from the wording, the subjects had been dealt with time and again in the press. One of these experts, Ducros, said that on two occasions he had invited Dreyfus to visit the artillery shops at Puteaux where the most secret gun-parts were manufactured, and that he had not come.

Finally Esterhazy appeared. He had bargained for and received a safe-conduct. He lodged at a religious house. All his former backers deserted him except Drumont and a few Nationalists. Through these he asked Freycinet to relieve him of the duty of 'professional secrecy'. Freycinet, seeing the threat, sent him a letter engaging him to refer compromising questions to himself. To the court Esterhazy said nothing, except that he had been supported by the General Staff until Cavaignac resolved to have his head, whereupon he had been deserted by cowardly and ungrateful superiors. He refused to say anything about his alleged relations with Sandherr, and as to the *bordereau*, he replied that since the first court-martial attributed it to Dreyfus, and the second had found the document was not his work, he had nothing more to say. As soon as his evidence was completed, he left the country.

At the end of December the Appeal Court had directed the legal authority at Cayenne to send a commission to The Devil's Island to examine Dreyfus as to his alleged confession to Lebrun-Renaud. The commission's report with the prisoner's indignant denials was received before the Chamber had discussed the removal of the case from the Criminal Appeal Court.

The committee on Lebret's bill was presided over by a Deputy of long legal and political experience, Renault-Morlière. Of the eleven members, eight and the chairman looked on it as an outrage. Either the judges were innocent of the charges brought against them, or they should be subjected to legal proceedings. According to Lebret's plan, all tribunals would be at the mercy of any journalists whom they displeased. 'Principles are not violated with impunity'. In the Chamber Renault-Morlière fought hard for rejection. 'You are killing the very idea of justice in the country'. A few followed him. Dupuy defended the extraordinary bill on the ground that the case was extraordinary, while Lebret uttered a sentence which became notorious in French parliamentary history: 'Gentlemen, think of your constituencies'. Few others spoke, and none of the leaders. The Right, the Progressists and most of the Radicals voted for the bill, and it was passed by over a hundred majority. There still remained the Senate.

Chapter Ten

The Death and Funeral of Félix Faure

On the evening of 16 February Félix Faure, his labours for the day finished, was entertaining a certain handsome Mme Steinheil in his private office. About 6.45 p.m. the chief of his civil secretariat, Le Gall, heard screams coming from the President's room. Entering, he found that the President had suffered a cerebral haemorrhage and was unconscious. The lady was extracted from the dying man's clutches, patched up and sent off by a private side-door. Doctors were called, but the case was hopeless. Félix Faure expired shortly before ten o'clock, without having regained consciousness.

It was all very awkward. The discreet recitals of Le Gall and other members of his staff were discounted by the gossip of the Palace servants. Editors gave versions of what had happened according to their taste and political colouring. Drumont attributed the unhappy man's death to a Delilah in the pay of the Jews. Looking to the future, Clemenceau, with more than usual brutality, wrote: 'Félix Faure has just died. It means not a man less in France. I vote for Loubet'.

This was the fourth President in succession who had terminated his period of office prematurely. The Members of Parliament were by now inured to the hurried election prescribed by the Constitution. It had not needed Clemenceau's finger to point to the obvious candidate, Emile Loubet, President of the Senate, 61 years of age, from peasant stock in the region of Montelimar, of which he had been Maire for nearly thirty years, thoroughly Republican, calm, simple and experienced. The only charge that had ever been made against him was that in 1892, when Prime Minister, he had done his best to circum-scribe the scandals surrounding the death of Baron Reinach, and earned thereby the hatred of the followers of the dead Boulanger, the Nationalists. Without seeking the office, he became the candidate of the Senate, and then of the main body of Republicans. Méline refused to stand, but did not dis-courage his supporters from putting him forward.

Since Loubet was known to be in favour of revision, there were the usual libellous and insulting articles in the *Libre Parole* and the *Echo de Paris*, by Drumont, Lemaître, Quesnay. On 19 February, at Versailles, Loubet was elected by 483 out of 812 votes cast. Méline was given 279, while Cavaignac, Deschanel, Dupuy, Rochefort, and a few more together received 50. On his drive from the Saint-Lazare station to the Elysée the new President was hooted by Déroulède's leaguers, Guérin's anti-semites and the followers of the Duc d'Orléans. Bicyclists fol-lowed the state carriage yelling 'Panama' and, since he was supposed to be pro-English, 'Oh, yes'. Loubet, however, was full of courage and confidence. 'The Republic will not founder in my hands', he said that evening. 'They know it, and it maddens them'.

Dupuy offered Loubet his formal resignation, which the President refused. The Chambers voted to give Félix Faure a State funeral on 23 February, to be attended by representatives of all the State institutions: after a service at Notre Dame, the funeral cortège would march to Père-Lachaise for the inter-ment.

If Félix Faure's term of office was something of a vulgar comedy, his final curtain belongs to farce. There were now two revolutionary groups contending for the right to take charge of a parliamentary system they abhorred and had no prospect of overturning; Déroulède's Ligue des Patriotes and the Royalist followers of the Duc d'Orléans—the followers of the Bonapartist candidate, Prince Victor, preserved the greatest discretion. Between these, waiting to join whichever was successful, hovered Guérin and his anti-semites. Déroulède had perhaps talked himself into believing that a *coup de force* might sweep away the whole of the parliamentary racket. This *coup* would receive its impulse from the populace backed by the Army.

For some time he had been sounding generals to lend themselves to his schemes, should the occasion appear. The only one who appears to have taken him seriously was the embittered Georges-Gabriel de Pellieux, who was to command a column of troops in the funeral procession.

Déroulède hoped that, at his signal, Pellieux would march his brigade to the Elysée Palace, thrust Loubet forth amid popular acclamation and allow the Ligue des Patriotes to form a provisional and dictatorial Government, in which no doubt would sit his own friends Marcel Habert, Deputy for Rambouillet, Lasies, Deputy for Condom—both Nationalists—Maurice Barrès, ex-Deputy for Nancy, and Thiéband, the journalist who practically invented Boulanger.

André Buffet, the chief agent of the Duc d'Orléans, had made scarcely any preparations. His assistants were young aristocrats, wholly inexperienced in affairs, who took to conspiracy as lightheartedly as they went racing. They hoped that, as soon as the situation in Paris had turned to anarchy, they would only have to bring on the claimant for the monarchy to be restored. They expected assistance from Guérin, now in the Duke's pay, and that the Army, of which they knew nothing, its reality obscured for them by the traditional myth, would do the rest. One of them had sounded Déroulède to find out if he would join them; but Déroulède, as Republican as any Socialist, replied that if the Duke appeared he would himself arrest him. Further, Déroulède had no use for Guérin, and looked jealously on his anti-semite leaguers as desirable recruits to the Patriots.

On 23 February Déroulède and his fellow-conspirators were all ready. Their intention was to meet the troops as they marched back from Père-Lachaise to their barracks in the Rue de Reuilly, at the Place de la Nation; then, taking their General, Pellieux, by the hand, to march on to the Elysée Palace. Pellieux, who had not been taken into Déroulède's confidence, seems to have heard of the scheme only on the morning of the parade, and realised that he would be involved in an adventure not at all to his taste, with the prospect of being lodged in the Cherche-Midi before nightfall. He recoiled with horror. At Notre Dame he quietly told Zurlinden that

there might be trouble. Zurlinden supposed he had the wind
up, but eventually agreed to let him break off from the main
column, with the battalion he was leading, before he reached
the place of rendezvous. Hence Pellieux led his men to Vincennes and, avoiding the centre of Paris, betook himself
quietly home.

Déroulède had taken up his position with Habert, Barrès,
Guérin and some 200 followers in a side-street at the entrance
to the Place de la Nation. There was not a policeman to be
seen; Dupuy, in spite of warnings, had massed the police at the
Elysée, the Préfecture and the Ministry of the Interior. As the
column of troops approached the Place de la Nation, Déroulède
perceived that the General at the head was not the expected
Pellieux, but Roget. It was too late to turn back. With his
friends he rushed at Roget and shouted wildly: 'Follow us,
General, have pity on the country. Save France, save the
Republic. Follow us to the Bastille, to the Hôtel de Ville. To the
Elysée, General!' His followers tried to fall in behind Roget,
cutting him off from the leading troops. The crowd, who had
not the faintest idea what it was all about, shouted '*Vive l'Armée,
Vive la République*'. The band of the leading regiment struck up
the Marseillaise and with immense gusto hundreds of cheerful,
well-liquored citizens joined in. Roget's horse took fright and
he had some trouble in keeping his seat; besides, he was slightly
deaf and in the pandemonium could not hear what the gesti-
culating Déroulède was shouting. He devoted his energies to
staying in the saddle and getting the regiment back to barracks.
He led them down the Boulevard Diderot, and at the gates of
the Reuilly barracks beckoned to the regimental sappers to
clear the crowd out of the way. Still at his side, Déroulède was
screaming: 'Save France, General. Not that way; take the road
into Paris'. Roget spurred his horse and swept into the courtyard with Déroulède struggling to get hold of the bridle. They
were followed by some dozen of his adherents who were carried in by the weight of the leading battalion. The gates were
closed on the crowd, leaving Lasies, Barrès and Guérin outside.
Roget, when he at last gathered the meaning of the extraordinary exhibition, requested Déroulède and his friends to go
home. Déroulède refused for himself and Habert (both of

whom now displayed their Deputy's scarves, which they wore under their overcoats), but sent away the others, saying grandiloquently: 'Go, tell Paris that I am a prisoner of the Army, under arrest among the soldiers for whom I have sacrificed myself'. He knew only to well that if he was shown out into the street, he would be the laughing stock of Paris.

Roget was in considerable perplexity; he knew the touchiness of the Chamber in defence of its members. Eventually, after consulting his immediate senior, he reported to Zurlinden, who passed the news on to Dupuy. Dupuy took his time to think out the easiest course. At last, at one o'clock in the morning, Cochefert of the Sûreté took delivery of the two unsuccessful but loquacious conspirators, charging them merely with 'trespassing into a barracks at the head of a crowd of demonstrators and refusing to depart, in spite of the orders of the military authorities'. It was an insult. Déroulède insisted that it should be inserted on the record that 'he had gone to the Place de la Nation to seduce the troops to an insurrectionary movement and overturn the parliamentary Republic'. Then he and Habert went off to the police-station.

The Royalist conspirators, who had been hanging about all the evening waiting for Déroulède and the troops, went home to bed, and André Buffet telegraphed the expectant Duc d'Orléans that it was useless for him to cross the border.

Chapter Eleven

United Appeal Courts

The police-court proceedings against the infatuated revolutionaries saw the examining magistrate attenuating the offence and the prisoners struggling to swell their crime. Déroulède wanted his case to be treated as treason and to be taken before the High Court of the Senate. He was unsuccessful: the prosecutor and examining magistrate calmly ignored his insults to the President of the Republic and the Government. The prisoners were remanded for the Assize Court.

Simultaneously Dupuy moved against the Leagues under the Law of 1834, as 'unauthorised associations of more than 20 persons', and in order to demonstrate his impartiality ordered the prosecution not only of the Ligue des Patriotes, the Anti-Semitic League and the Jeunesse Royaliste, but also that of the Ligue des Droits de l'Homme. The courts merely fined each 16 francs. They continued to exist.

The bill to dismiss Lucie Dreyfus's appeal from the Criminal Appeal Court and to transfer the case to the three courts came before the Senate on 27 February. The debate lasted three days, and the proposal was fought hotly by the most respected Republicans. They repudiated the Government's suggestion that the transfer was dictated by reason of State; they claimed that it was a violation of elementary principles. On the last day, 1 March, Waldeck-Rousseau said that the Government talked of pacification, but that this was not the time to diminish the authority of justice. 'We Frenchmen were once hungry for justice. Now it has been possible to declare, and without a shudder running through the whole country, that *raison d'état* can outweigh justice to the individual. You talk of opinion. I answer; let us talk of justice'. Nevertheless the bill was passed by a majority of 20.

Two days later the Criminal Appeal Court, in defiance as it seemed of Parliament, finally put the charges against Picquart —save for two minor ones unconnected with the Affair—back to the civil court of first instance. Picquart was re-transferred from the Cherche-Midi to the Santé.

Meanwhile the First President of the united Courts, Mazeau, had selected as *rapporteur* Ballot-Beaupré, the successor of Quesnay to the presidency of the Civil Appeal Court and a man of integrity and balanced judgement. The records of the proceedings of the Criminal Appeal Court were printed, in an extremely limited edition, and given to the judges. However, the Criminal Appeal Court had ordered the communication to the defence of the evidence it had heard, and Lucie Dreyfus's counsel, Mornard, had legitimately shown this to Mathieu Dreyfus. He in turn showed it to Rodays, now back at *Figaro*. By devious means the whole was copied and printed in *Figaro* day after day during April. A great number of people, hitherto dependent on rumour and false reports, were suddenly enlightened.

On 27 March the new judges demanded the delivery of the Secret File. It was brought to them by Colonel Chamoin, head of Freycinet's secretariat. Having examined it and found, as had the Criminal Appeal judges, that it contained nothing incriminating Dreyfus, one of the judges asked Chamoin whether they had received the whole dossier, whether there were not some other document inculpating Dreyfus directly: he appears to have had in mind the rumoured letter of the German Emperor. Chamoin replied that the file contained everything.

During April and May the courts heard other witnesses who had now come forward. Among these was one of the experts of 1894, Charavay, who had then, somewhat against his better judgement, allowed himself to be persuaded by Bertillon that Dreyfus was the writer of the *bordereau*. He now volunteered that had he seen Esterhazy's writing he would not have failed to say that he was the writer. Lépine, Préfet of Police in 1894 (now returned from Algeria), testified that the police evidence that Dreyfus was not a frequenter of gambling-houses or brothels had been given to the War Office, but not presented to the court-martial. Delcassé informed the court in writing that the German Ambassador had come to him to tell him that Schwartzkoppen admitted corresponding with Esterhazy by *petit bleu*. And du Paty, shown Cuignet's accusation against him, was allowed to rebut it.

But the most important witness was Captain Freystaetter, the junior member of the 1894 court-martial. For a long time Freystaetter had been convinced that Dreyfus was guilty. He had gone on active service to Madagascar soon after the trial. It was not until early in 1898 that he began to have misgivings. Cavaignac's declaration in July had puzzled him. Henry's confession and suicide opened his eyes. He had returned to France in January 1899, determined to say what he knew. The usual delays between government offices prevented his being heard before mid-April, and by that time another judge of 1894, Gallet, had told what he knew. One difficulty lay in the way of hearing Freystaetter. The court had decided by a majority that it had no right to ask the judges of the 1894 trial what, in the privacy of the judges' room, had motivated their finding. During Freystaetter's evidence efforts were made by individual members of the Appeal Court judges to discover if other evidence than that given in the public hearing had been communicated to Maurel, Gallet and the others; each attempt was cut short by Mazeau. Then one of the judges asked whether in evidence Henry had spoken of the *canaille de D* letter. Freystaetter replied: 'Only the *bordereau* was discussed at the [open] hearing'. It was a vital admission.

By the time they had heard all the witnesses and had read all the evidence, the judges from the other Courts had in the majority reached the same conclusions as their brothers of the Criminal Appeal Court. The latter sat through the proceedings in dignified silence, trusting to the professional integrity of the newcomers to support them. They were to be justified.

During the proceedings a new quarrel blew up between Delcassé and Freycinet, over Cuignet's impudence in contesting the Foreign Office version of the Panizzardi telegram and his charges of bad faith. Delcassé took the matter up with Freycinet, who had blandly accepted Cuignet's interpretation. A small, energetic quick-tempered southerner, already convinced of Dreyfus's innocence, Delcassé was not going to permit his department to be insulted by a creature of the War Office. He was very sharp with Freycinet, and sent Maurice Paléologue to the Appeal Court with the full record of the deciphering. Paléologue ended his demonstration of the documents by saying: 'The version in the War Office file is not merely erroneous, it is false'. Freycinet twisted and turned, assisted by Cuignet, for a couple of months before the matter was straightened out.

But Cuignet was not to escape the consequences of his vaporous intelligence. Early in May, Georges Duruy, a professor at the Polytechnic, had been hissed by his students for having written articles in which he begged the Army not to support so obvious a rascal as Esterhazy. Freycinet, frightened by Drumont, had suspended Duruy. Attacked for his weakness in the Chamber on 5 May, he had no serious defence and was violently heckled by the Radicals, formerly his supporters. He promptly repeated his familiar disappearing trick; he resigned, on the ground that he felt he no longer had the necessary authority to remain in office.

Then, during the debate on his resignation, the Nationalist deputy Lasies produced in the Chamber copies of the correspondence between Freycinet and Delcassé during March and April. Krantz, who had taken Freycinet's place, recognised that the only person to have read the correspondence was Cuignet, who promptly confessed that he had taken the copies and shown them to the deputy. Krantz at once relieved him of his appointment and left him 'at disposition', roughly the equivalent of half-pay.

On Monday 29 May Déroulède and Habert appeared at the Assize Court. The charge had been watered down to simple provocation against the security of the State. As before in the police court, both judge and prosecutor deflated the claims of the defendants. They allowed Déroulède to parade his extravagances in the box; they heard his witnesses—Barrès, Lasies, Syveton and Quesnay—extol Déroulède's 'symbolic action' and their own association with him. They permitted the denunciation of the President of the Republic. But there was no cross-examination of either defendants or witnesses, and in due course the jury acquitted the prisoners.

On the same day the united Courts began the hearing of counsel. They heard Manau the Procureur-Général, Ballot-Beaupré the *rapporteur*, and Mornard for Lucie Dreyfus. All three men were agreed that there had been a miscarriage of justice, all three were equally convinced of Dreyfus's innocence. But there were difficulties as to the line to be adopted. It was open to the court to reverse the finding of the court-martial and order the liberation of Dreyfus without retrial, 'if the annulment of the verdict leaves nothing in existence which could be qualified as a crime or delict'. This was the course recommended by Mornard. On the other hand, Ballot-Beaupré and Manau, on a detail of legal technicality, considered that the judges should send the case back for retrial. This course was approved also by Clemenceau, since a verdict of 'not guilty' by a court-martial would make the victory all the more resounding. Further, Lucie Dreyfus wanted this, as it had always been her husband's desire to be cleared by his peers (in 1894 he had refused to allow Demange to plead an erroneous wording in the indictment). Mornard bowed to her wishes.

The Appeal Court was crowded with journalists and sight-seers. The 46 judges in their scarlet and ermine heard in silence Ballot-Beaupré's long exposition of the case, the whole story of the four years since the arrest of Dreyfus, with the evidence marshalled and discussed. His great difficulty lay in the fact that, to secure a retrial of Dreyfus by his peers, he must produce a new fact which threw doubts on the verdict of 1894. He could not bring forward the illegal communication of documents to the judges, since that would force the court simply to annul the judgement without retrial. In his attempt to find this new fact he had other difficulties. He could not claim that Henry's oral testimony in 1894 was false, since that could not be proved without a trial of Henry, and Henry was dead. The evidence of the handwriting experts was still too conflicting to shake the authority of the *res judicata*. He laid these considerations before the court. (Perhaps it is well to remember that before both Courts, except for questions asked by the judges for the purpose of elucidation, there had been no cross-examination of witnesses, and no confrontation of contradictory witnesses.)

He turned to the 'new facts' on which he was calling for the case to be sent back for retrial. First, there was the distortion of what were claimed to be admissions. The documents listed in the *bordereau* were purely hypothetical. The only fact established was that there were other spies and that the leakage had gone on after Dreyfus's arrest. The only remaining question was still the principal one, asked at the beginning and now almost forgotten. 'The *bordereau*, the principal basis of both accusation and condemnation, is it, yes or no, in the hand of Dreyfus? Gentlemen, after profound consideration, for my part I have reached the conviction that the *bordereau* was written, not by Dreyfus, but by Esterhazy'. A great sigh went up from the audience, and several of the judges wept.

Ballot-Beaupré went on to examine Esterhazy's evidence before Ravary, and showed that he had lied. Before concluding, he spoke of the dangerous defenders of both Dreyfus and the Army, which, 'thank God, is above these discussions . . . its honour surely does not require that a man innocently condemned should be incarcerated on The Devil's Island'. He did not ask the court to find Dreyfus innocent, but to find that a new fact of a character to establish innocence had arisen. The audience could not restrain their applause, and Mazeau did not attempt to check it.

After Mornard had spoken, the court adjourned for two days to consider its judgement. This evening, as a result of the accusations made by Cuignet before the Court of Criminal Appeal, Zurlinden, on orders from Krantz, had du Paty arrested and sent to the Cherche-Midi. It is said that when Picquart had been transferred back to the Santé two months earlier, he had remarked: 'It's to make room that I'm being taken from here: it won't be long before du Paty fills it'.

No one knew that, during this crucial hearing of the appeal, Esterhazy in London was being interviewed by a bright correspondent of the *Matin*. On the morning of 3 June there appeared a report of the interview, in which Esterhazy announced: 'I am going to tell the whole truth; it was I who made the *bordereau*. Yes, I who wrote it at the request of Colonel

Sandherr, my superior and my friend. . . . Billot, Boisdeffre, Gonse, knew that I was the writer of the *bordereau*'.

Mazeau considered that the united Courts must return a unanimous verdict if public opinion was to be pacified. The majority of the judges could not simply impute the *bordereau* to Esterhazy, since this would destroy the basis of accusation against Dreyfus and would be the equivalent of a reversal of the original verdict: there would then be no grounds for a retrial. A small minority—six of the 46 judges—allowed reluctantly that revision could not be withstood but fought over the wording of the judgement. They attempted what was little less than blackmail. They insisted on the insertion of the reason for a retrial, the secret communication of the *canaille de D* letter. This would inculpate Mercier and embarrass the military judges at the second court-martial. The majority conceded the point.

As was to become clear later, this left the new court-martial free to hold Dreyfus the writer of the *bordereau*, or alternatively to decide that Esterhazy was the writer, but that the documents had been furnished by Dreyfus. Almost at the head of the long judgement, appeared:

Whereas the communication [of the *canaille de D* secret piece] is proved, at once by the deposition of President Casimir-Perier and those of Generals Mercier and Boisdeffre.

Since, in the first place, President Casimir-Perier has stated that he had it from General Mercier that the exhibit containing the words '*ce canaille de D*', then regarded as referring to Dreyfus, had been laid before the court-martial.

Since, in the second place, Generals Mercier and Boisdeffre, invited to say whether they knew that the communication had been made, refused to answer, and thereby have implicitly admitted it. . . .

The disappointment of the anti-revisionists, who had believed that the united Courts of Appeal would reject Mme Dreyfus's application, caused an explosion of rage. Denounce as they might, the anti-revisionists could scarcely be taken seriously in their claim that all 46 judges had been paid by the Jews. Drumont wrote more shrewdly: 'An army which cannot defend its honour against a gang of Jews will not be able to defend the country against a foreign invasion. If we could have found a shadow of manhood in a pair of red trousers, we should have won the battle. We found nothing, nothing, nothing, only congratulations and handshakes'. But Drumont was becoming a bore. For the rest, the stock of Déroulède was waning, and though a few generals, most of them on the retired list, made martial noises, no anti-Republican could seriously rely on any one of them. The only thing the young Monarchists could think of was to make a scene. The day after the delivery of the judgement was a Sunday, when the President of the Republic would appear at the races at Auteuil. A number of young gentlemen proposed to hoot him when he appeared. Since they were indiscretion itself, their intentions were soon known to the ubiquitous Célestin Hennion of the Sûreté. As before at the funeral of Félix Faure, the Minister of the Interior, otherwise the Prime Minister, made the mistake of putting the police anywhere except where they were needed. Loubet, on his arrival at the racecourse, was greeted with shouts of 'Down with Loubet! Resign!' and shortly afterwards a gentleman rushed up the steps of the presidential box and knocked Loubet's top-hat over his eyes with a walking-stick. The assailant was thrown from the stand by two generals and fell into the hands of the police. He was identified as the Baron de Christiani. 'The good Trublion,' wrote Mme de Clermont-Tonnerre, 'having lunched well and spurred on by a bellicose lady, had betted he would hit President Loubet and shout "Down with Panama"'. The well-dressed mob cheered their champion and joined battle with the rapidly mobilised police. Some hundred were arrested. Loubet said no more than: 'I'm not hurt; all the same, it's a lesson'.

Dupuy and the Préfet of Police had failed to protect the President. Some believed that Dupuy's laxness was deliberate, that he intended to sicken Loubet of office as he had sickened Casimir-Perier. On the other hand, Combarieu, Loubet's chief civil secretary and an ex-Préfet believed that it was due to ignorance: that Dupuy was ambitious and calculating but did not know the administrative ropes. It is possibly the wisest comment. In fact Dupuy had failed to bring about the pacification he had worked for, and the policy of treating as childish exhibitionism demonstrations against public officials was now looked on as unforgivable weakness in a man hitherto regarded as both tough and hard-headed.

The Chamber met on the day after the attack on Loubet, and Dupuy was faced with an interpellation on the scene at Auteuil. For the moment he succeeded in turning the wrath of the Republicans from himself to the Royalists; then the debate veered.

The judgement delivered two days earlier had to all intents accused Mercier of illegality in the Dreyfus court-martial. The Minister of Justice had no alternative to taking action against the former Minister of War. Lebret had therefore addressed to the President of the Chamber of Deputies a letter in which, after quoting the passages from the judgement, he stated that Mercier's action appeared to fall under a section of the Criminal Code, and that under the Constitutional Law of 16 July 1875 it was open to the Chamber to direct the opening of proceedings against him before a court instituted by the Senate. The Chamber should therefore be seized of the matter and required to decide as to the steps to be taken.

Early knowledge of this letter permitted the Right to switch the debate away from the Auteuil incident and to attack Dupuy. Cassagnac asked whether Dupuy, head of the Ministry in which Mercier had sat, was about to hand his late Minister of War over to the law. Another member of the Right suggested that Dupuy, under the theory of collective Cabinet responsibility, himself stood in danger. In any event the Appeal Court's judgement was not the end of the case; there was the retrial, and until that was concluded no proceedings could be taken. The Chamber passed a vote rebuking the 'hateful machinations of the Royalist and clerical reaction', and at the same time one of confidence in Dupuy: only a handful of the extreme Right opposed the first part. The assembly then passed to the discussion of Lebret's letter.

There was considerable perplexity regarding the interpretation of the Constitutional law: should the accusation proceed from the Government or from the Chamber? Ribot raised the point and then sat down. Dupuy, Lebret, Brisson, Poincaré and

Barthou remained silent. A private member moved the adjournment until the conclusion of the second court-martial. The Socialists offered an amendment in favour of charging Mercier. The adjournment was accepted by the Chamber. Lastly, in an attempt to wipe out Cavaignac's (and its own) blunder, it voted the *affichage* of the Appeal Court's judgement. At the end of the debate the press of both Right and Left were at one in the opinion that Dupuy must go.

As for the Auteuil scandal, Christiani was sentenced to four years' imprisonment, and seven other demonstrators got a few weeks and minor fines.

The real danger, of which some were aware, was not discussed, at least openly. The Appeal Court in its desire for unanimity had included the damning passage on Mercier. At the retrial of Dreyfus the unhappy officers nominated as judges would in fact have to decide between Dreyfus and Mercier: in freeing the Jew they would condemn the General. Behind this lay the question, for the Government and for the Republicans, what would be the reaction of the Army if Mercier were sent for trial? Short-sighted Dreyfusards expected the triumphant acquittal of Dreyfus; the longer-headed were disturbed. Monod sent on to Reinach a letter from an officer which ran: 'Since the law does not require the military judges to state how they arrive at their conclusion, Dreyfus will be condemned . . . he will suffer the revenge of the Army for the insults of the press'. The great fault, which the early Dreyfusists had avoided, the identification of the Army with a dozen army officers, became all too apparent. The transfer of the case from the particular matter to the general plane had robbed the case of its precision and had brought in allies interested less in freeing Dreyfus than in forwarding their own political aims.

This might have been less serious had the Government been strong. It was not. Reinach attributes its weakness to the activities of the Radicals over 20 years, and to those of the more recently arrived Socialists, both of whom now asked for strong government, meaning thereby a Government supported by themselves and dependent on them. But he forgets that since the foundation of the Republic it had been a cardinal point that it was the Chambers, particularly the Chamber of Deputies, which ruled. Once only had the Republic seen a strong Government—Ferry's of 1883–85—which had been bowled over in a few hours on an unconfirmed telegraphic despatch. The condition for the survival of a Government was fear, real or imagined, of what would result from its fall, a panic such as occurred in October 1885, in January 1889, and was about to re-occur. As soon as the danger passed, the antipathy to a strong Government returned.

Fear had arisen now as a consequence of the somewhat plebian demonstration of the young Royalists on 4 June. Dupuy had not reacted vigorously, and on 5 June had evaded the issue. Cassagnac on that day asserted the manifestation to have been that of the 'People' against the Republic itself. No reply to this grotesque claim came from Parliament: the challenge was taken up, not by Deputies, but by the small Socialist groups of Paris. It was rumoured that the Royalists intended to repeat their behaviour at Longchamps on the following Sunday. The *canaille* prepared to meet them, and prudently they stayed away. Dupuy, however, this time took precautions: large bodies of police and soldiers, the gendarmes and the Republican Guard, were all on hand. From early morning a vast crowd surged towards the racecourse. When Loubet arrived he was greeted with a mighty roar. Otherwise the day passed without disorder, save for a few scuffles with the police on the way home. On the morrow, 12 June, the Chamber passed a motion implying no confidence in Dupuy. He re-signed.

In this account of the major movements during the months of May and June two lesser but important incidents remain to be recorded. On 9 June the case of Leblois and Picquart came before the ordinary criminal court. Before passing to judgement the court ordered Picquart's release from the Santé: in all he had spent 348 days in detention. On 13 June the court found no case against the two accused. Picquart thus had nothing more to fear from the military on the matter of Leblois, the Secret File and the connected charges. All that remained were the two minor affairs. Zurlinden moreover assured him that he would not be once more arrested and confined in the Cherche-Midi.

11 *General de Boisdeffre*   12 *General Gonse*

13 *Group at Rennes: l. to r. Cuignet, Coupois (greffier), Mercier, Cavaignac,*
Roget; at back, General Deloye

14   *Demange and Paléologue*   15   *Labori and Picquart*

16   *Lauth*   17   *Gribelin*

Immediately after the delivery of the judgement of the Court of Appeal, a cruiser was despatched to Cayenne to bring back the man who had been in solitary confinement on The Devil's Island for more than four years.

Chapter Twelve

Waldeck-Rousseau

On Deschanel's advice, Loubet invited Poincaré to form a Government. 'With more scruples and less determination,' wrote Clemenceau, 'Poincaré is another Dupuy.' For all his honesty and his strictness, Poincaré was not a man of bold imagination. Instead of discarding the men who had failed, he sought them. Brisson and Bourgeois both refused. Ribot promised his help. For the key post, the Ministry of War, he thought of Casimir-Perier, who had resigned his seat. Casimir, knowing that the Chamber would not accept him unless he were a member, declined. Poincaré began bargaining with the Radicals and some members of Dupuy's Ministry. The Radicals told him clearly that they would not combine with Ribot nor, above all, with his friend Barthou, on whom Poincaré insisted and whom they distrusted. Millerand suggested that he invite the Socialist Viviani, whose talents Poincaré esteemed. Poincaré refused to include a Socialist, and then, tiring of bargaining office against office with the Radicals, threw in his hand. His indecision in negotiation had wasted time and increased the tension. He advised Loubet to ask Waldeck-Rousseau, the only figure he could see with the integrity, authority and energy to draw together the fragments of the Republican groups.

Since 1885, when the defeat of the Ferry Ministry, in which he had been Minister of the Interior, drove Waldeck-Rousseau from office, he had taken little part in politics. As a Senator he had hardly spoken, except for his speech against Lebret's bill in February, and had devoted himself to his legal practice, though outside Parliament he had in 1897 played some part in founding the Progressist party. He might be called an enlightened conservative. On one side he was a moderate but unimpeachable laïcist, on another he had been the promoter of the legitimation of trade unions. Moreover he was a revisionist. At no time had he ever shown himself a doctrinaire, far less a fanatic. A cropped head, a short moustache, calm and immobile features, gave the impression of great self-containment and perhaps capacity. 'He has a horror of politics,' wrote Galliffet to the Princess Radziwill; 'he prefers water-colours, in which he is very talented, fishing, shooting, and the position of being the leading barrister in Paris.' Undoubtedly a sense of duty—he had no need of ambition—led him to answer Loubet's appeal.

His intention was a Cabinet which should embrace all good Republicans. In this he would take the place of danger, the War Office, and to strengthen himself he proposed to appoint as the chief of his military secretariat a soldier against whom the Army could utter no reproach: General the Marquis de Galliffet, Prince de Martigues.

Galliffet was now sixty-nine and retired. Slim and upright though limping from old wounds, he had a bronzed red face, the features and impassivity of a battle-axe. His fame was widespread as the leader of the last forlorn charge of the remnants of Margueritte's cavalry division at Sedan, with his cheerful reply to General Ducrot: 'As often as you like, sir, as long as one of us is left'. His caustic and ribald tongue was equally well known; he spared neither himself nor the aristocratic society from which he came. His single passion was the efficiency of the Army. It was Gambetta's care of this that had made Galliffet a Republican from the seventies, and he had never wavered in his loyalty. He had quarrelled with Boulanger, whom he despised, and at the enquiry on Picquart he had spoken warmly on his behalf: both actions had earned him the hatred of the Nationalists. One other thing damned him. During the bloody week of May 1871 he had been the executioner of many Communards. Possibly the story was exaggerated, but it remained as a legend in Paris. He had never troubled to deny it.[1]

[1] At one of the Bixio dinners in November 1899 he said that his A.D.C. told him it was said that he had had 35,000 Communards shot. 'That's a lot. How many do you think I had shot?' 'Perhaps 200'. 'Well, it's useless to say 200; that will need explaining. 35,000 needs no explaining'.

At some point—the date is uncertain—Waldeck-Rousseau invited Arthur Ranc to become Minister of the Interior. Ranc refused. As always, he preferred to work behind the scenes.

Then, on Reinach's and perhaps Ranc's advice, Waldeck invited Millerand. Millerand at this time was Jaurès's right hand. Originally a follower of Clemenceau, he had joined the Socialists in 1893. Unlike his leader Jaurès, he was not an eloquent speaker. His speeches were invariably appeals to reason—he was a member of the Paris Bar—and contained no fanciful flights. Until Henry's suicide he had been an anti-Dreyfusard: since then he had been a strong partisan of revision. He was at this time a convinced Socialist: his speech at Saint-Mandé in 1895 in favour of Collectivism had given him the reputation of a dangerous man. But he was in fact without prejudices. Alone perhaps of the Socialists, he was evolving from intransigent opposition towards statesmanship. A broad, heavy-shouldered man, with the head of a bull and a thick mat of dark hair: 'He looks like a docker', said Caillaux. Millerand accepted the invitation.

Having secured what he considered two key men, Waldeck then invited the three members of the Dupuy Cabinet who had opposed Lebret's bill—Delcassé, Delombre and Leygues—and at the same time offered Poincaré the Ministry of the Interior. But these asked for more portfolios for their friends, including that of War for Krantz, an anti-revisionist. Waldeck gave up hope and retired.

Loubet hastily summoned Léon Bourgeois from the Hague, but Bourgeois, having failed to secure Galliffet, refused. Loubet thereupon once more pressed Waldeck, who received some vague promises of Radical support from Bourgeois, and at the same time was being urged on by his fellow-Senators. Beginning again, he took both Millerand and Galliffet, now making the latter War Minister, and transferring himself to the other danger-point, the Interior.

The Socialist groups, when Millerand told them of the offer to himself, were on the whole in favour. But Vaillant, while not objecting to Millerand's acceptance, refused to give him the blessing of his group. None, not even Millerand, as yet knew of the inclusion of Galliffet.

This time Waldeck had no difficulties over his team. He included Delcassé and Leygues from Dupuy's old Ministry, both of whom were members of Poincaré's group. The rest were men who had never held office, but they included one retired ambassador, Decrais, and one ex-governor-general, de Lanessan. Two—Caillaux at Finance, and Baudin at Public Works— had been members of the Chamber for only a year, and both were under 40. Millerand was given the Ministry of Commerce. It was a Ministry of talents, but it was inexperienced. From Waldeck's point of view this was a merit; in his own house he would be master. To head his secretariat he appointed Demagny, a tough, hard-headed Préfet, trained by Constans in 1889–90.

As soon as the names of the Cabinet were announced there was a scream of horror from all sides. Méline's Progressists declared that the admission of a revolutionary, Millerand, was the surrender of the citadel and that they would at once attack. Many leading Radicals went up in flames at the prospect of Galliffet, but the Socialist Radicals decided to back the Government. Vaillant and his twelve Blanquists broke away from the other Socialists when these proposed to support a Cabinet containing the executioner of the Communards. The Right, of course, called it a Dreyfus Cabinet sold to Reinach.

The great question for Waldeck was how far the rank and file of the Chamber would be swayed by these pronouncements, how blind they would be to the consequences of his immediate fall, to the anarchy which would follow, and again, how much part would be played by personal egotism and ambition.

On his return home on the evening of the day he took over the Ministry of War, Galliffet found Boisdeffre there, and immediately told him that while he and Gonse could never again be employed, they would not be touched. 'No reprisals, I have made it a condition'. Boisdeffre thankfully accepted the reprieve. Recently he had asked his confessor, Father du Lac, for his blessing on one who was awaiting the firing-squad.

The Cabinet came before a threatening Chamber on 26 June. Poincaré, Barthou and Aynard, a strong Catholic but a Dreyfusist, had worked, and were still working, among the Progressists to secure deserters from Méline. The entrance of the new Ministry was greeted with a howl. As they walked to the Government seats, the Nationalists, the Extreme Left and part of the Radicals welcomed the hobbling Galliffet with shouts of 'Murderer'. (Later he said: 'Pourquéry de Boisserin called me "assassin" for three-quarters of an hour. I answered: "Assassin? Present" '). In his declaration of policy Waldeck said very little. He asked for nothing but for justice to be permitted to fulfil its task in entire independence. He was at once attacked by interpellations. Mirman, an ambitious Radical professor, dragged up all the gutter slanders of the past against individual Ministers. As a Government supporter, Viviani answered: 'These men came when the others fled. There are not three policies before us: there is defence of the Republic; there is treason. Choose'. And he complimented Millerand on having understood the meaning of responsibility.

The report of Waldeck-Rousseau's reply in the Official Journal transcript is little better than fragments, such was the tumult that beset him. A few phrases were caught at intervals in the pandemonium. He stood for an hour attempting to say some 800 words, and at last left the tribune.

Pelletan had declared that between Galliffet and the Right he would not vote. Brisson—a haggard, sick man—climbed to the stand. 'And I will tell you why I shall not abstain! The Government proposes to defend the Republic. I give it my vote. I ask all those on whom I may have any influence to vote, I do not say for the Government, but for the Republic'. It is said that he raised his arms and made the Freemasons' sign of distress.

The Chamber voted. More than 60 members abstained, but the Ministry got home by the narrow majority of 25. A week later, on 4 July, Parliament rose. For three months—the months during which Dreyfus was to stand his second trial—the Cabinet was safe.[1]

[1] In the Senate the Government declaration was read by Monis, Minister of Justice, and accepted by an overwhelming majority. Waldeck-Rousseau told Clarétie that Brisson saved the government. Some called it a Galliffet cabinet, others a Reinach one. 'These designations . . . left most mysteriously hidden the most decisive of influences. It should be synthesized and called "The Ministry of the Unministrable and invisible Arthur Ranc".' (Capéran, Louis, *L'anticlericalisme et l'affaire Dreyfus, 1897–1899*, p. 296).

Chapter Thirteen

Up to Rennes

1

On 9 June Dreyfus was taken on board the *Sfax*. Although no longer a convict he was still in custody. He was placed in a cell but was allowed to exercise twice a day on deck. He had no communication with the ship's officers, though one lent him books and at the Cape Verde Islands gave him a newspaper in which he read of the arrest of du Paty.

The Government (still Dupuy's pending the formation of its successor) had originally ordered the *Sfax* to Brest, but fearing demonstrations diverted the cruiser to Quiberon. The *Sfax* was off the coast on the evening of 30 June. At midnight, in drenching rain and a strong wind, Dreyfus was transferred by pilot-boat to the shore, where he was taken over by the director of the Sûrêté, Viguié, and brought in the utmost secrecy by train and carriage to Rennes. The train was delayed at a level crossing. The man in charge of the gates asked who was in the train and on being told, answered: 'Qui ça? Dreyfus?' Mocked for his ignorance, he replied that he did not read the newspapers, they cost money. At this date, he was typical of rural France. Dreyfus reached Rennes while the city was still sleeping, and was taken to the prison. A few hours later Lucie Dreyfus, thanks to Mme Waldeck-Rousseau, was shown into his cell. It was the first touch of humanity he had received for nearly five years. Thereafter she saw him daily, and a little later Mathieu Dreyfus and his other brothers were admitted.

He had borne his 50-odd months of confinement on the grim rock with immense fortitude, but they had taken their toll of him. Solitary confinement and the silence of his jailers had robbed him of the faculty of ready speech; he could not easily recall words, and after listening for ten or fifteen minutes he was

unable to follow what was being said. Furthermore, he knew
next to nothing of his own story. The censorship had forbidden
all mention of his case in the letters from his family. He knew
only of Henry's suicide and the arrest of du Paty. He had never
heard of Picquart, or Scheurer-Kestner, or Zola. All the confusing detail of the past four years had to be explained and made
familiar to him before the opening of the court-martial. He
appears to have recovered fairly rapidly, although he suffered
from the northern climate. It is doubtful whether he was really
fit to stand his trial in August.

On 3 July he had his first interview with Demange. Demange
had brought with him Labori, who had begged to be allowed
to support him in the defence. Mathieu Dreyfus believed that
the younger lawyer would be an admirable complement to the
prudent and circumspect Demange. It was an error of judgement. It soon became apparent that the differences in temper
and temperament between the two lawyers extended to differences over the strategy and conduct of the case. Demange had
learned something of courts-martial; he advised circumscrib-
ing the case within the question left open by the Appeal Courts'
judgement, the exact discussion of the material evidence and no
hostility to the witnesses. Labori itched for a dramatic thundering battle. The two counsel were soon at cross-purposes.

2

While the advocates were discussing the documents with
Dreyfus, the anti-revisionist world was busily engaged in the
spreading of rumour. Quesnay de Beaurepaire had a seemingly
inexhaustible store of inventions, none of value and many
ridiculous: any rogue with a story, plausible or implausible, was
able to gain his ear, frequently also his purse: by the end of July
he had a list of witnesses prepared to offer the most damning
testimony against Dreyfus. In contrast to Quesnay's publicity,
Mercier, according to the Dreyfusards, was quietly circulating
the story that he had in his possession one of the photographs of
the invincible document: the *bordereau* annotated by the
Emperor William. No one admitted having seen it; many professed to know someone who had. It was widely rumoured

that Mercier intended to produce it: he did not deny this.

The two members of the Government officially involved in the case—the Prime Minister and the Minister of War, Waldeck and Galliffet—were agreed that no governmental pressure must be exercised on the court, and that no directions as to the conduct of the case, other than adherence to the questions left by the Appeal Courts, must be given to the military prosecutor, Major Carrière. 'We are agreed', wrote Galliffet, 'in wishing the Dreyfus trial to be judged in perfect freedom. As Minister of military justice, I could have sent general directions to the *parquet* of the court-martial. I renounced my right. The more they fling themselves at Dreyfus, the better his chance of acquittal, if he is innocent'. And again: 'Even before the court has been constituted, the president is committing irregularities, which would permit all annulments if Dreyfus is condemned. At other times I would easily intervene, but in the present circumstances I must act carefully lest the Government be suspected of partiality'. Though it was within the rights of the Government to order Carrière to drop the charges against Dreyfus from the indictment, he could take them up again in his opening address to the court. His orders, in fact, were to avoid touching on any point on which the combined Appeal Courts had given a decision: on these he was to call no witnesses, 'under penalty of excess of powers and [consequent] annulment'.

This scrupulous prudence was perhaps unwise. Furthermore, Galliffet would not even appoint a civil legal adviser to guide Carrière. The anti-Dreyfusards filled the gap by sending him the Nationalist lawyer Jules Auffray.

The Dreyfusards had persuaded themselves that the trial would be a mere formality, leading to a triumphant acquittal. Many of the more violent were looking forward to the reprisals they would exact. Galliffet warned Reinach of the clumsiness of his allies, 'too susceptible, too much in a hurry'. And the more experienced Waldeck was far from sure. On 16 July he wrote that the accused had only a few chances. Even these would be reduced if the Dreyfusard journalists continued to abuse the Army, and if the lawyers did not confine themselves to the matters left open by the Appeal Courts. Galliffet believed that the military judges, 'with not a single ill thought, would incline to give their preference to the soldiers' evidence'.

The anti-revisionists jeered at the Dreyfusards, who had always called for full light on the case, for accepting the Government's directions to the commissioner not to wander outside the questions left by the Appeal Courts. Clemenceau, in touch with the ardent Labori, was foolish enough to accept the challenge and to claim that all questions relevant to the case should be reviewed. Nothing could have been more rash. For example, the combined Courts had rejected the testimony of Lebrun-Renaud and held that the story of Dreyfus's confession was without foundation. The question therefore should not be touched, and Carrière had subpoenaed no witnesses. The defence committed the colossal blunder of calling Lebrun-Renaud, and thus re-opened the question.

At the same time Carrière made his own intentions clear by summoning all the witnesses hostile to Dreyfus, but not those, such as Freystaetter and Hartmann, who before the Appeal Courts had testified in his favour. By the time the court-martial sat, the judgement of the Appeal Courts was as good as forgotten.

3

Outside the narrow field of the legal proceedings, the Government had acted promptly from the hour the Cabinet was formed. The leading government counsel, who had behaved so weakly, as it seemed, at the trial of Déroulède and Habert, were transferred to places of less influence. Lépine was re-appointed Préfet of Police in place of Charles Blanc, who had signally failed to protect Loubet. Galliffet dismissed Zurlinden from the military governorship of Paris, and Brugère, who had been attached to the military secretariats of Presidents Grévy and Carnot, was given the post. Roget was transferred from his brigade to another at remote Belfort. Several senior generals who were rash enough to make speeches implying that it was the duty of officers to be hostile to the Government were either removed from their appointments, reprimanded or told to hold their tongues.

Before the fall of Dupuy, Zurlinden had given instructions to proceed against du Paty. This unhappy man had now become the scapegoat for all the sins of the War Office. He was charged with the forgery not only of the *Blanche* and *Speranza* telegrams and of the *Blanche* letter, but also even of the *faux Weyler* and the *faux Henry;* the last on the accusation of the now quite cracked Cuignet. In addition, he was accused of communicating the *canaille de D* letter to the *Eclair* in 1896, of giving the still un-identified 'liberating document' to Esterhazy, and finally of anything else 'that might be discovered'. All the charges were found baseless in a couple of days. He was freed, and wisely retired to a sickbed, from which, such was his foolishness, he wrote privately to Mercier insisting that the version he had given to Gonse a year earlier from memory of the deciphering of the Panizzardi telegram was correct.

Almost simultaneously a War Office enquiry into the activit-ies of the deceived Pellieux in the Esterhazy case led to his transfer from Paris to Quimper.

By this time the personnel of the Statistical Section had changed completely from the days when Picquart first saw the *petit bleu.* Henry was dead, Picquart a civilian. Lauth had returned to his dragoon regiment in November 1898, Junck was awaiting the court-martial before being sent to Madagascar. Gribelin had been transferred to the less exciting climate of Dunkirk. But the new members were no less resolute to defend the Section. It was now headed by Major Rollin, who had served on it six years earlier, with Captain Mareschal—he too had fallen under Henry's spell: he had accompanied the body of the suicide to Pogny churchyard—and Captains François and Fritsch. Against Picquart to a man, they were filled with the tradition of the Section and rancorous against their enemies.

4

'Defence of the Republic' had been the theme of the Prime Minister's speech on 26 June, and of those who supported him. The words had been eagerly seized on by his opponents, who had tried to show that, by the inclusion of a Socialist as Minister of Commerce, Waldeck-Rousseau was in fact compromising, indeed betraying, the Republic he pretended to defend. On both sides the speeches were like Captain Boldwig's estate—all very high and mighty and noble. But had they any validity? Was the Republic in any danger, and if so from whom?

As has been seen, in dealing with Déroulède, Dupuy had refused to take him seriously, and Dupuy's contemptuous attitude had been adopted by the more serious press. The patriotic agitator had taken the slight very ill: he would show them that he was not a man to be trifled with. The adjurations of his friends made him all the keener to start again. He believed that there was mass discontent. That there was discontent is possible, but its remedy was not to be had through Déroulède. In the Army there was anger at the abuse from anti-militarists. Marchand was touring France making speeches against Delcassé's weakness which had led to the evacuation of Fashoda. Mercier was becoming the pillar of the Ligue de la Patrie Française. In June Déroulède was approached by an agent of the Assumptionists, who offered him the help of their Catholic electoral committees, 'Justice-Egalité'. In the same month he received from the friends and agents of the Duc d'Orléans offers of support, collaboration and cash. It went against the grain that he, a Republican, should accept help from the Royalists; nevertheless he hardly repulsed them, and they decided to put all they could at his disposal, and to leave the disentangling of the alliance to the future. The Bonapartists followed them. It was a repetition of the Boulanger episode of 1888–89, but Déroulède was not '*un brav' général*', but merely a battered minor poet with an uncontrollable tongue and a weak voice.

During the spring Jules Guérin of the Anti-Semitic League had purchased—with, it is said, money supplied by the Duchesse d'Orléans—a house in the Rue Chabrol, near the Gare du Nord, which he had fortified. It was here that during May and June the Royalist committees and a number of Deputies of various political shades met. So inept were they that they were quite unaware that among the conspirators were several police spies. Déroulède himself was a fountain of indiscretion. Moving from platform to platform, calling on his audiences, many of which seem to have been rigged, to recognise the auspicious hour, to come down into the street and revolt, he was convinced that he had a national following. The cheers he was given by happy holiday-makers at the Longchamps review on 14 July persuaded him that he had the people behind him. He assumed that the Army was with him, although he had not secured the support of a single general; for that matter, no general could be sure that he would be followed by either his officers or his men. Déroulède went on noisily preparing his stroke.

On 4 August he appears to have warned his friends and the Royalists that he would 'march' either on the day when Mercier gave his evidence at Rennes or on the day of the verdict. He himself remained in Paris and saw to the mobilisation of brigades of patriots about the city, but he seems to have given no warning to a single one of the men he expected to appoint to high office when his *coup d'état* was accomplished. The trial at Rennes began on 7 August, a Monday; Mercier was to testify on 12 August.

Warned by Lépine of what was on foot, on 10 August Waldeck summoned a nervous Cabinet and rapidly obtained their approval of the steps he intended to take. That evening he and Lépine compiled the list of those to be arrested. At dawn on 11 August the majority, some eighty in number, were taken in their beds, Déroulède at the top of the list. Thiébaud, the Bonapartist, got away over the roof. Habert, who was not sleeping at home, went into hiding. Guérin, also not at home, fled to 'Fort Chabrol' and barricaded himself inside with a group of his leaguers. André Buffet, the pretender's chief agent, was recognised trying to cross the frontier and arrested. The single Royalist deputy involved, Ramel, was left at liberty.

So concentrated was public attention on what was happening at Rennes that this police operation caused not a tremor of excitement. Few believed in the existence of a plot. Indeed, with all the Royalist and Nationalist deputies still at large, with no move from any army officer, it was a little difficult to believe in. The sole sign of trouble was Guérin and his fourteen braves in the Rue de Chabrol. For several days they were left alone, it being believed that they would surrender to the police: they spent the time marketing. When summoned on 15 August, Guérin made a bombastic refusal. Waldeck rejected a suggestion that the house should be stormed. On 20 August two groups—one of Anarchists who had no contact with Guérin, the other of anti-semites—rioted in the neighbourhood, and the police had a rough ride before breaking up the mobs. From that date the Fort became a sight for idlers and tourists. Nationalist papers tried to work up sympathy for the garrison; but no one was roused save Cardinal Richard, who foolishly and unavailingly visited the building on 1 September. The water was cut off, and on 20 September, eleven days after the Rennes verdict, after forty days, Guérin surrendered, the garrison being on the point of rebellion from the stench.

The satisfactory aspect of the business was that, by forestalling Déroulède, Waldeck had ensured tranquillity during the trial. Did he seriously believe that the Republic was in danger? Probably not; the whole thing was too fatuous; but very properly he was taking no chances. The greatest sufferer appears to have been Galliffet. Several members of his club—the Union —had been arrested. 'Although nothing more than a soldier Minister, I am obliged to share the responsibility for all actions of the Ministry to which I belong. It isn't possible to belong to a club whose members are arrested—it's not clubbable. That seems to me so obvious that I've sent in my resignation, from a club of which I've been a member for 33 years'.

Chapter Fourteen

Rennes

1

It has been said that the choice of Rennes as the place for Dreyfus's re-trial was made by Dupuy from a malevolent desire to make it difficult for Dreyfusards to attend in strength, and thus proportionately increase the weight of the Nationalists present. The accusation is probably without foundation. Rennes was within reach of Paris, but not too easy reach; it was within range of a number of ports, which would allow the rapid transfer of the prisoner from shipboard to jail: it was not likely to offer opportunities for rioting. The headquarters of an army corps, the seat of an archbishopric, of a university and of the main Court of Appeal for Brittany, with a population of some 70,000, it was a quiet, stately eighteenth-century city—it had been burned in 1720 and rebuilt in uniform style. Some think its aspect severe, but in summer the creamy stucco of the walls catches and throws back the sun, making it a city of light. 'In this antique city', wrote André Siegfried about 1910, 'the nobility of Upper Brittany . . . find the aristocratic atmosphere they enjoy. Their sons attend the law schools; army officers discover a fashionable garrison. The Boulevard de Sevigné, the Rue de Paris, constitute a small-scale Faubourg Saint-Germain, in which the nobility lives apart and isolated. The upper-middle classes of tradition, another aristocracy to-day almost extinct, scarcely mix more in the life of the town. . . . And the religious atmosphere of the West, the penetrating sound of bells morning and evening, the preoccupation with the affairs of the Church, haunting even to its enemies . . . invade the whole encircling air'. Rennes was reactionary, and anti-Dreyfusard. Life had been made very difficult for two professors at the University who had taken the wrong side. Scandal was cried when Lucie Dreyfus took rooms in an hotel: she was forced to remove herself, and at last was taken in by a humane woman, who later was made to suffer for her charity. Mercier, now on the retired list, was the guest of another retired general, the Comte de Saint-Germain, the same who presided over the enquiry which had condemned Picquart in February 1898.

2

The commander of the Tenth Army Corps, General Lucas, had wisely ordered the court-martial to be held in a room in the ordnance stores, which would have limited the audience to the shorthand-writers. Under the violent protests of Labori and the journalists, he was compelled to move the court to the Lycée, to a room large enough to accommodate several hundred. By August 1899 there was scarcely a country not passionately absorbed in the Affair. Writers, politicians, and distinguished journalists from all over the world descended on Rennes. From France there were MM. Jules Clarétie, Jaurès, Viviani and Maurice Sarraut. There was M. Maurice Barrès, who so recently had declared that the case was beneath his notice, now quivering with bilious hatred and ready to believe the worst of anybody. There was Mme Marguérite Durand of the *Fronde*, accompanied by the beautiful revolutionary, Mme Sévérine. The *Daily Mail* sent G. W. Steevens, sometime Fellow of Balliol and brilliant war-correspondent, *The Times* W. R. Fullerton, and representing a Vienna paper was Karl Liebknecht, the revolutionary German Socialist. Several crowned heads had sent their private observers, and towards the end of the trial there came from England, on behalf of Queen Victoria, the Lord Chief Justice, Lord Russell of Killowen. But alas! above the medley of passionate partisans, officers, Socialists, Nationalists, reporters, politicians and crooks, hovered those impish mouthpieces of Anatole France and Peter Dunn, M. Bergeret and Mr Dooley, who were to make the French the laughing-stock of the civilised world.

The officers appointed as judges were, with the exception of the president, all gunners, capable of understanding the technical evidence—a contrast to the trial of 1894. The president,

Colonel Jouast, was on the point of retiring from the Engineers, a brisk old soldier with an enormous flowing white moustache and an eyeglass, who beneath a peremptory manner concealed a balanced mind. The rest—Lt.-Col. Brongniart, Majors Merle, de Bréon, Profilet, Captains Parfait and Beauvais—were, so far as was known, little interested in politics or religion, except de Bréon, a believing and practising Catholic whose brother was a priest and a Dreyfusist. Only Beauvais, a dark, round-headed man with black protruding eyes, appeared to be seriously interested in the case; later he said that he alone had studied the dossier, sitting up until two or three in the morning and rising again at five to refresh his memory. None the less, they had all read much about the case and had discussed it. Being officers, they naturally took the side of the Army, and knowing little of civilians distrusted them. From the beginning their minds were loaded with suspicion and to a great extent with doubts as to the good faith of the Courts of Appeal.[1]

The prosecuting officer, Major Carrière, a dull and obtuse man, being about to retire, had begun a new career by becoming a law-student: he was somewhat in the state of a first-year undergraduate, but outside the court he was enthusiastically coached by the violent Nationalist lawyer Jules Auffray, who, like Labori, saw himself as a dynamic politician, a view shared by the electorate only once in thirty years. The War Office representative, Galliffet's liaison officer, was Colonel Chamoin, perfectly upright, but completely lost in the maze of procedure and the wilderness of documents. Delcassé sent Paléologue to represent the Foreign Office.

The disagreement between Demange and Labori as to the conduct of the case had already become acute before the opening of the trial. Demange, from his experience of the first court-martial, well aware of the contrast between High Court judges trained in the weighing of evidence and untrained officers with their rough justice, perhaps also sharing Waldeck-Rousseau's opinion as to the unlikelihood of an acquittal, believed that the wisest course was to keep the case rigidly within the circle of Alfred Dreyfus and the *bordereau;* it was better to fill the minds

[1] De Bréon was probably more suspicious than the others. He had been the victim of the forger in the La Boussinière case, referred to on page 29.

of the judges with doubts than to rouse their hostility by irrelevant appeals to public opinion, or great abstract principles. Labori, on the other hand, apart from his desire to repeat the personal success he had enjoyed at Zola's trial, thought that the strategy should be to dramatise the case, to shake and excite the audience, to appeal to the world and overwhelm the judges with the force of public opinion—in short, not to seek justice for one individual but to challenge the Army system. In spite of the efforts of Mathieu Dreyfus to harmonise their respective strategies, their differences were in the end to weaken the defence.

3

The August heat in Rennes is not conducive to prolonged clear thinking. Only the mornings were to be devoted to the trial, from 6.30 to noon. In the bare classroom of the Lycée the judges sat behind a table on a raised dais, while, for some unexplained reason, General the Comte de Saint-Germain, Mercier's host, sat behind them, squat, apopletic and objurgatory. To the left of the judges was the seat for the defendant, and behind his chair sat his counsel, Demange, plumply benevolent, and Labori, an excited greyhound. Facing the judges were the shorthand-writers and the audience, chiefly journalists virulently hostile to each other.

At seven o'clock on the morning of Monday, 7 August, Alfred Dreyfus, wearing the uniform of an artillery officer, was led in. The moment was dramatic. Here was the man over whom many had quarrelled for long months, over whom families were split, over whom friends and lovers had parted, but whom few had ever seen in the flesh. 'There came in', wrote Steevens, 'a little old man—an old, old man of thirty-nine, a small-statured, thick-set old man in the black uniform of the artillery. Over the red collar his hair was gone white as silver, and on the temples and back of the head he was bald—a rather broad large-featured face, with a thrusting jaw and chin. It was not Jewish until you saw it in profile. The eyes under the glasses were set a trifle close together'. It was a hard face until the sweetness of his smile changed it completely. This description of a neutral may be put beside that of an enemy, Barrès. 'Dreyfus seems to me to-day completely inoffensive. Either because he has suffered much sunstroke, or because he is progressing towards general paralysis, or again, he may possibly have some creeping affliction; he is done for. Certainly his defenders, the Laboris and Picquarts, are much more dangerous. He no longer has the slightest intelligence; he is a puppet'.

After the clerk of the court had read the formal documents, the witnesses were told to retire. Colonel Jouast then asked the accused a number of questions as to his guilt, the *bordereau* and the documents mentioned in it, of which naturally he knew nothing, and about the details of his private life. Jouast pressed him closely on the matters he might have known and the information he might have had. Dreyfus answered briefly and clearly with his habitual military courtesy. He denied at some length his alleged confession to Lebrun-Renaud and recalled his refusal, to du Paty, of Mercier's overtures.

The court rose soon after ten o'clock and went into secret session for the examination of the now gigantic Secret File. This occupied the next four days. It was not until Saturday, 12 August, that the hearing of the long list of witnesses, more than a hundred, began.

The Rennes court-martial was not a trial: it was a spectacle, sometimes a farce. All the important evidence had already been heard by the Appeal Courts. That which was added was of little moment. Several witnesses had volunteered or been pressed by Quesnay de Beurepaire. The earlier witnesses once more repeated their old stories with variations. Casimir-Perier came first, followed by the War Ministers and the generals; Cavaignac, in a grey frockcoat and a Muller cut-down, 'a tiresome prig with his eternal protestations of Roman virtue', still clinging to the alleged confession, says Steevens; Billot struggling to prove that Picquart wasted the secret service-funds on frivolous investigations. There was Roget, 'this white Mephistopheles', with his waxed moustaches, his jaunty air and his inexhaustible loquacity; 'he obviously intends to make his career by getting Dreyfus condemned, and since he alone is not defending his actions, it looks the worse'. There was Freycinet with his little fluting voice, talking vaguely of the thirty-five millions which the Syndicate had brought into France, but totally unable to provide the slightest evidence: 'As we all know', wrote Fullerton, 'he is incapable of giving an honest yes or no'. There was Boisdeffre, still dignified and courteous in spite of his disaster. There was Gonse, now on half-pay, refusing responsibility for anything, lying and lying again to cover his errors, giving his friends away generously, driven to admit that he had falsified testimony, but claiming that it had no importance, driven again to admit that so little had he thought of Dreyfus's confession that he had never mentioned it to Picquart. There was Cuignet, bursting with crack-brained theories. There was Picquart, 'slouching up to the bar in an ill-fitting morning-coat. . . . Without hesitation or confusion he explained the case for seven hours and a half'. There was Bertulus, vividly recounting his interviews with Henry, and suddenly checked by Mme Henry's cry of 'Judas!' There were Lauth and Junck, both tall and athletic, giving their evidence for the fifth or sixth time without hesitation, doing their utmost to discredit Picquart. Lauth, remarked Steevens, was cool, ready and resolute: 'If he was lying, he was the master liar of the world'. But by this time none of these men who had so often told their tale was consciously lying; they had written and learned their parts, and their roles had become second nature to them.

Beyond these there was a confusion of minor characters. A number of officers embroidered to their taste chance conversations with Dreyfus. A colonel appeared who had once got mixed up with a spy: after some time it was discovered that his story had nothing to do with the case. A gentleman testified that he was shown round Potsdam Palace and in the Kaiser's private room he saw a newspaper with the words written on it in large letters, 'Captain Dreyfus is a prisoner'. Does he know any German? He does not. An officer told how, meeting Dreyfus accidentally on a station platform, Dreyfus asked, 'Any news?' it was highly suspicious. Another man stated that he had told Cavaignac of meeting Dreyfus in Brussels, that sinister city of spies, and that Cavaignac had pressed him to testify. Dreyfus readily agreed that they had met, at the time of the Exhibition. When was that? In 1886!

A retired officer insisted that he, Dreyfus, and all the staff learners of 1894 had known as early as 17 May that year that they were not going on manoeuvres. He and Roget quarrelled openly, but he made a deep impression on the audience. There was a group from Mulhouse come to assert and to deny that Dreyfus attended German army manoeuvres. There were now ten handwriting experts, each with his own system, all contradicting each other. There were the commissioners from the Sûreté, Tomps and Cochefert. Cochefert owned that, had he seen Esterhazy's handwriting, he would have warned the Minister of War to be very careful. Tomps related how Henry prevented him from talking to the spy Cuers at Basle and how later, in order to discredit Picquart, he tried to make Tomps say that the copy of the *bordereau* printed in the *Matin* had not come from Teysonnières. Tomps also demolished the Statistical Section's story that Picquart, in order to help Dreyfus, had put in hand the shadowing of another man; the order had come from Sandherr. Out of the testimony of these two men was to grow an underground quarrel between the Section and the Sûreté, with political consequences.

Once more the artillery experts Deloye and Hartmann met, and Hartmann had the better of the controversy. Colonel Cordier, now retired, cheerful and irreverent, smelling of absinthe, told the court what he and Sandherr really thought of Henry, and explained the methods of the Section, to the dismay of the audience. At the end a half-witted cunning Austrian adventurer named Cernusky was introduced by the efforts of Quesnay. After a good deal of argument he was heard *in camera*, when it was found that all he could offer was a rag-bag of lies.

Two well-known personages did not appear, Esterhazy and du Paty. From London Esterhazy first said he would come, then said he would not, since the court-martial was resolved to acquit Dreyfus: besides, he had no money. During the trial he sent letter after letter from the National Liberal Club, or from 40 Upper Gloucester Place, to Roget, who, after the first, handed them unopened to Jouast. Eventually he addressed Jouast directly, in a letter full of threats and abuse. Hence, in place of his oral testimony, his empty deposition before the Court of Criminal Appeal was read.

Du Paty, armed with medical certificates, stuck to his sick-bed, and there submitted to an examination by a representative of the War Office. He merely repeated his earlier statements, and since he was neither examined nor cross-examined, his deposition contributed nothing.

One figure dominated the trial—that of Mercier. He gave his main evidence on 12 August, and thereafter he remained in court, ready to protest, ready to intervene, ready to confront. By August 1899 he had lived with the case for nearly five years. He had long convinced himself that Dreyfus was guilty and that he, Mercier, had, by his action in 1894, saved the country. 'He has become hallucinated', wrote Galliffet on the evening of 12 August. 'He thinks France is incarnated in his person . . . but all the same he is an honourable man'. To Labori, who had carelessly used a term implying that he was being examined as an accused person, he haughtily took up the word: he was an accuser. Until the Courts of Appeal stripped him of the weapon of silence, he had never admitted the truth about the com-munication of documents to the judges of 1894. Now, although he cunningly tried to imply that Sandherr was the artisan of the scheme, he did not hesitate to justify what was done. He led up to his dramatic moment carefully. While dealing with the documents, he mentioned here and there pieces of gossip which tended to show that the Kaiser took a personal and active interest in espionage. Then came his major declaration. Casimir-Perier, he said, had referred to the 'somewhat unusual' approach of the German Ambassador: 'but he did not say that he, the President of the Republic, the Prime Minister and I, waited from eight in the evening until half an hour after mid-night in his office at the Elysée, to know if peace or war were to issue from the exchange of notes. I had ordered the Chief of Staff, General Boisdeffre, to wait for me at the War Office with the officers required, should need be, for the despatch of the telegrams ordering the preparatory measures for mobilisation to be put in hand. You see that we were within measurable distance of war'.

Casimir-Perier insisted on being heard and indignantly tore the story into fragments. Mercier had seen him on the evening of Dreyfus's degradation, the night of 5 January, but his inter-view with Münster had taken place on 6 January. And on 6

January Boisdeffre was not in Paris. In any case there had been
no controversy likely to lead to war. Moreover Dreyfus had by
now been condemned. Unabashed, Mercier merely said that if
it was not on 5 or 6 January, then it was some other date. He
hit on 12 December, but on that date Casimir-Perier had not
yet been told anything about Münster's remonstrations with
Hanotaux. Mercier refused to give way. The 'historic night'
had certainly occurred, and he called on Boisdeffre to support
him, which in due course Boisdeffre did. Few seriously believed
the story, and yet some residue of it remained to perplex.

On other matters Mercier was equally reckless. Having
at last been driven to admit the illegal communication of documents in 1894, he denied that the Panizzardi telegram was
among them, but included Panizzardi's letter about the French
railway organisation written three months after Dreyfus's
degradation. And he suddenly produced a new document: a
copy of a letter alleged to have been written by the Austrian
military attaché, Schneider, saying that the German and
Italian military attachés admitted Dreyfus's guilt. As soon as he
heard of it, Schneider from Vienna telegraphed his denial of
what he claimed to be a forgery. By that time Mercier's statement had been accepted. On a statement by Freystaetter that a
shell had been mentioned in the biographical note on Dreyfus,
Mercier turned the question on to the mention of a particular
shell. At the same time he did his utmost to blacken the honour
of the honest Freystaetter. On the statement of another officer
that he had lent Esterhazy a primitive form of director in 1894,
Mercier turned up with a director of 1899 to demonstrate that
anyone could procure one. Fertile in invention, resourceful,
rusé, he continually widened the battle-front, staging ambushes,
mounting counter-attacks, always in the breach. The yellow,
lined face never quivered, never expressed disturbance. The
thin lips never hesitated. The slow, passionless monotone of the
voice never changed. Unscrupulous as he had been, he never
flinched; he remained what he was, a bold soldier and a mono-
maniac. Perhaps his adherents recognised a touch of lunacy in
the unshakeable fighter. 'He sees nothing', remarked one
journalist, 'lost in endless reflection'. By now he believed what
he had scarcely believed five years earlier. At the end of his

first morning's evidence he turned towards Dreyfus and said:
'If the slightest doubt had entered my mind, I should be the
first to declare and say before you, to Captain Dreyfus, that I
was mistaken in good faith'. Dreyfus rose and cried: 'That's
what you ought to do!' and on Mercier attempting to continue,
said huskily: 'It's your duty!' Amid the excited hubbub of the
audience Mercier coldly repeated his sentence. By that small
demonstration, early in the proceedings, he put the trial in its
true perspective. The verdict must be for Dreyfus or for Mercier.

One card only he did not play, the famous photograph of the
annotated *bordereau*. The anti-Dreyfusard editors, Drumont,
Rochefort, Meyer of the *Gaulois*, all called on him to produce it.
He did nothing. If—which is doubtful—the photograph existed,
Mercier was certainly wise enough to know that it would be
destroyed as evidence in half an hour: much better allow it to
live on in rumour.

4

Only those who knew the case intimately could have drawn
any conclusions from the chaos of facts, fictions, truths, half-
truths, opinions, suppositions and contradictions. Sometimes
the audience heard evidence of fact, sometimes evidence of conjecture, sometimes evidence of evidence of an opinion. English
journalists, used to the strict interpretation by High Court
judges of what is and is not permissible, sat aghast as hearsay of
hearsay was poured out by garrulous witnesses. The audience
heard of the secret dossier, documents from it were quoted or
mis-quoted, but its contents still remained a mystery. The proceedings were without reality.

Jouast, secretly convinced that Dreyfus was innocent, and
therefore more indulgent to the witnesses for the prosecution
than to those for the defence, failed to keep the hearing to the
point. No doubt he was unskilled, but he was not helped by
counsel. Labori was absent for the second week. In the early
morning of 14 August, while on his way to the court, accompanied by Picquart, he was shot in the back by an unknown
young man, who fled before hands could be laid on him and
vanished into the countryside. No one came forward. The

Chouan does not betray. Labori's wound was not severe and he was able to return on 22 August. His subsequent conduct of cross-examinations was not calculated either to bring out the truth or persuade the judges. His attacks on witnesses, his apostrophes, undoubtedly rubbed them up the wrong way. Demange, quieter, more deeply read in the case than Labori, secured better results. 'Like a *maître d'hôtel* offering the turbot', wrote Barrès, 'he presented his remarks to Zurlinden and Chanoine, who did not see the trap beneath the parsley, and when he had shown them the horror in the dish, with what an air of good temper he drew the attention of the judges'. The transcript of the proceedings reveals that neither counsel was a skilled cross-examiner. It may well be that the mediation of the judge between counsel and witness, as Lord Russell of Killowen remarked, often made their questions ineffective, yet a skilled cross-examiner could have done much better than they in fact did. But the root of their failure lay in their permanent dis-agreement as to strategy, Labori wishing to dominate and bully the hostile witnesses and demonstrate to the audience that they were liars, Demange aiming to throw such doubt into the minds of the seven judges that they would find the charges not proven.

Day after day Dreyfus sat patiently listening to witness after witness. He was a sick man. He could eat little and lived chiefly on milk. He was often shaken by fever. And it is probable that his battered mind often failed to follow the bewildering non-sense which was being retailed from the witness-box. Once or twice he was driven to protest against some wilful distortion. Once (it was on the question of whether he had attended German manoeuvres) he asked for a question to be repeated, hesitated over his reply, and, according to Steevens, left an impression of imperfect frankness.

In the fifth week little was left except small fragments of argument between experts on minor points. Labori, theatrical as ever, attempted to secure the testimony of Schwartzkoppen and Panizzardi, and receiving no replies, telegraphed to the German Emperor. All that was returned was an official note drawing attention to the formal denials of Münster and Bülow in 1894, 1895 and 1898, that at no time had any German agent had contact with the accused.

On 7 September Carrière for the prosecution asked for a verdict of Guilty. Labori gave up his right to plead. Demange addressed the court on 8 and 9 September. 'Before he had spoken two sentences', wrote Steevens, 'you saw that here was a master. Not a great emotional orator, but a great pleader, a master of his business, which is to persuade'. He spoke for seven hours and was never monotonous. Lord Russell thought that Demange was mistaken in treating the evidence as honest; that to confine himself to treating the question of Dreyfus's guilt as not proven was unjustifiable, and that he should have appealed to public opinion. Russell was surely wrong. Courts-martial, as much in England as in France, up to 1914 and after, were travesties of judicial tribunals, and moreover at Rennes the appeal, the real appeal, was not to any public, but to seven army officers whose minds were burdened with army sentiment.

Demange ended at noon on 9 September. Carrière asked to reply and spoke after lunch. It is said that he consulted Jules Auffray, and that Auffray, guessing that the judges, or a majority of them would shrink from sending Dreyfus back to The Devil's Island, and would therefore acquit, suggested to Carrière a middle course. Thus in his reply, instead of merely asking for the usual sentence, which would have sent Dreyfus back to The Devil's Island, Carrière reminded the judges that they could, if they wished, add a rider of extenuating circumstances.

Demange made a brief rejoinder. Dreyfus, asked by Jouast if he had anything to add, could only utter a few broken sentences: he was innocent . . . the honour of his children . . . The court retired.

Only those versed in the case could have given a decisive verdict of Not Guilty. The French in the audience were partisans, their minds already long made up. Among the neutral observers, Russell seems to have thought the prosecution's case not proven, Liebknecht believed Dreyfus guilty, Steevens was unable to make up his mind. The judges had listened through five weeks to the confused medley of testimony. They were not lawyers, they were not even skilled, as were the reporters, in listening and observing. Now they must declare. On all sides they had been watched. It was known that de Bréon had been worked on by his Dreyfusist brother, the priest; he was seen frequently going to church to pray: he was known to be racked by conscience: his old friend, one of the leading Royalists, Villebois-Marueil, had attempted to reason with him. Major Merle was in tears at the end of Demange's speech. Major Profilet, on the other hand, although a poor man with three daughters, was believed by the anti-Dreyfusards to be perfectly reliable: 'We are sure of him, although he's poor'. Jouast throughout had shown himself favourable to the prosecution witnesses and rough with those of the defence.

After the judges retired there was a long pause. Everyone knew that the verdict was in doubt. What in fact occurred is known from Captain Beauvais, who about the middle of 1901 confided in a friend, who passed the story on to Syveton. There appears to have been no discussion before voting. Jouast started, according to convention, with the junior officers. Beauvais, a dyed-in-the-wool anti-Dreyfusard, and Parfait voted Guilty. So did Merle and Profilet. De Bréon: Not Guilty. Brongniart then said Guilty. Jouast had apparently expected Brongniart to vote the other way. He burst out: 'What! you think there are proofs? You think there are even indications?' and himself put down Not Guilty. Parfait, it is said, then suggested that they should start again. Jouast refused, since it would be illegal; but he at once took up the question of extenuating circumstances. Beauvais—rightly, since he believed Dreyfus to be guilty of treason—fought fiercely for twenty years' imprisonment, Jouast for five, which would have meant immediate release. At the end of an hour's heated discussion, Jouast secured five votes for the rider of extenuating circumstances, and an agreed penalty of ten years' detention.

They returned to the courtroom a little before five. Scarcely able to master his voice, Jouast delivered the verdict—Guilty by a majority of five to two. The audience seemed stunned; there was no demonstration. Demange and Labori burst into tears. Dreyfus, waiting in another room, was informed of the verdict by Labori, Demange being too overwrought. He said simply: 'Console my wife'.

5

It has been suggested by Reinach that those who voted Guilty were swayed by the introduction in secret, by or through Mercier, of the photograph of the *bordereau* with the notes and initial of the German Emperor. In support of this he cites the accounts given to Mornard and Jaurès by a Dr Dumas, of conversations with Major Merle in 1902. Even though one refrains from calling in question the good faith of Merle's questioner, who was a passionate Dreyfusard, nothing solid emerges from the conversations. Merle admitted that what had led him to a conviction of Dreyfus's guilt was not entirely the facts that had appeared '*au grand jour*'. The phrase might apply merely to those parts of the evidence heard *in camera*, and have no reference to the photograph. Dumas relates that he spoke of the photograph and that Merle seemed 'stunned and frightened' and answered: 'Nothing of that kind should be mentioned; it might get abroad'; and: 'Don't talk about it: I don't wish to speak of it'. ('*Il ne faut pas parler d'une affaire pareille; elle pourrait monter sur l'eau*'. . . . '*Ne parlez pas de cela; je ne veux pas en parler*'.) Merle in his deposition of 19 May 1904 gave a somewhat contrary version of the conversations.

There is, however, no need to go deeply into the allegation. The answer lies in the behaviour of the court itself. If the photograph was shown to the judges and accepted as genuine, how was it that Jouast and de Bréon voted for acquittal, and how then did Jouast persuade three others to join with him in the rider of extenuating circumstances? The account of what happened, given by Beauvais implies that the usual court-martial procedure was followed; that is, the president without discussion passed immediately to the vote. There is no place here for the insinuation of the photograph; nor does Beauvais, the hot anti-Dreyfusard on the court, mention it. The only alternative possibility is that it was shown to a few uncommitted judges privately outside the walls of the court, but strangely in that case it was not shown to the obviously wobbly de Bréon. Furthermore, why was Auffray so uncertain at lunch-time on the last day that he persuaded Carrière to draw the attention of the judges to the possibility of extenuating circumstances?

Again, the rider of extenuating circumstances—what extenuating circumstances could there be for a guilty traitor?—could have been accepted by Brongniart, Merle and Parfait only if in their hearts they knew that they had voted from motives other than those of pure justice.

It is unlikely that the evidence, either that which was true or that which was false, played an influential part in the condemnation. The verdict sprang from the inescapable dilemma which faced the judges: Dreyfus or Mercier. The ethos of the Army lay in the belief that one's senior is always right and must be implicitly obeyed. Whatever their personal feelings, they must vote for Mercier.

Moreover there were personal considerations. There was the pressure of wives, dreading the social ostracism that would follow acquittal. Jouast was on the point of retirement: he had nothing to fear. All the others knew that their future careers depended on the verdict they gave; on it depended accelerated or delayed promotion. Beauvais in his account said that Profilet, in spite of being a poor man with three daughters, could be reckoned on to vote against acquittal. Profilet voted for condemnation and against extenuating circumstances. It is said that the Army was influenced by religion. This Republican opinion is denied by both officers and priests; and the one judge who was a sincerely religious man, de Bréon, voted Not Guilty.

The pressure on the judges to recondemn Dreyfus came not from any weight of evidence, but from their fear of inculpating senior officers. Soldiers, filled with the spirit of hierarchy and solidarity, filled too perhaps with hatred of the civilians who attacked the Army, they could only vote for Mercier. They should not be blamed. The case, as Georges Sorel says, in *La Révolution Dreyfusienne*, was vitiated by its very nature.

6

Of the many interested parties not present at Rennes, none waited for the verdict more anxiously than Galliffet and Waldeck-Rousseau. Galliffet, receiving a daily report from his representative, Colonel Chamoin, had foretold a condemnation

almost from the beginning. 'I believe that Labori, by his continuous outbursts, has done his client the worst of service. All
my reports confirm this impression. . . . In the judgement,
Dreyfus matters little to me; you know that I've never known
anything about his case, and he has never seemed to me a
sympathetic character. What alarms me is that France will be
condemned by Europe: it will be painful to me to think that the
cradle of every liberty will be accused of not tolerating one'.
It is said that Waldeck-Rousseau desired an acquittal. As an
individual he may have done so: he certainly dropped well-
intentioned remarks to Reinach, but perhaps they should be
discounted. For, as Prime Minister, however much he may have
believed in Dreyfus's innocence, he could see the consequences
of a verdict of Not Guilty. Galliffet had already written to
Princess Radziwill that he would support Mercier in all
circumstances, but Lebret's letter of 5 June to the President of
the Chamber, containing the charges against Mercier, had only
been adjourned pending the decision at Rennes.[1] If the Government, faced by an acquittal, re-opened, as it must do, the case
against Mercier, Galliffet would resign and the Government
would then be defeated, with incalculable consequences. The
best, indeed the only, solution likely to bring peace was the
'condemnation of favour', that is condemnation by four votes to
three, which would permit the prisoner's liberation and bar
attempts to re-open the case. It might be an injustice; it would
at least solve the political problem.

On the day before the verdict—Friday, 8 September—
Galliffet wrote to the Prime Minister at length on the consequences of a second condemnation. What he said may be
briefly resumed as follows. If Dreyfus is condemned by a large
majority, the revising court, in case of appeal, will, from solidarity with the Army, refuse to recognise errors of law or procedure.
If, as Waldeck seems to think, the matter then goes to the civil
Courts of Appeal, there will be the verdict of two courts-martial
against the verdict of two Courts of Appeal. Every foreign
country will condemn us with extreme severity, but many
revisionists, tired of the struggle, will accept the verdict. 'Let us
not forget that in France the majority is anti-semite'. Thus on

[1] See page 210.

one side there will be the whole Army, the majority of French-men (leaving apart the Senators and Deputies) and all the agitators; on the other, the Cabinet, the Dreyfusards and the foreigner.

Neither Galliffet nor anyone else could have known whether the majority of Frenchmen was anti-semite: indeed, the great majority, outside what may be called more or less intellectual circles, seems to have been indifferent. It was, however, at once made very clear that the foreigner was anti-French. The Italian and German Foreign Offices had already shown their resent-ment at some of Mercier's allegations against their representa-tives. 'It is just to say', wrote Lord Russell, 'that, in its com-ments during the actual sitting of the court, the British press, from *The Times* upwards or downwards, almost without exception have indulged in such partisan comment as would have earned for their editors at the hands of English judges prompt committal to prison, had any such comments been made during a trial pending in England'. The Germans, Dutch, Belgians, Italians were no less explosive. In many foreign cities French consulates were besieged and stoned. A number of hostile journals suggested that the Paris Exhibition of 1900 should be boycotted. The French began to think that their only friends in the world were the Russians, and even they were doubtful. In England, Valentine Chirol, under the pseudonym of 'Verax', himself of Catholic upbringing, started a corres-pondence in *The Times* with a violent attack on the Catholic Church and Catholic education. In the United States Mr Dooley gave his friend Hennessy an uproariously funny travesty of the 'historic night' of General Mercier.[1]

---

[1] 'I dhreamed that I see th' German Impror playing a Jews-harp (Cries iv "Abase Rothscheeld!" an' sensation.) I woke with a vi'lent start, th' per-spiration poorin' fr'm me rugged brow. "Cap Dhryfuss is guilty," I cried. But no, I will confirm me ividence. I darted into me r-red pants. I dhruv with fury to th' home iv Madame Cleepathry, th' cillibrated Agyptian asthrologgist an' med'cin woman . . . I tol' her me dhream. She projoosed a pack iv cards. She tur-rned a r-red king an' a black knave. "Th' Impror Willum and Cap Dhryfus," I says in a fury. I burst forth. I had Cap Dhryfuss arristed. I dashed to th' prisident. He was a-receivin' rayfusals f'r a new, cabinet. "I have found th' thraitor," says I. "Hush!" says he. "If th' Impror hears ye, he'll declare war," he says. I was stupefied. "Oh,

7

Waldeck-Rousseau's problem was not one of justice. Dreyfus's counsel had considered filing an application to appeal on a number of legal grounds. It was perfectly certain that it would be rejected by the military revising court. After that an application to the Appeal Courts could come only from the Minister of Justice. But this would at once demonstrate that the Government was taking sides, and as Galliffet had already pointed out, such action would merely restart the whole weary circle of trials: 'a third court-martial would condemn him six to one, a fourth unanimously. It is in the state of mind of the Army; one can't hide it from oneself.' The War Minister was moreover highly disturbed by the general unrest and indiscipline among the officers: whatever solution was found, it must be one that did not inflict a further injury on their *amour-propre*.

Waldeck consulted Lucie Dreyfus's counsel, Mornard, as to whether there was any means of quashing the verdict without recourse to a third trial. Regretfully they could find no method. The only release possible was by way of pardon. Would it be politically possible? On this same morning the members of the court-martial met and unanimously agreed to forward a memorial to President Loubet asking that the ceremonial degradation, required by the law, should not be repeated.

On this same Sunday a group of Dreyfusards met at the office of Ranc's *Radical*. Reinach, knowing nothing of the consultation of Mornard by Waldeck, said that the only way out was by Presidential pardon. Clemenceau and Jaurès were bitterly opposed; they wanted the prisoner to appeal and endure his trials until an impartial court appeared. Clemenceau declared that when the whole people had been roused in defence of justice, it was immoral to ask it to be satisfied with an act of mercy. Reinach was supported by several journalists returned from Rennes, who said the soldiers expected pardon and were not hostile to the idea. On the next day Mathieu Dreyfus, now

---

my beloved counthry!" I cried. "Oh, hivin!" I cried. They was not a minyit to lose. I disbanded th' ar-rmy. I ordhered th' navy into dhry dock. I had me pitcher took. I wint home an' hid in th' cellar. F'r wan night Fr-rance was safe.'

18 *Reinach*

19 *Dreyfus gives evidence*

E. L. D.

20   *The rehabilitation: Dr*
with General Gillain and
Major Targe

21   *Demange's final appeal*
judges

back from Rennes, said that his brother would not survive his sentence and that an immediate pardon was necessary.

Reinach and Mathieu therefore sought the Prime Minister. Waldeck welcomed their approach and agreed to a pardon as soon as possible, provided Dreyfus withdrew his appeal. Mathieu at first refused on the ground that his brother would be left open to the charge that he had accepted a just condemnation. Millerand, who now became the link with the Cabinet, persuaded him to yield. Jaurès, under the weight of the solid proletarian common sense of his party-paper's editor, Gèrault-Richard, gave way, and in the end Clemenceau, growling, surrendered.

One further difficulty had to be overcome. Loubet, in a speech on 24 August, when he thought an acquittal certain, had rashly said that all would accept the verdict. Naturally he shrank from so precipitate a *volte-face*. The pardon was postponed for a week. Galliffet also insisted that, while he would propose the act of clemency, there must be initiated a bill of amnesty for the generals and other officers involved. Otherwise he would not answer for what might occur in the Army.

On 19 September, in response to a formal letter from the Minister of War, Loubet remitted the balance of the sentence on Alfred Dreyfus and cancelled the order for his degradation. To the disgust of the Dreyfusards, the Minister's letter foreshadowed an amnesty for the other actors in the case.

On the same evening Dreyfus was brought by the Director of the Sûreté to Nantes, where he met Mathieu. A day or so later he reached the house of one of his sisters near Carpentras, to begin his convalescence. In accepting the President's act of clemency, he nevertheless claimed the right to use every means in his power to establish his innocence.

Also on the same day Scheurer-Kestner, who had given so much to the cause of justice, died at Luchon.

Two days later, on 21 September, Galliffet, without consulting the Cabinet, sent directly to the Corps Commanders and to the newspapers, a manifesto:

The incident is closed! The military judges, surrounded with the respect of all, have given their verdict in complete

I

independence. Unreservedly we defer to their judgement. Equally we defer to the action which a sentiment of deep pity has dictated to the President of the Republic. There should be no question of reprisals whatever.

Therefore I repeat, the incident is closed. I ask you, and if it were necessary I should order you, to forget the past in order that you may think only of the future. With all my comrades I heartily cry, '*Vive l'Armée*', which belongs to no party, but to France alone.

The incident was far from being closed, as a large number of people hastened to tell him.

Chapter Fifteen

The Politics of Liquidation

1

At Carpentras, Dreyfus endured a slow convalescence from the physical and mental ordeal to which he had been subjected. He was wracked with rheumatic pains; for two years he suffered from fevers and nightmare. To the anger of the majority of Dreyfusards, he refused to lend himself to the campaign against the generals or the Army. His single desire was to be acquitted by his peers and to be re-incorporated in the service. He had given Mathieu Dreyfus permission to withdraw his appeal against the Rennes verdict only after much argument, and he intended to pursue his rehabilitation with all the means open to him. The more violent Dreyfusards, whether crusaders or opportunists, were disgusted that, by his reluctance to be made the spearhead, he was denying and deserting his supporters. Clemenceau, exasperated that his principles and his ambitions should both be thwarted, was outraged: 'Dreyfus may busy himself with Dreyfus; well and good. We, we think of our country dying under the implacable evil of the Roman sect and under the imbecile brutality of a sword which is powerless against the foreigner'. For the younger idealists from the University, who had fought the anti-semite gangs in the street, Charles Péguy wrote bitterly: 'We might have died for Dreyfus; Dreyfus has not died for Dreyfus'. Dreyfus refused to be either bullied or persuaded to abandon his aloof and dignified stoicism. To Julien Benda he once remarked: 'These people who are always groaning over my sufferings oppress me. I like to talk objectively about my case'. And Benda adds: 'I understood his condemnation'. Far more important for the victim than these summons to violence was the need to discover the new fact which would permit him to lodge an appeal to the civil Appeal

Courts. Only after long and cruel disappointments was he to discover the clue that would lead him through the maze of legal procedure befogged by politics, and reach the centre.

2

The pardon was no more than the preliminary act in the process of cleaning up after the Affair. During September Galliffet and Waldeck-Rousseau were carrying out a number of operations for which no parliamentary sanction was necessary. The Prime Minister rejected Méline's request that he should summon the Chambers. There was urgent work to be done. Moreover he must study the new situation and settle his policy.

Before the conclusion of the Rennes trial, Galliffet had considered the suppression of the Statistical Section. Lauth and Junck were back with their regiments: the officers who had succeeded them had become inoculated with their tradition, now sanctified by the martyrdom of Henry; their practices had been divested of all respectability by the revelations of Mercier, Roget and Gonse at Rennes. Furthermore, in what they believed to be the interests of the service, they had monkeyed with the funds at their disposal; they had financed the abduction of Bastian before the Rennes trial, and they had played some part in the introduction of the lunatic buffoon, Cernusky. Faced with dissolution, they put up a strong case for survival, and Galliffet, to his subsequent chagrin, was persuaded to allow the Section to live. He contented himself with minor reforms. On 13 September he relieved Henry's successor, Rollin, of his duties and replaced him by his junior, François. On the same day he handed the duties of counter-espionage over to the Sûreté, where they were given to Commissioner Tomps, the hated detective who had refused to enter into Henry's schemes. The Section was henceforward confined to the business of providing information regarding foreign military developments, but was forbidden to deal directly with foreign agents. Furthermore Galliffet prohibited any future touching of the Dreyfus case.

A fortnight later, on 29 September, he published a decree stating that, in future, promotion to the rank of general was reserved to the War Minister alone. Formally, it was merely the reaffirmation of the earlier practice. Galliffet's action was intended not only to cow the senior officers, but also to reassure Republicans of his own unimpeachable republicanism.

On the day before Loubet signed Dreyfus's pardon, Waldeck laid before the Senate the cases of the men arrested on 12 August. In their preliminary examination, the senators decided that there was sufficient evidence to warrant the charge of an attempt against the State by some 20 of the prisoners; the other 45 were released. The trial took place before the High Court of the Senate between 9 November and 4 January, in a series of noisy hearings. It was soon evident that there was no substance in the plot, and that no serious preparations had been made except by the adventurer Guérin. Déroulède, his friends and witnesses, all joined in a long and dreary act of *cabotinage*, insulted the senators and behaved like ill-bred children. In the end the great majority of the 'conspirators' were acquitted, somewhat contemptuously. Déroulède and André Buffet were condemned to ten years' exile, and Marcel Habert, who surrendered in December and was tried later, to five. Guérin, the Duc d'Orléans's mercenary, the only formidable member of the group, was given ten years' imprisonment, which was commuted to banishment in 1901. It was the end of Déroulède as a force.

3

Superficially the situation of the Cabinet appeared precarious. Its majority in June had been very narrow. Since then nothing had occurred that seemed calculated to increase it. Save Waldeck, not one of the Ministers had any personal following, while the enormous range from the conservatism of Galliffet to the socialism of Millerand made the Cabinet highly vulnerable. To weld a majority in the Chamber, it was necessary to take account of the claims of the Socialists and to make some concessions to social welfare. It was no less necessary to smooth the susceptibilities of the Radicals with their insistence on individualism and the principle of private property. At the same time, since the support of the Progressists who had backed the Government in June had been given rather from disgust at the blunders of Méline and Dupuy than from love of the Cabinet, it was necessary to avoid taking up any of the peculiar doctrines of the Radicals and Socialists, for example the adoption of income-tax.

On the other hand, the Cabinet had been put in to clear up the Affair and to bring the restless army officers back to normal behaviour; the Army also must be smoothed and brought to order. Pacification of a kind might be secured by a general amnesty covering the generals, but the restoration of discipline could not be achieved in a moment. Galliffet himself was far from being loved. His rough sallies over many years had made him enemies. His comments on soldier politicians, such as Billot, were well-known. His well-advertised belief that the Army was rotten did not encourage corps commanders to love him. His no less well-advertised distrust of the Russian Army and the Russian alliance could not fail to make him odious to the circles in which Freycinet and Hanotaux moved. He had relieved two generals, Négrier and Zurlinden, of their commands. He had sent Roget to a garrison far away from Paris: 'General Roget talks well, but he talks too much', he was to tell the Chamber in November, and it is unlikely that he minced his words in private—he did not in his letters—in speaking of the Right's hero, Mercier, 'this raving lunatic'. By the Left, this aristocrat, the executioner of the Communards, would be supported only just so long as he remained the enemy of the Right.

A further difficulty was Millerand. In spite of his undoubted capacity, he had to prove at once that he was still a Socialist and yet not one.

The situation, however, was less insecure than it appeared. In spite of their divisions over Millerand, the Socialists perceived that they could for the first time become part of the Government forces. The case had done much for them. As Reinach remarks with great truth: 'There sprang up a whole bourgeois Socialism, a whole university Socialism, which dates, which emerges, from the Affair'. They could look forward to becoming the Government party, and to everything that goes with that position. 'Never did men adopt quicker the good and bad practices which are contracted on the fringes of power,

when power's responsibilities and profits are shared. As long
as their association with the Republicans lasted, never were
politicians more politic, never opportunists more opportun-
istic'. Although three months later the delegates at the Socialist
Congress voted the resolution that no Socialist should partici-
pate in a bourgeois Government, the party in the Chamber
would not fail for another five years to uphold a Government of
the class enemies. 'Everything', wrote the disillusioned Dreyfusard Charles Péguy, 'everything begins with a *mystique* and
ends in politics. Founders come first, but the profiteers come
after them'.

Much the same was to be said of the Radicals. On the one
side they hated the Socialist doctrine. 'If the Collectivist society
became a reality', said Camille Pelletan, 'I should be the first
to escape from it'. They remained impenitently individualists,
and as individualists their tendencies were divergent. In reality
few Radicals were embarrassed by questions of doctrine. Their
electors were not the proletariat of the great industrial cities,
but the shopkeepers, artisans and peasants of the country
towns, who would vote for the man they knew and would
accept from him the vaguest of declarations.

Thus, on facing the Chamber on 16 November, Waldeck-
Rousseau put forward what amounted to a very moderate programme. The Chambers gave him a vote of confidence by a majority of upwards of 100, four times greater than the vote of June.

Having obtained his vote of confidence, Waldeck now proceeded to what he hoped would be the liquidation of the
Dreyfus case. On 17 November, in the Senate, he tabled an
amnesty bill; or rather since an amnesty bill for a number of
minor crimes, put forward in the previous year by Dupuy's
Government, was still under consideration by the Senate committee, he tacked on to it a supplementary paragraph covering
all crimes and misdemeanours connected with the Dreyfus
case, or included in a prosecution relative to any of the trials.
Further he added another clause to extinguish all pending legal
actions connected with the case.

As would appear later, it was a casual, almost skulking
method of proceeding. Moreover it was grossly unjust, since it
covered all the illegalities and irregularities of the past five years,

but deprived the most injured of all means of redress. As if to underline the odiousness of the proposal, all cases of Dreyfus-ards against civil parties were immediately adjourned: Rein-ach's case with the widow Henry, Picquart's against Vervoort of the *Jour* for printing a faked photograph of him in con-versation with Schwartzkoppen. From the Dreyfusards went up a howl of protest, immediately answered by another from the anti-Dreyfusards, since Waldeck-Rousseau refused a suggestion from a member of the Senate committee that the amnesty should be extended to Déroulède and his co-defendants, now appearing before the High Court of the Senate. The project indeed resembled the Act of Forgiveness and Oblivion of Charles II, forgiveness of enemies and oblivion of friends. Regardless of the fact that all the Dreyfusard journalists were fulminating, the anti-Dreyfusards developed the theme that Picquart and Reinach were the authors of the scheme.

In January 1900 were held the elections for the renewal of a third of the Senate. Mercier was invited to stand by the Right politicians who practically controlled the electorate in Loire-inférieure. With characteristic audacity he accepted the in-vitation, but made it a condition that he should not be expected to join in the ordinary party struggles: he would stand as a Nationalist and patriotic candidate. The Breton nobility, Royalist and Catholic, with behind them a century of rebellion against the Republic, humbly accepted the terms of the arrogant Republican and free-thinking general. He obtained some 70 per cent of the votes. His election was perhaps less significant than the defeat of three Dreyfusist senators, Ranc, Thévenet and Jules Siegfried. The country was not yet con-verted to Dreyfusism.

The Senate, its hands full with the Déroulède case, did not hurry itself over the amnesty proposal, and after the New Year the Budget, as usual not passed by the beginning of the financial year, occupied most of its time. Waldeck-Rousseau, having succeeded in getting the legal actions touching on the Affair adjourned, did not press the matter, it may be from his distaste for the inevitable irritation its discussion would cause. The Senate committee, however, at the end of February dis-covered a flaw in the procedure which effectively prevented the tacking of the Dreyfus amnesty clauses on the earlier bill. Further, it was pointed out that an amnesty applied only to the already condemned, not to the innocent. Thus on 1 March Waldeck laid a new bill which extinguished all proceedings on criminal charges, other than murder, but did not cover civil cases. 'The question', he said, 'is not to judge or absolve actions accomplished; it merely prevents parties from reviving a painful conflict'. Picquart and Reinach once more protested that they, innocent of crimes, would get no redress, while Dreyfus from Carpentras memorialised the chairman of the committee that the extinction of the actions meant that evidence which might reveal a new fact, permitting him to lodge an appeal, would never come to light.

By now the public, weary of the Affair, indifferent whether justice were done or not, was looking forward to the opening of the Paris Exhibition in April. The Senate committee agreed with the public, and with one dissentient accepted the bill. They too were getting bored.

Before the bill could be discussed by the Senate, there were changes in the political situation. On 1 May were held the municipal elections. Although in the provinces the new councils were almost wholly Republican, in Paris there was a landslide to the Right, or rather to the Nationalists. This may have been due to the generally bad administration of the hitherto favoured Radicals and Socialists, who quarrelled on principle with the Préfets of the Seine and of the Police, found jobs for their friends, and raised the cost of living by adding to the level of the *octroi* dues. Or it may have been the reward of extensive bribery by two Nationalists, Edmond Archdeacon, railway director and racehorse-owner, who popularised his political speeches by giving racing tips in the peroration, and Boniface de Castellane, who had married Anna Gould and enjoyed spending the Gould millions. In the upshot, of the 80 seats on the municipal council, 45 were won by Nationalists, a fact which added gall to the repeated Nationalist claim that the Government did not represent France.

In the same month a more unpleasant crisis arose. The Statistical Section, anti-Dreyfusard to a man, had ignored Galliffet's injunction against meddling in the Affair. By chance they had run across the fact that Commissioner Tomps was in touch with a group of foreign agents, and after much involved negotiations succeeded in getting hold of two letters written by Tomps which might be interpreted as indicating that, in an attempt to defame the General Staff, he was busying himself in the Dreyfus case at the very moment when the Government was preaching appeasement. François tried to get his seniors to take up the matter, but Lacroix, Gonse's successor, thought the letters unimportant, and having in turn reported to his chief, Delanne, told François to file the documents and do no more. Furious at their failure, the officers of the Section ignored his orders and pursued the matter.

A second attempt by François had no better luck. Delanne again said the case had no interest and dropped François's report on the fire. As it happened, one of the foreign agents involved, arrested and threatened with extradition, applied to the Minister of the Interior, Waldeck-Rousseau, who communicated with Galliffet. The latter at once realised that his orders were being disobeyed, and that the Section must be cleaned out. He immediately returned François and another to their regiments, and maintained Captain Fritsch only to hand over to their successors. Fritsch, another man to be poisoned by the Dreyfus virus, had photographs taken of the two Tomps letters and handed prints to Le Herissé, deputy for Rennes, one of Boulanger's former adherents, now a Nationalist. The Right, the Nationalists and Méline's followers believed they had enough matter to detach sufficient deputies from the Government majority to bring about the defeat of the Cabinet. On 22 May a formal accusation was made that the Government intended to re-open the Affair. After Waldeck-Rousseau had replied, the question was brought to a head by a motion inviting the Government to oppose any re-opening, from whatever quarter the proposal might come. During the debate Humbert charged the Government with lying, and brought up what had been learned from the officers of the Statistical Section, and finally referred to the Tomps letters, of which both Waldeck and Galliffet were in ignorance. The motion was passed, and later Galliffet was shown the photographs by Le Herissé. He promptly ordered an investigation. Delanne interrogated Fritsch, who now realised what he had done, burst into tears and cried: 'I have committed an act of madness'. He was at once relieved of his appointment, but Galliffet had to meet the Senate and the Chamber. With the former he had no trouble: he explained what he called Fritsch's crime and there was no debate. He came before the Chamber on 28 May.

Already, as has been seen, Galliffet had had doubts as to the survival of the Government. The doubts had grown. As recently as 16 May he had written to a friend of the dangers arising from the cleverness of the Nationalists in showing up the weaknesses of the Government, its sympathy for the Dreyfusards, its lack of persistence in pressing for the amnesty, its minor but irritating persecution of the Church. He ended: 'The Cabinet has suffered the consequences of the association of Millerand with Galliffet. It should have got rid of one or the other at the re-opening of the Chambers in November. . . . The departure of either would have indicated the definite orientation of the Ministry'.

On 28 May he apologised to the Deputies for his ignorance at the previous session of the two Tomps letters. He assumed full responsibility, declined to follow the interpretations which had been put on the documents, and condemned Fritsch for dereliction of duty. He desired that the Army should be kept remote from politics. 'It still suffers from the fact that 15 years ago an adventurer [Boulanger] was forced on it: it will not let another be imposed'. 'If you need someone responsible, let it be me'.

After the usual calumnious and insolent attacks of the Nationalists, Waldeck-Rousseau spoke in support of his War Minister. No doubt tired, no doubt bored with the humbug of this unworthy farce, he allowed himself to drop the word 'felony' in connection with Fritsch's conduct—Fritsch in a less tumultuous season would have been awaiting court-martial. Galliffet took umbrage at the word. 'There are things a soldier can say, which he cannot bear to be said by a civilian', he wrote to a friend the next day. He scribbled a note of resignation and hobbled out of the Chamber; thereafter he was seen no more. As he explained to his correspondent, he could not rebuke the Prime Minister, but he could not in the circumstances remain in office. 'My authority, laboriously and progressively built up over eleven months, would have been too much weakened . . . while to accept the public apologies of Waldeck-Rousseau and give way to Loubet's persuasion would be to return to a hostile Chamber, the Right hostile from ingrown habit, the Left because I could not be forgiven for my departure yesterday . . . Waldeck-Rousseau, who at first was in agreement with me, has fallen under the destructive influence of Millerand; he gets daily more deeply under it. Every day the need to hold his majority together obliges him to take a step forward in the programme of the Socialists and Anarchists'.

For an hour it looked as if the Government would be beaten. Bourgeois, realising the emergency, rallied the weakened morale of the ministerial forces by calling on them to defend the Republic, to unite against 'the eternal enemies of civil liberties'. He proposed a vote of confidence, which was carried by a small but sufficient majority, but it was noticeable that Barthou voted with the Right, and that Poincaré scrupulously abstained.

Nevertheless the Chamber, save for the small intractable body of Dreyfusards, had made it abundantly clear that it was unwilling to reconsider the Dreyfus case, or to make any move towards the victims of military justice to vindicate their honour or obtain redress.

Waldeck-Rousseau may have been wrong in delaying to press for the amnesty. The error, if it was an error, is understandable. As a private person he was convinced that at least two judicial crimes had been committed, which he wished to see repaired: but as Prime Minister his duty was to prevent the anti-parlia-mentary forces from creating parliamentary anarchy, and in all circumstances legality must be preserved, even if justice could not. He could get no support from the Right; he must lean, unwillingly, on the Left. It was not, as Galliffet complained, that he was influenced by Millerand, but that he must have the Socialist support: he was therefore willing to accept reforms proposed by his Socialist colleague so far as they were purely administrative developments, and not revolutionary measures. He would, for example, support Millerand's bill for shorter working hours for women and children, because legislation on these lines had been several times voted by Parliament, though in practice it had been ineffective. On the other hand, he would not countenance Millerand's proposals to enforce arbitration in strikes between owners and employees, because that would be both novel and contrary to prevailing opinion. Forced to prefer order to justice, he was thus impotent to act towards the victims of military justice as he would have liked. *Raison d'état*, as much as his own sentiments, made him desire revision of the case. *Raison d'état* equally forbade him to re-open it.

On the suggestion of Bourgeois and Brisson, the Commandant of the Polytechnic, General André, was appointed to succeed Galliffet. From the Radical point of view he was all that could be desired: Republican, Positivist, and anti-clerical, though not a Freemason. As a Minister, and particularly as Minister of War, he was entirely unsuitable. Far more widely read than most soldiers, he was at the same time muddle-headed, unmethodical, self-confident and obstinate. He looked on himself as a reformer; indeed, some of his reforms—the raising of the pay of junior officers, the putting in hand of heavy guns—were admirable: but his intention to republicanise the Army, which was impossible and perhaps undesirable, required a man of tact and presence. He had no tact, and his odd, gloomy features and tall, ill-balanced body were comic rather than impressive. Clemenceau nicknamed him the spouting whale.

4

The amnesty bill was discussed by the Senate on 1 and 2 June. Waldeck defended it simply on the ground of necessity. 'The amnesty', he said, 'does not judge, it does not accuse, it does not acquit; it ignores'. In the tiny minority against the bill only four Republicans voted, on the ground that innocent men were being deprived of justice: they were all old men from the days when the Republic was untried and unstained. The *affichage* of Waldeck's speech was voted by a huge majority.

The Chamber, having, only six weeks earlier, urged the rapid passage of the bill, now dilly-dallied. The committee disagreed and the bill was held over until after the summer recess. It did not reach the order of the day until December, when it occupied four confused sittings. The Right demanded the inclusion of the Déroulède group and the exclusion of Reinach and Picquart, the authors of all the ill, while the defenders of justice also asked for their exclusion on the ground that they were innocent. Some of the Left attacked the generals, others Méline. Waldeck spoke three times. In his last speech he said: 'I know well the sentiments which some among you have obeyed. The wound inflicted by some acts, either too arbitrary or too inhuman, has re-opened, and you have listened only to the inspiration of your conscience and the counsel of your indignation . . . I do not condemn these reactions, which I myself have felt. . . . But there are moments when one must turn to the future and take less account of the aspects which impugn the guilty than of the state of affairs which has created them'. The bill was carried at 2 a.m. on 19 December in an almost empty House. A few days later the amended bill passed the Senate.

Chapter Sixteen

The End of the Affair

1

Neither Dreyfus nor Picquart had subscribed to the amnesty;
but, while Dreyfus contented himself with stating that he would
continue to pursue the establishment of his innocence, Picquart
took up a public attitude of extreme hostility to Waldeck-
Rousseau. The Prime Minister wished the Conseil d'Etat to
deal immediately with the appeal which Picquart had lodged
in February 1898, in order that he could be restored to the
Army, promoted to the rank he would now have reached, and
given a command. Picquart replied by withdrawing his appeal,
and published an open letter in which he forcefully restated his
grievances, claiming his right to be tried by court-martial,
asserting that the interests of the country required that he should
have justice. Like so many others, he had by now become
poisoned with the Affair: he accused Waldeck of bargaining
for Dreyfus's pardon, hinted that the Prime Minister knew
more about the attempt on Labori's life than had been made
public, while at the same time he was letting 'the real enemies
of the country' escape unscathed.

From December 1900 onwards, the Dreyfusist group fell out
among themselves. Labori had taken umbrage that Mathieu
Dreyfus had accepted his proffered renunciation to plead at
Rennes, and protested that if he had been allowed to speak the
verdict would have been an acquittal. He quarrelled with
Mathieu who, after a long struggle to reason with the vain
lawyer, broke with him. Later Labori quarrelled with Reinach,
who gave up employing him. Labori took to saying that he had
been ill-paid for his trouble, and finally allied himself with
Picquart. Alfred Dreyfus had come to Paris in November and
had written Picquart a letter asking to be permitted to thank

him in person for all he had done. Picquart would not even acknowledge the letter. His former anti-semitism stirred in him; it is said that he took to reading the *Libre Parole*. He associated only with Clemenceau and Labori, who was planning to re-open the Affair in order to satisfy his political aspirations and to make trouble for Waldeck-Rousseau. In an attempt to heal the breach between his brother and his counsel, Alfred Dreyfus called on Labori on 22 December. Picquart was present. He and Labori were harsh and insisted that Dreyfus should no longer accept the advice of Mathieu or Demange but put his case in their hands. Otherwise he could no longer look for their support. Disillusioned, Dreyfus refused.

2

The prime difficulty in the way was the legal point that, to win an appeal, a new fact, vital to the decision of the judges at Rennes and unknown to them, must be submitted. Search as they would, the Dreyfus brothers and Reinach could discover no new fact. They had hoped, by enquiry of the judges at Rennes, to discover that the famous annotated *bordereau* had either been shown or at least spoken of in secret. Jouast refused to speak. Merle, as has been seen, dodged the question and denied the words attributed to him by the Dreyfusard emissary. All that existed was the current rumour that Mercier had a photograph of the document in his possession, and a volume of newspaper paragraphs, none of which could be adduced as influencing the verdict.

Mathieu's patient detective work wasted much time. It was not until the spring of 1903 that a move was made. The action then arose out of the elections of May 1902, a matter wholly extraneous to the case. Syveton, treasurer of the Ligue de la Patrie Française, had been elected over a prominent Radical in the Paris Bourse constituency. During the campaign, Jules Lemaître, picking up the rags of a falsified quotation from the letter Galliffet had written to Waldeck-Rousseau at the end of the Rennes trial, had produced a poster referring to the Govern-ment as 'the foreigners' Government'. On these grounds a parliamentary enquiry into the conduct of the election was set

up. The report of the committee, which favoured the validation
of Syveton, came to the Chamber in April 1903. Jaurès had
been told of Mathieu Dreyfus's search. Now the power on the
Delegation of the Left, he saw in the debate on the Syveton
report an opportunity to raise the question of the annotated
bordereau. 'He saw, as an artist', wrote Reinach, 'the fine speech
he would make, which would go echoing round the world and
down in history, and the fine scene, while as a politician he
calculated the effects of his action: Nationalism definitely con-
quered and dishonoured, and a thrust to the heart of the
Church party'. Unfortunately for his plan, and for Dreyfus, the
Chamber were thoroughly sick of the Affair they had hoped
was safely buried.

The debate on Syveton began on 6 April. By working in the
wording of the election poster, Jaurès successfully reached the
discussion of the annotated *bordereau*, but none of the Nationalists, not even Millevoye, who had first publicly given the terms
of the letter, accepted the challenge. Nothing emerged, and the
debate wandered. There were sharp passages of arms between
Cavaignac and Brisson over the resignation of Pellieux, much
noise from the Left; and Lasies once more trotted out Cuignet's
obsession that the Foreign Office had falsified the Panizzardi
telegram. The single relief was a promise by the War Minister
in the Combes ministry, General André, to have a further War
Office enquiry into the Dreyfus documents. In deep boredom
the Chamber unseated Syveton.

Unfortunately Jaurès tried to carry the matter further. Once
again a storm blew up. The Radicals were restive at Jaurès's
persistence. On the eve of the day on which Jaurès was to speak
Ferdinand Buisson came to see Dreyfus. 'He told me of the disquiet of many minds in the Chamber over Jaurès's intervention. The Left groups were far from happy over the importance
he was acquiring and the fact that he wished to drag them in his
train without consulting them'. The Socialists and Radicals
thus welcomed a resolution to leave the case within the judicial
sphere. But by ventilating the question of the annotated
bordereau Jaurès had succeeded in demonstrating that the
mythical document had no existence, and thus deprived it of
its character as a possible 'new fact'. Nevertheless, on the advice

of his counsel, Mornard, Dreyfus himself applied to André for an enquiry into this and also into the Cernusky evidence.

3

André entrusted the investigation to a member of his personal staff, Major Targe. For the first time since the War Office had occupied the Rue Saint-Dominique, a thorough search of its files was carried out. This alone occupied six months, but it brought its reward. A number of reports to the Statistical Section tending to demonstrate Dreyfus's innocence, which the Section had carefully suppressed, were discovered, of which the most important was a letter of April 1895 from a spy named Lajoux, giving a recognisable description of Esterhazy as the officer in the pay of the German War Office. Several notes from Schwartzkoppen came to light, relating to the purchase, at 20 francs each, of sections of the large-scale plans. Further it was discovered that, to hide the identity of certain agents, Henry, with the aid of Gribelin, who now decided that truth was the better part of discretion, had falsified the registers, that he had amassed a secret fund to be employed on unavoidable ends, and that from Guénée's notes he had put together a file on the characters of leading politicians, generals and journalists.[1] It was also discovered that on the chargesheets against Esterhazy given to the president and vice-president of his court-martial the date of 1894 had been erased with the intention of absolving him of the accusation for all time. One document on artillery, which had disappeared, and was therefore presumed to have been handed to the Germans by Dreyfus, turned up in the private file of a deceased officer. But possibly the most revealing discoveries were: (a) true copies, made by Gribelin and signed by Sandherr on the very day of its receipt, of the letter from Panizzardi, stating that he was about to receive details of the French railway organisation, showed it to have been written on 28 March 1895, three months after Dreyfus had been condemned, whereas the date of the original had

[1] This secret fund had been discovered immediately after Henry's death, but nothing had been said about it: the money had simply been put back to the War Office general secret fund.

been removed by Henry, and March 1894 substituted: (b) a true copy of the letter from Panizzardi, quoted by Cavaignac in his speech to the Chamber in July 1897, saying that 'D' had brought many interesting things, showed that the original initial was not 'D' but 'P'. Now for the first time the file of documents dealing with the case was put together complete and in order.

It was not until 19 October that André submitted to Combes a full report, in which he was careful to make no recommendation. Combes promptly handed it over to the Minister of Justice, who at once sent it to the consultative committee. The committee unanimously decided that there were grounds for revision, and on Christmas Day, 1903, the Procureur-Général was instructed to submit the Rennes verdict to the Court of Criminal Appeal.

Baudouin, the Procureur-Général, approached his task with an open mind, expecting to find at least some reasonable ground for Dreyfus's second conviction. As Picquart had been staggered in 1896, so now was Baudouin. Yet his task was an involved one: it was not until 8 March 1904 that he was able to produce his summary before the Criminal Appeal Court, now presided over by Bard. The Court decided in favour of full revision.

Once more the witnesses were summoned. Once more they were cross-examined by the judges—Mercier, Gonse, du Paty, Picquart and the rest. Some witnesses who had never yet been seen were secured. Maurice Weil, much suspected of being Esterhazy's accomplice, who had carefully avoided appearing at Rennes, was somewhat roughly handled: his dossier from the War Office showed him to be a coward and a parasite but contained nothing criminal, and nothing of interest came out. Old Bastian, no longer protected by the Statistical Section, half-witted, illiterate and wildly anti-semitic, made scenes, but her evidence was valueless. She, however, produced a series of letters from Henry making appointments. Albert 1, Prince of Monaco, recounted a private conversation with the Kaiser, who had once more reiterated the statement that the Germans had never dealt with Dreyfus. Finally two committees of experts examined the relevant documents. One, of senior artillery officers, affirmed that no gunner could have written the *bordereau* and that the famous secret manual was in fact not confidential. The other, composed of savants including the great mathematician Henri Poincaré, destroyed once and for all Bertillon's system, and established Esterhazy as the writer of the *bordereau*. It was nearly the end of November before the last witness was heard. It remained for one of the judges to write and present the report on the evidence.

4

One of the more puzzling questions at the end of the Affair is that of the enormous lapse of time between the setting up of the War Office enquiry by André in April 1903 and the delivery of the judgement of the united Appeal Courts in July 1906. Is it to be accounted for by the normal 'law's delays'? While the period up to the conclusion of the evidence is not unreasonable, the 19 months between November 1904 and June 1906 are not explained by the fact that the first two *rapporteurs* appointed by the Criminal Appeal Court fell sick. There is a gap of more than twelve months between the appointment of the last *rapporteur*, Moras, and the meeting of the united Courts.

Georges Sorel in his pamphlet review of Reinach's history, *La Révolution Dreyfusienne*, suggests that the obstacle was Cavaignac. But by the end of 1904 Cavaignac was wholly discredited and moreover was a dying man: he died on 25 September 1905. Even if Sorel's belief were true, there remain nine months between the death of Cavaignac and the first meeting of the united Courts on 18 June 1906.

Sorel's second suggestion seems more realistic, that during much of the time private argument was going on as to whether the courts should send Dreyfus for a third court-martial or break the Rennes verdict once and for all. By this time no one could trust a court-martial, however competent its members. The Army had not only retained its former prejudices, but had now suffered the Two-Year Service Law. A new court-martial with a sixth rehearsing of the hundred witnesses would revive all the old hatreds. On the other hand, there was the legal question whether the United Appeal Courts could produce technical grounds for refusing to return Dreyfus to military justice. The sole ground on which they could do so was if no crime had been committed, or, materially, if the despatch of the *bordereau* to Schwartzkoppen was in itself not a crime. Baudouin attempted to adopt this thesis by accepting Esterhazy's statement that he had written the document on the order of Sandherr. The united Courts, when they came to deliver judgement, rejected Baudouin's proposition. It is probable that the judges felt the justice of the plea, put forward by Mornard on behalf of Dreyfus, that it was absurd that the verdict of a junior tribunal composed of extemporary judges, who, without being required to state their reasons, merely said Guilty or Not Guilty, should be placed above the reasoned judgement and verdict of the highest court in the land.

It is still more probable that the delay was prompted by political considerations. The year 1905 was occupied with the unpleasant conflict with Germany over Morocco, which in June led to the virtual dismissal of Delcassé from the Foreign Office and the even more difficult negotiations leading up to the Algeciras Conference. There is no doubt that Rouvier, the Prime Minister, who took over Delcassé's office, was considerably agitated: the last thing he can have desired was a revival of the Affair. Further, at the same time Parliament was struggling with the Laws of Separation. The Dreyfus case would add fuel to a raging fire. By the end of 1905 a general election was once more in view. Until this, which would take place in May 1906, was out of the way, it would be most impolitic to allude to the case. It is surely significant that the united Courts began their sittings within a month of the conclusion of the election.

This may be purely fanciful. The delay may have been due merely to administrative difficulties which no official was in a hurry to solve. Certainly during the three months before the elections the judges were fully occupied in dealing with a mass of voters' registration appeals. The answer will perhaps never be known.

5

During the long delay Clemenceau in the *Aurore* and Picquart

in the *Gazette de Lausanne* continued to campaign for pure
justice: Dreyfus must not be judged by civilians but by his peers,
and if his peers once more condemned him, so much the worse
for the Army and for France, and the fight for yet a fourth
court-martial would begin. Picquart had now become a bitter
anti-semite: 'the better share of the booty [of the Affair] has
gone to the Jews—they have been pushed up, particularly in the
Army'. No Nationalist could have gone further: Picquart even
achieved quotation by Drumont.

So far as Clemenceau was concerned, he lost interest in
Dreyfus as a stick with which to beat the Government. In
March 1906, two months before the election, Rouvier was
defeated and resigned. Armand Fallières, who had succeeded
Loubet in the Presidency of the Republic in January, found an
interim Prime Minister in the ageing Radical, Brisson's Minister
of Justice, Sarrien, 'the post to which the Car of State is hitched
when the horses are tired'. Sarrien invited Clemenceau to join
the Cabinet—the first time such an invitation had ever been
extended to him.[1] He took as of right the Ministry of the Interior, at the moment the key Ministry, and at once his opinions
were transformed: he wanted no re-kindling of fires on the eve
of the election. 'While I am Minister', he said, 'not a church in
France shall be closed'. The elections passed off quietly, with
an increase in the Radicals and a heavy defeat for the Nationalists.

The three Appeal Courts met on 18 June and continued to
sit until 7 July, the Criminal Court presided over by Bard, the
Court of Petitions by Tanon, who had led and persuaded the
united Courts in 1899, and the Civil Court by Sarrut, who had
been one of Scheurer-Kestner's advisers. On this occasion there
was no first-night crowd, just a few old Dreyfusists and the
journalists: above all there were no police. In turn Baudouin
the Procureur-General, the *rapporteur* Moras, and Mornard for
Alfred Dreyfus, made their long submissions. Moras held that
the writing and delivery of the *bordereau* was a crime and that
Dreyfus was not the criminal. He submitted to the judges three
new facts as a basis for revision: the substitution of the letter

---

[1] In 1887 he had been invited to form a Government by Grévy who was
being forced out of the Presidency by the Chamber, and had refused.

'D' for 'P', the falsification of the date of the Panizzardi letter on railway organisation, and the recovery of the missing report on artillery. He claimed that Dreyfus had not written the *bordereau*, had not confessed to Lebrun-Renaud, that the annotated *bordereau* had no existence, and that the Foreign Office version of the Panizzardi telegram was correct. Nevertheless, he proposed that Dreyfus should once more be tried by court-martial.

As soon as it was published in the press, his report was greeted with a yell of protest from the minor participants in the Affair— Cuignet, du Paty, Gribelin and Gonse. (The last incidentally challenged Picquart: they met on 6 July, Gonse missed, and Picquart did not fire). Boisdeffre and Mercier were silent. Drumont summoned the latter to speak—to reveal, as he hoped, the photograph of the annotated *bordereau*. Mercier wrote a long letter protesting against minor details in Baudouin's speech; it had no fire, and Drumont replied bitterly: 'You have not spoken; you have made a pretence of speaking'.

On 12 July Ballot-Beaupré, the *rapporteur* of 1899, on behalf of the judges read their full reasoned judgement. Each fact was examined, document after document analysed, charge after charge rebutted. Not a fragment of the original accusation was left in existence. The courts therefore broke and annulled the verdict of the Rennes court-martial, which had been erroneously and wrongfully delivered. It was noted that Dreyfus had declared that he would forego any pecuniary indemnity which the Code allowed him; further, that the judgement of the courts should be printed at the public expense and posted up in Paris and Rennes.[1]

6

By the anti-Dreyfusards the verdict was accepted with sneers and resignation. Drumont groaned: 'To think that I have battled for years for the Staff and General Mercier! I really do

[1] It is doubtful if the annulment without re-trial could be justified in law. It is severely criticised in *Recueil Sirey* for 1907 (pp. 1–49). A defence of the judgement appeared in Dalloz, *Jurisprudence Générale;* the author is believed to have been Sarrut, President of the Civil Appeal Court, and therefore prejudiced. But surely, if ever *raison d'état* was justified, this was the occasion.

not know why so many Dreyfusard civilians have seemed to take
military men for great captains'. Among the politicians the Left
at once adopted postures of justified virtue. The Senate, which
had formerly treated Scheurer-Kestner and Trarieux with
hostility and contempt, passed a vote recognising the civic
excellence of the two dead members, and decreed that their
busts should be set up in the lobby. It is fair to say that the
Right opposed and the Centre abstained.

As for Dreyfus and Picquart, the Cabinet was perplexed what
to do with them. Obviously reparation must be made, but not
exaggerated. Dreyfus, who had refused to make himself a
political symbol, was to be promoted to the rank of major, which
he would normally have reached in 1903, and given the fourth
grade of the Legion of Honour. Since he had refused a financial
indemnity, this reparation was scurvy. Picquart's was a more
difficult case. Unlike Dreyfus, he had taken to political journalism. During 1903–4 André had made an effort to restore him
by a special bill in the Chamber, and had failed. The new
Minister of War, Etienne, proposed to promote him to the rank
of Brigadier-General as from 10 July 1903, which would place
him in the seniority he would probably have reached. Special
laws for the reintegration of both men were necessary. Etienne
introduced them in the Chamber on the day before the recess,
13 July. Both bills were passed by majorities of over 400. Except
for one speech—that of the only intelligent member of the Right,
Denys Cochin—the debates were commonplace. Cochin took
up some violent criticism of the anti-revisionist Right, uttered
by the *rapporteur* Messimy, and pointed out that the great
number of the deputies who had opposed revision were not, like
himself and his party, opponents of the Government and the
regime, but dyed-in-the-wool Republicans. Were not Dupuy,
Cavaignac, Billot, Méline, defenders of the Republic? Was
General Mercier a Jesuit? He protested at the campaign against
the Army, the volume of abuse of the whole officer body. In
vain the Left tried to shout him down and threw insults at
individuals; he was telling them what they wished to forget—
that for political gains neither Radicals nor Socialists had dared
to declare for the cause of justice, that they had accepted
Cavaignac, that even after Henry's confession and suicide, when

it was plain to reasonable men that revision, which did not imply recognition of innocence, was necessary, they had by their votes confirmed Dupuy's tergiversations. It was true, and now these late-comers had ridden to power on disreputable calcula- tion. The righting of an injustice had been due, not to them, but to the patient and courageous obstinacy of a handful of men who had undergone obloquy for their refusal to accept *raison d'état*. Founders lead, but the profiteers are on their heels.

In the Senate the debate took a different turn. Mercier, defeated, still fought on. He asked to be allowed to explain why he could not vote for the reintegration of Dreyfus. He claimed that the united Appeal Courts had acted irregularly in that they did not know, could not have read, all the evidence. When indignant exclamations smothered his words and the President invited the assembly to allow the General to offer his defence, he at once riposted that he was not an accused, and that his conscience—the word raised cries of derision—did not allow him to vote for the bill. He was answered by one of the early Dreyfusards, Delpech. 'If we desired to extend our need for justice, there is one man who should take the prison cell of the honourable victim whose innocence, after long and terrible sufferings, was yesterday confirmed. That man, sir, is you'. Mercier attempted to continue the struggle, but the patience and courtesy of the Senators were worn out. He was shouted down and the bills restoring Dreyfus and Picquart were passed.

On 22 July a small parade was held in one of the minor courts of the Ecole Militaire. In the presence of a few friends, under the eyes of a guard of honour, Dreyfus was decorated with the Legion of Honour.

7

It had taken nearly twelve years from the arrival of the *bordereau* at the Rue Saint-Dominique to establish the innocence of one accused man. During that time a number of men who had worked either for or against revision had passed away— Scheurer-Kestner, Trarieux, Waldeck-Rousseau, Grimaux, Cavaignac, Cordier were dead. Billot followed them in 1907, Galliffet in 1909. Déroulède, after vain struggles to re-enter

Parliament at the end of his exile, died in 1914. Guérin, of the Anti-Semitic League, such is the irony of our existence, died in 1910 of pneumonia resulting from his attempt to save a drowning boy from the Seine floods.

Roget was refused promotion, and retired in January 1908. He stood for the Chamber as a Nationalist in 1914 and was defeated. He died in 1917. Both Lauth and Cuignet retired. Both were living in 1935, still convinced that Dreyfus was a traitor; Cuignet even published a book about the case and helped Cavaignac's daughter in her account of the case. André died in 1913, but Boisdeffre lived on in silence until 1919. Mercier, the indomitable, got himself re-elected to the Senate in 1906 and remained a member until 1920: a year later he died, at the age of eighty-eight. Du Paty, retired from the Army, was restored at the end of 1912 to the command of a territorial regiment by Millerand, now Minister of War. The protests that rose from the Left forced the rash Minister to resign. In 1914 du Paty was offered a lines-of-communication appointment. He refused and enlisted in the 16th Chasseurs-à-pied. He was then given back his rank and commanded an infantry regiment with skill and great gallantry. In September 1916 he died of wounds received in action, aged sixty-three. In November 1914, at Jaffre's request, supported by Poincaré and Millerand, he was given the ribbon and commanded an infantry regiment with skill and gallantry. In September 1916 he died of wounds received in action, aged sixty-three.

Schwartzkoppen had retired in 1908. In October 1914 he was given command of a brigade and took part in the heavy fighting at Notre-Dame-de-Lorette in the following spring. Owing to a serious fall from a horse in October 1915, he was on the sick list for a year, after which he was appointed to the command of a division on the eastern front. Here he was taken ill and brought to Berlin, where he died on 8 January 1917. On his deathbed he suddenly cried: 'Frenchmen, hear me! Dreyfus is innocent! It was all just intrigue and forgery. Dreyfus is innocent'.

Drumont lost his influence. Anti-semitism went out of fashion: the aristocracy no longer relished his puritanism, and were now marrying more and more into Jewish families. The circulation of the *Libre Parole* declined. Tentative offers to buy it were made by Charles Maurras, the rising hope of the enemies of the Republic, but the negotiations came to nothing. In the winter of 1917–18 Drumont died in poverty.

Bertillon was an obstinate man. Long before his death the finger-print method for the identification of criminals had been adopted by the police of western Europe. Bertillon resisted any change in France and maintained his own anthropometric system. Similarly he refused to admit he had made any error in his attribution of the *bordereau* to Dreyfus. It is said that in consequence of his attitude, he was never given the Legion of Honour, to which his long service and his reforms in police administration had undoubtedly entitled him. He died in February 1914, and the Préfecture of Police promptly went over to the finger-print method.

The career of Esterhazy followed its fantastic and obscure course. Having been condemned *in absentia* to three years' imprisonment in 1899 on Christian Esterhazy's charge of false pretences, he did not return to France. At intervals from London he abruptly intervened with letters to notabilities, but he was no longer useful. For some time he lived with a French-woman who kept a *maison de rendezvous*, but in the end she turned him out, and he disappeared from view. At some time in 1904 Etienne Lamy, the very Catholic editor of the *Correspondant*, put Judet, now editor of the *Eclair*, in touch with a man called Fitzgerald, who, as a good Irishman, hated the English. Judet, himself anglophobe and detesting Delcassé's *rapprochement* with the British Government, went to London and arranged with Fitzgerald for a series of articles under the heading *l'Angleterre Inconnue*. He apparently failed to recognise in Fitzgerald the famous Esterhazy, and thus for some time, under Judet and his successor Trogan, the Uhlan continued to lambast the country which sheltered him. About 1906 he retired to Harpenden, where he acquired a house and assumed the name and style of Comte Jean-Marie de Voilemont. He also acquired a wife and is said to have lived by selling foreign tinned foods. He wrote much. He survived until 1923 when on 21 May he expired and was buried in the parish churchyard.

Two months after his restoration to the Army, Picquart was appointed to command an infantry division, but a month later, in October 1906, Clemenceau succeeded Sarrien as Prime Minister and remained in office for three years of chaotic opportunism. With characteristic levity, he appointed Picquart Minister of War.

No great reforms can be attributed to Picquart's term of office. Those he attempted appear to have been met with the hostility of his brother generals and often ignored. His own resentments still swayed him. He refused to promote Roget. He would do nothing for Dreyfus. He never lived down his past and always suffered embarrassment when faced by officers who could not forgive him. He was eventually appointed to command the Second Army Corps at Amiens, where in January 1914 he was thrown from his horse and a few days later died. He was a complex and difficult character, a courageous and honourable man, reserved to a fault, very conscious of his own great qualities and inclined to think that they had been insufficiently recognised. But a man who overcomes his innate and deep-rooted prejudices, who breaks his own career on behalf of a betrayed, innocent, deserves our profound respect.

Joseph Reinach did not easily live down the reputation his enemies attached to him for his share in the case. He did not win back his constituency of Digne until 1906, and lost it for good in 1914. During the war he became the military commentator of the *Figaro* under the pseudonym of Polybe, much in favour with that Catholic, patriotic and combatant general, Charles Mangin, but regarded by British G.H.Q. as a pestilent nuisance. He died in 1921. Long before that his *éloge* had been written in shining words by a Catholic Dreyfusist, who himself died in battle. In *Notre Jeunesse* Charles Péguy wrote: 'Alone he, Reinach, was of a political and social depth, of an order of greatness at least equal to that of Jaurès. . . . Of our whole headquarters, we see that he alone did not weaken before the Dreyfusist demagogy. . . . And this is even more remarkable in that he has throughout his career been a politician. . . . This is the highest praise I know of a man . . . that this politician, wealthy and powerful, had at many turns the political virtues of a poor man. Of what non-Jew can so much be said?'

Dreyfus remained what he had always been, a strictly honourable soldier. He had never lent himself to political adventurers.

He was even heard to say that the abuse of Mercier was exaggerated. After a short period in the Army, he resigned and went on to the reserve. During the 1914–18 war he was recalled to service and commanded an ammunition column with efficiency. He died in 1935, a quiet old gentleman. During his later years he liked to play bridge. One evening his partner remarked that a certain X had been arrested for espionage, and then, realising the tactlessness of his remark, added that he did not suppose there was anything in it. Dreyfus, calmly dealing, rejoined: 'Oh, I don't know; after all, there's never smoke without fire'.[1]

[1] This anecdote was given to me by Marcel Abraham (1898–17.2.1955), Inspecteur-Général of the Service universitaire des relations avec l'étranger, at Nice in December 1953, he himself having been playing at the table.

Short Selected Bibliography

Le Procès Zola devant la Cour d'Assises et la Cour de Cassation, 2 vols., 1898.

La Révision du Procès Dreyfus (devant la Cour de Cassation), Vol. 1, *Instruction de la Chambre Criminelle:* Vols. 2 and 3, *Instruction des Chambres Réunies, Debats*, 1899. (This prints also the Ormescheville *rapport* of 1894 and also the proofs of the evidence of the witnesses for the prosecution at the 1894 court-martial.)

Le Procès Dreyfus devant le conseil de Guerre de Rennes, 3 vols., 1898.

Révision du Procès de Rennes. Enquête de la Chambre Criminelle de la Cour de Cassation, 3 vols., 1908.

Desachy, Paul, *Bibliographie de l'Affaire Dreyfus*, 1905.

André, Gen. L. J. N., *Cinq Ans de Ministère*, 1907.

Barrès, Maurice, *Scenes et Doctrines du Nationalisme*, *1*, 1902.

Baumont, Maurice, *Aux Sources de l'Affaire. L'Affaire Dreyfus d'après lès archives diplomatiques*, 1959.

Benda, Julien, *La Jeunesse d'un Clerc*, 1936.

Benda, Julien, 'Regards sur le Monde Passé in 264', *Nouvelle Revue Française*, 1 September 1935, pp. 413–24.

Blum, Léon, *Souvenirs sur l'Affaire*, 1935.

Brisson, Henri, *Souvenirs: Affaire Dreyfus*, 1908.

Dardenne, Henriette (Caraignac's daughter), *Lumières sur l'Affaire Dreyfus*, 1964.

Dreyfus, Alfred, *Souvenirs et Correspondance*, 1936.

Dutrait-Crozon, H. (Ps. of Colonels le Parent and F. Delebecque), *Précis de l'Affaire Dreyfus*, 3rd edn., 1938.

Esterhazy, Major Walsin-, *Les Dessous de l'Affaire Dreyfus*, 1898.

Guillemin, Henri, *L'Enigme Esterhazy*, 1962.

Lazare, Bernard, *Une Error judiciare*, 1897.

Leblois, Louis, *L'Affaire Dreyfus; l'Iniqité, la Réparation, les Principaux faits et documents*, 1929.

Paléologue, Maurice, *Journal de l'Affaire Dreyfus, 1894–99: l'Affaire Dreyfus et le Quai d'Orsay*, 1955.

Ranc, Mme C. Arthur, *Souvenirs et Correspondance, 1831–1908*, 1913.

Radziwill, Princesse, *Lettres de la Princesse de Radziwill au Général de Robilant*, 11, 1934.

Reinach, Joseph, *Histoire de l'Affaire Dreyfus*, 7 vols., 1901–8.

Reinach, Joseph, *Tout le crime*, 1899.

Schwertfeger, Bernard, *The Notebooks of Colonel von Schwartzkoppen*, 1931.

Sorel, Georges, *La Révolution Dreyfusienne*, 1909. (This is in fact a long review of Reinach's *Histoire*, above, published ten years after the Rennes trial.)

Steed, H. Wickham, *Through Thirty Years*, 1, 1934.

Steevens, G. W., *The Tragedy of Dreyfus*, 1899.

Thomas, Marcel, *L'Affaire sans Dreyfus*, 1961.

Index